Dot S

HITHER AND YON

Under a Lucky Star

PREFACE

Many of the travelogue sections of the book have been written from notes taken during our travels but they are not intended to restrict one of my main purposes which has been to show the reader how God has guided and protected me all my life. In retrospect of course wisdom reveals this to be true.

The earlier sections draw on memories that remain very clear and when notes were not made. With age our memories need all the help they can get!

Finally, I should like the reader to believe, as I do, that God has a sense of humour.

PART 1: WHILE I WAS SINGLE
AT HOME IN SUSSEX, 1941-50

My granny always said she thought I was born under a lucky star. I overheard her telling my mother this from my bedroom over the sitting room. Sound insulation wasn't very good in those days. Granny may have been right! In 1941 a bomb fell just outside the nursing home in Eastbourne where I was born on 31st. May and blew all the windows in. "Put the baby under the bedclothes" the nurse is said to have shouted.

I was baptised Dorothy Anne Sopper at the church of St. John the Evangelist, Meads on Sept. 21 1941, by Rev. W.H.M.Walton. Mother told me that I grasped her pearly necklace which broke, and the pearls scattered on the floor!

In my grandfather's house in Horley I remember hearing the wailing sirens and a cat coming in to warm up in my bed. Grandfather, my father's father, had died some years previously after a botched surgical operation, so I never knew him. Sadly, I was not to remember my father either as he died of T.B. when I was about 2.

All this doesn't sound very promising, but I have a few delightful memories of days at grandfather's house, playing around a large pond. It was a miracle that I never fell in, because I was

2

unsupervised when mother went off to work locally. I watched her disappear in the morning on her bike shouting "Don't get the sack" but I had no idea what that meant!

There were chickens to watch and eggs to fetch. I wore dungarees with pockets made from green blackout curtains. Invariably I fell bringing back eggs and the yolk would dribble down my dungarees. The eggs would be stored in a large jar of isinglass water.

There were trees to climb and birds' nests and eggs to discover. A wonderful freedom denied to most young children today.

There was a walk I used to take, with the son of a tenant, which took us through a farm, down avenues of chestnut trees which we beat to make the chestnuts fall; we climbed stiles and eventually arrived into a large area littered with shot, presumably from locals after rabbits. Many years later this field became part of Gatwick airport.

Two evacuees came to live with us. Chrissie and her sister, whose name I no longer remember, but I was convinced she was a boy. They fitted into the household well and became lifelong friends of my mother and me.

Alison, or Aison as I used to call her, was my grandfather's household cook and was from Scotland. She was a patient soul, especially when it came to lacing up my long boots as I sat on the kitchen table.

Aunt Ando, one of the five children of my grandparents, and about whom we will hear more as my story unfolds, was a terrific gardener, very strong and able to climb ladders to clip hedges, and she would tackle all the more difficult garden jobs.

Edward Bear was a good companion and was beautifully dressed by aunt Ando, who was clever with sewing machines and needle. She made him striped pyjamas, a red dressing gown with the initials EB embroidered on the pocket, and short blue trousers and a shirt for daytime wear.

The Horley period came to an end when my mother and I went to live with her mother, who had recently been widowed.

Knowing the financial situation of the two widows, a benefactor had left them a maisonette in Eastbourne for us to live in. This came with the adorable addition of a black Scottish terrier puppy, who we named Kirsty. She became my companion and confidante.

There was a small garden at the back of the property, which became our playground. The apple tree was perfect for climbing, and a retreat for me and Edward Bear. The local cats were soon sent packing by Kirsty, but not before they had ruined my little tent by spraying it with urine, the smell of which never washed away.

Just as mother was wondering about my education, an aunt of hers left her £300 in her will, and it was decided to use this to send me to an Eastbourne kindergarten run by three sisters. Here I was given an excellent start in life in many subjects, and one of the children from the school is still my best friend; we have both married and spent most of our lives apart, but we are now both living in Eastbourne in our old age.

After lunch at school, we had a rest on a blanket. No doubt the rest was much needed by the three sisters. For us it was a time to explore the physical differences between sexes! Of course, I knew all about this didn't I having witnessed the boys from the farm competing to see who could pee the farthest over the lake. Later, at my next school, I was confronted by a "flasher" on my way home.

Once a year, parents were invited to see what their little darlings had been doing. We had rehearsed the Mad Hatter's Tea Party. As I recall, I was the Mad

Hatter and, when the time came, I got irrepressible giggles and was quite unable to say anything at all!

The terrible winter of 1947 nearly put paid to me as I contracted whooping cough and mother had to trudge through the snow-covered streets looking for paraffin for a heater to help keep me warm.

My father had been a bit of a whizz at golf and played for the county of Surrey. Later, the various silver cups he had won were sold to buy my first bike. In those days it was possible to just leave the bike unlocked and never imagine that it might not be there later. What has happened to society? Aunt Ando taught me how to ride and mopped up my tears when I fell into the nettle beds. It was on this bike that I was allowed to ride along the seaside to kindergarten, or the front as we called it. It must have been nearly 2 miles. At this time motor traffic was minimal and not considered a worry for a child cycling to school.

One day, after a few hundred yards, I thought I was a bit chilly and realised I had forgotten my underpants!

MOTHER

My mother, born in 1917, suffered the death of her much-loved father when she was only eleven years old, and when brother Dick, her only sibling, emigrated to Brazil at a young age, this was another terrible blow for her.

Margaret, or Peggy as she was known in the family, was sent to school in Bolsover Road, Eastbourne, together with her two cousins, Rachel, and Dorothy (my godmother); they all developed chilblains in winter and had themselves to remove ice from the wash basins.

Mother learned to play the piano and was quite gifted. She also enjoyed acting, and in later years joined an amateur group that performed locally. Her memory was excellent. "Treading the boards" was something she would have loved to continue doing, but I believe this was frowned on by her mother.

After she married my father, she lived for a while with me and her in-laws and at Bayhorne and took a job at a garage in Horley until she moved to Eastbourne to be with her widowed mother. My father died of TB in 1943 at the age of 35. Looking back, I can now see how hard it was, and still is today, for a single parent to bring up a child.

Mother was strict over many things. She would not tolerate a failure to sit up straight at table, believing this would lead to a concave chest. I remember having a walking stick put between my shoulders at table on a few occasions, just to bring the point home. The fact that my father had died of TB, was always at the back of her mind.

She loved poetry and, because of her excellent memory, she would quote her favourite poems endlessly, usually whilst she was overseeing my bath or putting me to bed. Sadly, I never really appreciated them. She suffered from painful duodenal ulcers which flared up from time to time. She was operated on by a doctor, who decided to "see exactly what was going on inside" and left her the most enormous scar from the top to the bottom of her stomach. Nothing untoward was found. I believe her condition was due to a nervous disposition. If there was a cold going around, mother would catch it, and they were usually terrible colds, necessitating inhalations under a towel, and recovery took several weeks.

For her, time-keeping was a problem. "I'm coming" did not actually mean what it should! Granny would call out that lunch was ready, but mother would not appear until much later than we would have wished. If there was a letter to be posted to catch the final clearance of the post-box, she would dash off on her bike a minute before zero hour. Despite this, she managed to hold down a typing job at the Eastbourne Town Hall, which she had learned at the garage in Horley.

Shopping took forever, because mother loved chatting to everybody and hearing about their families. She was very personable and kind. She would happily shop for others when needed. The change always had to be scrutinized and the pennies counted out on returning home. She always kept the maisonette in Royal Parade very clean and she stoked the two sitting room fires with coal. The main boiler, in the kitchen, which she looked after worked well, but all this was a lot of work.

Mother was very good looking and had many suitors. Very unfortunately for her, the men she attracted were always married. So, I had "uncle" so-and-so who was taking us to Rye for a couple of days! One such visit proved very interesting because we met a lovely water colourist, Mrs. McIndoe, wife of the famous plastic surgeon – whose legacy can be seen at the Queen Victoria Hospital in East Grinstead.

Later in her life, when we were living abroad, mother was particularly vulnerable. Sadly, she became the victim of a con man, who I really believe she loved. He would disappear and she never knew where he went and could not contact him, but always had to wait for him to call. The whole saga became a heartbreaking affair for the whole family, especially when we learned that this man had relieved her of several thousands of pounds that she could ill afford to lose.

Mother was a devoted grandmother and loving mother, always encouraging me in whatever I tried to do. We always got on reasonably well, though I would not have called the relationship a very close one.

Peggy and Eileen, Edward's mother, were as different as chalk and cheese as they say. The two of them did their best to get on, and tip-toed round each other if there was any disagreement! But I shall never forget mother's outstretched arms to welcome us back to Eastbourne when we visited her. She invited us to stay with her when we began looking for a home in Eastbourne. It was thanks to her that we bought the flat in Bolsover Road which was to be our home for 18 years. Mother loved that spacious flat as much as we did, and sometimes came to stay. Once, when Edward was away, she was enjoying a jacuzzi bath; getting in was easy, but she soon discovered that she was unable to get out. It was impossible for me to lift her, so I was obliged to call 999, whereupon a couple of young firemen arrived and were happy to help!

In her later years, mother suffered from heart problems and because of this she was in and out of hospital several times. Eventually she was admitted when it was more serious and seen in

A & E; I never understood why she was not admitted to the heart ward. In the evening of March 11th. 2002, I sat with her as she complained that there seemed to be a huge weight on her chest, making it hard for her to breathe. A small amount of oxygen was administered through the nose, but it did not help much. I decided to return home to make our supper which was a big mistake. Why did I not call the hospital chaplain? Halfway through our meal a call came from the hospital to tell me to come. Mother was at the end of life. By the time I arrived, there were several staff around her bed, but it was all too late. Regret is something one must eventually come to terms with.

COUSINS

As background regarding the family, I want to mention my cousins. My mother Peggy's brother Dick, who had joined the Blue Funnel shipping company and been made manager of the business in Brazil, where he married a Brazilian girl called Winnie and had three boys. The eldest cousin John will come up several times in my story, his younger brothers were George and Tony. Dick sent all three boys to school at St. Paul's in London.

John married a girl called Asla and they had two children, Carina and Richard, but he divorced Asla and married Andrea with whom he had a daughter Natasha. John was a sun worshipper and loved sailing and diving; and, sadly, he developed skin cancer and died in 1994. He kept in touch with Asla after she moved to the USA.

He visited us in the UK and was kind enough to invite our daughter Melanie to visit him in Rio de Janeiro. My mother went out to visit him for a week or two, and at that time Edward stayed for a night when he was on a business trip to Colombia, which he reached by means of a Brazilian airline that offered an overnight stop in Manaus.

George was banker and married a girl called Nancy and they had two children, Christina and Susan. George, died of a heart attack on the tennis court at the age of 45.

Tony married a Swedish lady called Christine who had been an air stewardess with PanAm, and they had a son called Andrew who married an older Brazilian girl named Adriana and they provided Tony with a granddaughter called Clara.

Tony invited Edward and me to the most wonderful holiday in Brazil, and I will tell you more about that later. He and Christine were always very good about visiting us and, when mother was alive, we all met up in Devon for a holiday. Tony developed a rare blood cancer for which he sought many treatments and altered his diet drastically, but sadly it was all to no avail, and he died in 2021.

There were three other male cousins on my father's side of the family. A Sopper uncle emigrated to South Africa and married a local girl named Violet, and they had three sons: James, Tom and Harry. As far as I know these boys have not been to Britain, and I have never met any of the family. However aunt Ando made a point of visiting them all when she was working for the Red Cross in Swaziland. She told me that they were all very tall, that James had a granddaughter born in 2003 and that Harry had three children: Natalie, Samantha and Leslie. It seems very unlikely that we will ever meet.

FIRST STEPS ON FOREIGN SOIL

Mother decided it would be fun to go to Boulogne for the day taking a trip on one of the paddle steamers that left from Eastbourne pier. On the boat a rather mysterious gentleman sat beside us and from time to time partially lifted the lid of a box containing very black overripe bananas, bits of which he proceeded to cut off with a knife and eat. According to him one should always eat them in that state. The fact that he had put the knife in his mouth seriously shocked mother.

Boulogne was rather boring; we didn't get much beyond the harbour. However, we were brave enough to enter a shop and buy a few miniature bottles of liqueur.

The return journey was blessed by a magnificent summer thunderstorm with torrential rain and frightening fork lightening. No sign of banana man!

Although we set foot on foreign soil, we did not need a passport and it occurred to me that when we did not see banana man return on the boat that he might have chosen to follow a gallic way of life.

A VISIT TO PARIS, 1954

My second trip to France came about when aunt Ando invited me to join her on a trip to Paris, with one of her friends and a daughter my age who was going too.

We had an exhausting time rushing round all the usual iconic places, climbing the Eiffel Tower and marvelling at the strange sights and smells. I bought a bottle of red wine to bring home and nearly made it, but I dropped it in a London gutter before taking the train back to Eastbourne.

Ando's sister Catriona, or Giz as we always called her, often invited mother and me to London to a ballet or to Bertram Mills Circus. I think they were trying to make up for the loss of their brother, my father.

Giz used to go to London to work and nobody really knew what she did as she kept quiet about it. Later we learned that she was on the staff of SOE the Special Operations Executive. Its agents dealt with sabotage and subversion behind enemy lines, mainly in France. After the war Giz was awarded an MBE for her work. She belonged to the Special Forces Club in London and I remember going there to stay with her. She was Secretary of the Club for about 8 years.

THE BOY NEXT DOOR

This was the son, a few years my senior, of the owners of a small hotel which usually welcomed coach trips from the North. He also possessed a projector and some Laurel and Hardy and Charlie Chaplin films, and he kindly agreed to come and show them at my birthday parties. How we giggled and squirmed, and giggled some more -- until our stomachs ached. This was a huge success, so much so that the children didn't want to leave when their mothers came to fetch them.

There was plenty of entertainment around and mother scraped some money together to buy tickets to see Arthur Rubinstein, a Polish American pianist, who came to perform in Eastbourne.

Then there was Uncle Bertie at the bandstand just over the road from us, now derelict. He came on Saturdays in the holidays and was a popular entertainer for children. On the pier were the exciting slot machines and for a penny one could watch the skeleton in the bedroom or "What the Butler Saw".

I was allowed to hang out with a man who gave pony rides. Tony the pony was a docile creature and for sixpence he could be led up and down a green sward near the sea, which is now all tarmacked over for parking. Imagine nowadays allowing a young girl to spend the day helping someone like this. Unthinkable! There were often bus trips up to the top of the Downs for a walk with Kirsty.

A VISITOR FROM BRAZIL, 1957

This year I changed schools locally. Excitingly my uncle and cousins living in Rio de Janeiro came to visit. Mother's brother, Dick, had taken a job with a merchant shipping company that served Brazil and had moved to Brazil shortly after their father died in 1943. He married a local girl, and they were blessed with three boys.

One excitement that John, my eldest "Brazilian" cousin, and I shared was going to a 3D film. We must have been given special glasses to wear, and what a shock it was when we felt we needed to duck under the seats to avoid the Red Indians' arrows coming directly at us, and later having to lift our feet when it seemed the cinema was flooded. WOW! That was great entertainment.

LEARNING TO SWIM

As we are an island nation surely everybody should learn how to swim.

The sister of a friend finally taught me how to swim in the indoor saltwater baths that we enjoyed in Eastbourne. It was good fun there because there was a long slide. In the sea I had a large black inner tyre from a garage, and I used this to play around; Kirsty came to the beach with me, but she did not swim very much.

I was never blessed with much stamina, but later when at boarding school where all the normal swimming strokes were required, I eventually won prizes for style and later earned a "dolphin" badge which was mainly for mastering life-saving skills.

Sea swimming was always preferable to indoor pools and at the time of writing this (in my eighties) I am still able to enjoy a swim in the summer.

PETS AND THEIR CHARACTERISTICS

You have already met Kirsty our Scottish terrier. We were told she was of a very good pedigree, and this was apparently confirmed by the fact that the roof of her mouth was black.

She hated cats and always rushed into the garden barking to chase off any intruders. However, during a walk on the front, a cat ambushed her from a doorway, and she leapt sideways and took off faster than an Olympic sprinter!

Bones, preferably lamb bones, were a favourite treat and were eventually taken into the garden to bury. We would spy on her from the kitchen window as she was very furtive and didn't wish us to see where the interment took place. When Kirsty returned to the kitchen we would notice the mud on her nose and would say "Oh Kirsty, what have you been up to?" whereupon she would make a face which I thought looked like a guilty grin.

One day Kirsty dug up one of these bones and I was horrified to see it was covered in maggots. UGH! Had she already indulged? So off to the vet we went, and he assured me that dogs have very different stomachs from humans, and they are well able to cope with such things. No worries!

We also had a pet budgerigar, Joey. He was very

friendly and came out of the cage to fly around the sitting room. He loved to sit on a fork just as we were about to put it into our mouth during lunch. Then he would attach himself to Granny's newspaper and sit there shredding bits until the floor was covered in scraps of paper.

Finally, there was a tortoise. We named him Sir Ptolemy after a character in one of the Beatrix Potter books. He must have been about 15 years old judging by the number of lines on his shell. In winter, he would hibernate in a box of straw in the garden shed. Then in spring we would have to ensure that his lips were not sealed by offering tempting foods such as tomatoes, lettuce, dandelion leaves, flowers and grapes. He would come out to meet us if we called him and sometimes, he would bang his shell on the back door until we opened it.

One summer Sir Ptolemy began exploring the coal heap in a corner of the garden and digging there. His appetite became phenomenal. I came out to find him one afternoon and rushed straight back to mother calling "Mummy, come quickly, I think Ptolemy is dying!" He was puffing and blowing and seemed in distress. Soon the reason became apparent as an egg was deposited on the lawn. So,

Sir Ptolemy became Ptolemina. We carefully took the egg and placed it in cotton wool in the airing cupboard but, sadly, nothing ever came of it.

BOARDING SCHOOL, 1954-58

Mother and I attended church, usually an evening service, and it was at a time when my hormones were going ballistic, and I often felt like fainting during the service. This led to Christian connections. Mother and granny knew a delightful vicar by the name of John, who appreciated their circumstances. Because of those he suggested that I should sit an exam at a school where he was on the Board, and which offered six financially assisted places for children with one or no parents.

The result was a place at a school in Salisbury where John was later to become Bishop. Mother was so pleased and proud. At this time my faith grew and confirmation at the cathedral was a highlight of my time at school there. These were the years to be making lifelong friendships, which are so important in life. But I also began a wonderful period of association with the cathedral, and with the organist and his wife to be, who was my piano teacher. Occasionally I was allowed to go into the organ loft and turn the pages.

When the organist was courting my piano teacher, they used to drive around town in a three-wheeler and managed to squeeze a cello inside as well. Later I was allowed to attend their wedding in the cathedral.

Scholastically I did not excel, but I managed to pass enough exams. Mother would have liked me to go to university, but I really didn't feel it was my scene.

So, what was I going to do? The school turned out some brilliant brains and the usual supply of missionaries and nurses. But these options did not appeal to me.

LEARNING FRENCH IN SWITZERLAND, 1959

Once again, my lucky star came into action. A wealthy friend of my mother, who had a brother working in Switzerland suggested that we so there for a holiday and see whether I could find someone to teach me French. I think I had already felt an affinity with the French language, but my knowledge of it was quite limited.

Having arrived by car at night, the sight that greeted me in the morning quite took my breath away. The view across Lake Geneva from the eastern end was spectacular, looking towards the Rhone valley with the Dents du Midi, covered in the first snowfall of the year, sparkling in the sunlight.

We arrived in September and explored the option of a girls' school in Chateau d'Oex, but we discovered that all the housework including the washing up had to be done by the pupils!

I was already in love with the country having read the book "Heidi" by Johanna Spyri, and I had told Mother that when I married, I wanted my husband to take me to Switzerland.

The Mademoiselle that we found, and who I came to live with, was called Emilie, but we came to call her Mittie. She was a lady of later middle age and became like a surrogate mother for me. There was already a German student staying when I arrived. It was no picnic as we had to speak French all the time. Once I escaped to see a film in English, but upon returning was told to make a summary of it in French. Not much of an escape! All this was funded by mother's man friend.

The first three months were hard. To say nothing of the skiing. My skis were too long, and it was never going to be a sport for me. Infuriatingly, the English crowds who came out for a week or so and unlike me had lessons every day, seemed to be up and away very easily.

As the end of my year there approached, I thought I must do something before the money runs out, and I was advised to take a secretarial course -- which meant learning typing and shorthand in French, by the Aimé Paris method, so that's how my evenings were taken up.

I didn't want to go back to England yet, and I going to need a job.

Happily, Mittie knew someone in the Advertising Dept. of Nestlé, a multinational Company based in nearby Vevey, and he arranged for me to be called for an interview. Shaking with nerves when it came to the shorthand tests, I was surprised to find that I had been hired as a bilingual typist.

There were lots of young men and the place seemed a bit like a marriage bureau, so it was not long before I was going out with young Swiss, Italian and Greek men.

What a life! Excellent subsidised lunches in the Company restaurant and swims in the lake afterwards. My lucky star was shining brightly.

OBERAMERAGAU, 1960

A couple of ladies from the English church in Territet (Montreux) were going to drive to see the famous Passion Play in Germany which only took part every 10 years. They asked me if I would like to join them and combine it with my trip to England. Naturally I jumped at the chance.

But shock, horror! It was only when we were about to cross over the border from Switzerland into Germany by lake Constance that I realised I did not have my passport with me. We were booked into a hotel after what had been a long drive and from there, I telephoned Mittie to look for the passport and put it into the post a.s.a.p. Thanks to the efficiency of the Swiss postal service, the document arrived the next morning, so we could all breathe again.

Upon arrival in this small village, I was surprised to see that everybody, including the men, all had long hair. This was not the trend in those years. It was necessary for this play for which we had tickets, and which was due to start the following day and last all day.

The stage was open to the skies and various birds flew across from time to time. All the actors had been carefully chosen and it was considered a great privilege to be involved.

The life of Jesus enacted like this proved to be a very moving experience for me. There was a small problem which meant that I had to leave before the crucifixion – which perhaps was for the best – because I had to get transport to Munich to catch a train back to the UK.

During the long rail journeys home, I had plenty of time to meditate on all that I had seen and treasure the memories of that special time.

AN UNFORGETTABLE WALK IN THE ALPS

This came about in 1960 thanks to a delightful Scottish lady called Averyl, a longstanding friend of Mittie, and Averyl and her mother were resident nearby. She was a member of the Swiss Alpine Club and one day she asked me if I would like to join her and two friends from the Club on a walk, along with Bunny her dog.

This took place over a long weekend and started with a train ride down the Rhone valley to Sierre, followed by a bus ride up the Val d'Anniviers. We arrived at pre-booked lodgings and settled down for the night. Well before dawn I was awakened and told I must dress and get going! Breakfast was brought with us, and we set off and started to climb up through the forest until a suitable spot was found for breakfast, by which time the sun was coming up.

I had my skiing boots on, and they were very comfortable and very different from today's boots. They were made of lovely leather.

We continued up past the tree line, and onto the scree, and then took a left turn at which point Averyl pointed to a distant peak and declared that that was our destination. What? There was no turning back, and we kept going until we reached the Cabane de Tracuit refuge hut, by which time, having spent the day climbing steadily, evening was upon us, and we were into the snow.

Having eaten a meal offered by the cabane guardian we collected snow to brush our teeth and went off to bed. Next morning, we had to cross a glacier, which meant being roped to each other and to the dog. We had to continue to the little pimple of a mountain called the Bishorn (4,135 m. or 13,894 ft.) and return before the sun became too warm making the glacier tricky. At the summit we marvelled at the incredible view all around and a brandy bottle came out. If only I had had a good camera in those days!

Thank you so much, dear Averyl, for that amazing experience.

EASTER IN ROME AND TOURING ITALY, 1961

With an English friend and work colleague called Sue I decided to join a tour group for a few days break and we took the train, which went straight to Rome without any changes.

Upon arrival, Sue and I decided to break away from the group and explore the shops. I was looking for some shoes. Very soon a couple of young men hovered around us, and I heard one of them muttering about the "bella bionda", presumably referring to me as Sue was dark haired. They introduced themselves as university students of architecture, and, for some unaccountable reason, Sue and I decided that we were Swiss, so we spoke Vaudois (Swiss French with them).

It was clear that we were not going to get rid of them and they insisted they wanted to show us the sights. Before we knew it, we were taken to the Trevi Fountains, one of Rome's fifty monumental fountains. Sue reminded me that, because it was Lent, many of the famous statues around town were draped in mauve cloth.

Next, we were driven to the beach resort of Ostia, about an hour away, where we all sat on the sandy beach and chatted (in French). The young men were very respectful. Looking back and thinking about today's youth, such carefree interaction might be seen as unwise. Clearly, my star was on watch.

Back in town we were invited to a bistro, where I seem to remember the walls were lined with endless bottles of wine. I can't say who paid for the drinks or meals, but I feel sure Sue and I must have chipped in.

Whether or not we were in St. Mark's Square to hear the Pope's speech I can't recall, but on the whole, we have good memories of the trip.

In the summer of that year, Mittie and I decided to join a 10-day coach tour from Lugano taking us all round Italy. This took us to Milan, Genoa, Pisa, Florence, Siena, Rome, Naples, Sorrento, Capri, Bologna and Venice.

I climbed the Leaning Tower of Pisa and visited the Sistine Chapel in Rome. Capri in those days was a darling little island with a small square in the centre, where a tree had benches right round the trunk and a donkey carried loads around the place. When I visited years later, I was disgusted to see concrete everywhere with plazas and up-market shops selling the expensive things that one sees all over the world.

This amazing trip cost each of us about 300 Swiss

francs and included everything.

Of course, during holidays, I also visited mother and granny in the UK, and sometimes mother came out to Switzerland. This went on for nearly three years.

MEETING MY HUSBAND TO BE, 1961

An Englishman, called Edward arrived to stay with Averyl and when we met in the road I was surprised to learn that he had been one of Mittie's boarding pupils five years earlier, before returning to England to seek a first job. Most of those five years he worked for Unilever in its Head Office on the embankment in London. Eventually he approached his boss about a potential appointment elsewhere, but nothing came up except a mention of a possible move to Hull. This was not what he had in mind, and so he responded to an advertisement in the Daily Telegraph offering a career in the Far East. His mother had introduced him to bird watching as an eight-year-old, and he had been a keen birdwatcher for years and this seemed the perfect opportunity for him to see new ones.

It turned out that the company advertising was Nestlé and that he had been hired by the firm I was working for; and that he was to have some months of basic training before being posted to somewhere in Asia. He was delighted that Mittie could let him a room and we usually took the train to Vevey together.

After about 3 months he proposed marriage. However, I did not feel ready for that and in any case, it would have meant him having to forgo the job in Thailand which had been offered to him. In those days companies did not pay for wives on a first overseas assignment. We agreed on an unofficial engagement.

No, we did not make love before he left for Thailand. We were not brought up like that. It would have felt wrong. Call us prudish or whatever you like, but this is how it was.

Soon after Edward left for Thailand, I became restless and decided to go to Greece.

GREECE AS A NANNY, 1962

I travelled by boat overnight from Genoa to Athens, in November, and that was very enjoyable. When I arrived at the home where I was to stay there was a huge bunch of red roses awaiting me arranged, of course, by Edward.

This move was a mistake as I was soon to find out. The boy "O", aged two, had been so spoiled by a Greek nurse that he told me immediately "isse vromiara" ('you are a filthy pig'), or words to that effect and he tore out lumps of my hair!

Eventually when things had calmed down a bit we used to go for walks in the park and I drank tsai cognac (tea with brandy) to ward off the cold while O. played. We passed the Evzones on duty in their place at the Palace gates; they were wearing kilts, and they used to wink at me when I too was wearing a nice warm Scottish regimental kilt, lent to me by Edward before he left for Thailand. I was allowed to meet up once a week with other English nannies and we were soon a group of eight plus four university boys. They were a really proud bunch and were delighted to show us round the local hot spots.

The winter of 1962-63 was an extremely cold one in Europe, and there was plenty of snow in Athens.

My enduring memory of Athens was the smell of wet cement as there seemed to be plenty of construction work going on. After four months I came home to see Granny, who wasn't very well, and left another nanny to do battle with O.

WHAT NEXT? 1963

Thanks to aunt Giz, who lived in London, I landed a job and I lived with her from Monday to Friday when I was working and on Friday evening I would catch the train to Chichester and pick up a bus to Selsey to stay with my mother and granny, where they were living in a small draughty cottage near the sea with our dog Kirsty, who was now in her dotage. It was while I was in Chichester waiting for a bus that I heard on the news of the assassination of President Kennedy in November.

My work in London began when I joined an agency that found me some dregs of typing jobs in appalling places. One such job was near Tower Bridge in an office which would have been in place in a Dickens' novel; the manual typewriter was antiquated and the work unbelievably boring.

My last agency job was a temporary one at Martins' Bank in a splendid new building in St. James's Street, SW 1. Happily, the bank decided to pay off the agency and keep me on the permanent staff. Things were looking up. The bank had a cafeteria at its Hanover Square branch, and I found I could get there for lunch, and, in the evening, I walked back to auntie's flat in Belgravia, doing this I clocked up a fair few miles walking each week.

Although I was engaged and let everybody know it,

a young bank employee and I made friends and I used to ride on the back of his motor bike to attend events like concerts at the Royal Albert Hall.

Hand-written letters went back and forth between Edward and I. Edward's letters all about the exotic country he was in were all well written and interesting. Sadly, all of them were lost in a house fire, which you will hear about later.

In those days a call from Bangkok to England, which was expensive, required one to visit the main post office there and submit the request and wait for it when a booth would be made available. I think Edward must have made all the calls at his end. It was to be years before we had e-mail or smart phones. Even from Switzerland to England one had to book a call and wait, sometimes for ages, for a "slot".

So, we planned our wedding long distance with the dates set for the civil marriage on March 11th. 1965, and the Church wedding the next day. Edward always claims that he fixed it so that the anniversary would be exactly a week after his birthday!

Mother   Granny

Me Feeding the Chickens

Kirsty and Ptolemina

Me on Eastbourne
Beach

Me with the Pony

Aunt Ando   Averyl

Switzerland looking over Lake
Geneva towards the Rhone Valley
with France beyond

Mittie

Our Wedding Day

Cousin Tony and Christine

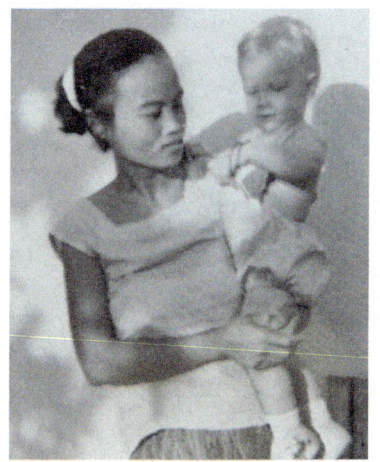

Ahmah Narlee
with Philip

Butter wouldn't
melt

Angkor Wat

Philip in school
uniform

Asia Minors

British school sports day

PART 2: OUR WORKING LIVES TOGETHER
MARRIAGE AND HOME LEAVE, 1963

The marriage had to be in Switzerland, of course, because of all the friends we had made there including those that we had worked with during our time in Vevey with Nestlé.

My mother came out to stay with Mittie and Edward's parents, Charles and Eileen, came over too. Sadly, granny was not able to come, but Edward before flying from England to Thailand in 1962 had gone to meet her in Selsey.

My wedding dress, which was made in London by Mrs. Kielbrianska, a Polish lady, was brought out by my friend Jane in the boot of her Triumph Herald. It was modelled after a picture I had seen in a Harrods catalogue. The material was 'duchesse' satin and the veil with acorns embroidered on it was a copy of one Princess Margaret had had. All our friends from our times in Vevey rallied round and several gave us special presents: I particularly remember a dish beautifully painted by Mrs. Walkinshaw.

The ceremony took place in the English church in Territet, and I was given away by the Head of the Advertising Department at Nestlé, where I had worked.

Edward has asked his friend Heath Houston to be best man, but Barclays Bank was unable to arrange to free him from the Caribbean, and so Paul Treuthardt, an Australian news correspondent who had married Gill Lydbury – a friend from Edward's time in Blackheath, when he was working at Unilever House stepped up.

The ceremony was followed by a special lunch at the Excelsior Hotel by the lake in Montreux, where Edward had spent the previous night.

We spent our wedding night in a hotel near the station in Lausanne as we would be taking a train to Davos early next morning for a week of winter sports. We were both sure we were a bit rusty so next day we hired a charming guide who, learning that we were on our honeymoon, said that she too had been married on March 13th. and so we headed to a restaurant where we ordered a bottle of champagne!

Our hotel was very comfortable, and we visited it again some twenty years later. One Swedish lady, the wife of a senior executive in one of the major lumber companies, insisted on giving us a tray decorated with a ski scene, and we still have it.

Next, we flew back to England and attended a small party in London at the United Services Club made possible by Maynard Goodall, Eileen's brother-in-law, who was a member. This allowed all our English friends and relatives, who had not been able to come to Switzerland, to celebrate with us and see our photos from the wedding.

Edward and I now had the rest of his three months leave to enjoy and to treat as part of our honeymoon and thus quite prolonged. We went down to the cottage in Brampton in Suffolk where Charles and Eileen lived. Some days later Heath Houston arrived, having escaped from Trinidad, and drove us up to Scotland, travelling up the A9 when it was still a single-track road with passing places.

We visited his parents and the west coast including the island of Handa and other places. He then drove down to stay near Brampton, and Edward took him to Buss Creek in Southwold, and to Walberswick and Minsmere, and after a few days they got up early with the objective of seeing 100 species or more of birds before bed; they actually saw 102 species.

Finally, after tearful farewells with our mothers, we set off on a slow journey back to Thailand via Beirut and Kashmir.

I was never very fond of flying, but it was

something I now had to get used to. The Boing 747 became my favourite plane as their landings and take-offs were so smooth.

BEIRUT, 1965

We were booked into the St. George's Hotel; this was beside the sea, which was looking rather more green than blue. A friend in Switzerland had given us the address of a Beirut family of carpet sellers to contact, which we did. In fact, the contact, George Oyachek, rented a shop on the ground floor in St. George's Hotel where he sold oriental carpets!

The welcome we were given was more than warm; it was exceedingly generous. Rachide, the driver he found us – perhaps a taxi driver from outside the hotel, donned a bernous or Arab headdress and cloak for the occasion. He loved to make remarks like "If Edward isn't nice to you just let me know", or "such a beautiful man is your husband, not like an English". I must mention a shop sign I noticed which read "Haute Couture – High Sewing"!

George took us to two different night clubs, where we saw some Arab belly dancers, the first club, part-way down a cliff by the sea, was called the Grotte Bleu.

We were also invited to George's home and he and his family wanted to hear all about our wedding and our planned onward travel. One reason for stopping in Beirut was to buy Indian rupees at a good rate of exchange, as these would make our next stop less costly, and with George's help a cooperative bank was found.

We made the essential visit to Baalbeck, in its valley further inland, to see the remains of six massive temples to three gods: Jupiter, Venus and Bacchus. This was very instructive. Two thousand years of Phoenician, Greek, Roman and Arab history were shown to us in the space of an hour or so. The ridge the car had to climb and cross was 5,300 ft. above sea level. Along the way we passed several nomads, some in the shade under canvas, others accompanied by a few bored looking camels.

Pan American Airways flew us to Teheran in a Clipper jet where we had to refuel at the airport, after which we took off for New Delhi, where we arrived at 3 a.m. local time. Nothing was open, and there were no seats after we had collected our bags, so we lay down to rest on the airport floor until our connecting flight.

The heat was so great I thought we would pass out. But at 6.30 a.m. a rather tired couple, feeling a bit sick, walked across to the Indian Airways desk and out onto tarmac for a Viscount to take to Srinagar – a two-hour flight. Myna birds and their calls are a lasting memory of the old Delhi airport.

KASHMIR, 1965

This is part of Jammu and Kashmir and there are unresolved issues due to territorial claims by Pakistan, and a border with China that is contested.

Friends had recommended that we stay on a houseboat and how exotic that was! To get to it we were driven from the airport to the town and then on to the lake shore through scenery which made us blink – doubly so as we were so tired. There were trees springing up out of water, cows with ribs looking as though they might pierce the skin, grim shops, mostly shacks, with goods half sitting in the muddy road, along with their owners, some smoking hookah pipes. Very few wore shoes, but they waded through whatever they had to.

We remember the lake as Nagin Bahg (but Nishat Bagh may be correct) which is a beautiful and very interesting lake which is half surrounded by pale green mountains, revealing an occasional snowy peak in the distance. The trees here are mainly chinar and willow, although a great many walnut trees are to be found elsewhere in Kashmir.

We were met at the lakeside by a shikara. Shikaras are everywhere. They paddle the local canoes. The taxi shikaras have couches, cushions, canapes, coloured curtains and comfort. They are the answer to coronary cases, as there is nothing so soothing as being paddled along rhythmically by two heart-shaped oars at the end of which sit dark skinned people crouched over dark-skinned toes.

They are not to be compared with the Venetian gondolas because they are much more peaceful: no music or cries of "look out" – for whatever might be being tipped on your head.

The paddled boat glides its way through floating gardens, rushes or willow trees. The little floating lake gardens contain rounded mounds and looked from a distance like Christmas puddings. Here they grow watermelons, which stand out as the mounds, as well as some vegetables.

We were rowed out to a houseboat named Sobra, and met by the Wangnoo family, who owned it (and live on an adjoining boat). The family had been in the travel business for three generations and had provided support for travel in the Himalayas by Teddy Roosevelt on foot and on horeseback.

It was raining and cold, so we were quickly handed warm cloaks, or phrans, which have just a slit for the head and long sleeves. One makes a tent around oneself with this garment, and within it below you there is central heating: this comes from a round wicker basket with a handle which contains a clay jar filled with hot charcoal. Very comforting!

There was a comfortable sitting area with plenty of cushions and we could watch the world go by, either when sitting on the upper part of the boat or inside below deck.

Now in an area like this you would think nothing much happens, and that spending money wouldn't be easy. However, there is never a minute's peace from eager merchants, who will glide past the windows in shikaras, and plead with you even during mealtimes unless you specify otherwise. Boats are laden with articles ranging from shaving cream to orange squash: "Salaam Saib Sir…. I got good Kashmir wools" or "Madam, you like and see my jewellery please?" There is no escape. He boards the boat and before you know it endless little parcels are untied, and the floor strewn with glistening trinkets, or brightly coloured hand-embroidered cloth. Of particular interest are the hand painted papier mache works and hand carved goods in walnut. Next, the hairdresser appears, but to wash where and with what? One doesn't ask. The flower merchant claims his name is Mr. Marvellous and he comes with his boat full of roses, cornflowers, red-hot pokers, yellow iris and daffodils.

Let me say a bit more about the boat itself. You step from a shikara onto a platform and then into the living room, which is very comfortably furnished and leads into the dining room. Next comes the galley from which steps lead up to the flat roof, where there are deck chairs. Beyond the galley comes the first double bedroom, then a bathroom (with flush!) and right at the end of the boat another double bedroom and bathroom. Planks run along both sides of all these crafts not only to enable the servants to trot back and forth without disturbing the inhabitants, but also to facilitate the punter's job when the boat is on the move.

But it is we who are on the move! One day we are taken to some formal Persian gardens, using a shikara to cross two lakes to get there. On another day we travelled by car about 30 miles to Gulmarg, which lies to the west of Srinagar. The name Gulmarg means "Flower meadow". We hired ponies for the trek up to 8,000 ft. above sea level, winding our way up through four kinds of different strongly scented pines. Edward, who had virtually never ridden a horse, managed somehow – but caused me much amusement, and produced even more inquisitive stares, by wearing the bernous he bought in Beirut. For me, coming over a precipitous path on horseback is like arriving on the edge of a ridge on skis, the only difference being that the horse knows what it is doing and the sooner one relies on its strong fetlock muscles the better.

The birds in Kashmir, particularly those around the lakes, seem to be so tame that even the most uninterested person surely cannot help but take notice of such examples as vivid coloured kingfishers as they dive tirelessly from early morning until dark using one's boat as their watch post. There were bee-eaters and rollers, and male and female paradise flycatchers flashing their long white or red tails in the willow trees, and there are yellow and black birds in the pine forest, all of them coming so close that using binoculars was almost unnecessary. This is birdwatching I enjoy.

11th June 1965. We have just returned from a two-day trip to the NE into the Himalayas to a place called Sonamarg, or 'Valley of Gold'. The trip began with a 55-mile car drive, following the river Siond steadily upwards, eventually leading to a grassy meadow and the hut in which we were to spend the night. We were accompanied by the driver, our houseboat man and guide, and one of the shikara paddlers serving as a porter.

Edward had a bad cold which didn't improve with the ever-increasing height. Nevertheless, some satisfactory birdwatching was done, and Edward reckoned we had seen total of eighty species.

Supper took place by candlelight in front of a log fire. The fire in our room was not so successful and simply smoked the room out. Afterwards a campfire was lit for our benefit.

The surrounding mountains and two visible glaciers were quite clearly illuminated by the moon. It was interesting to compare the vegetation with that of Switzerland at this height. Here we were situated on roughly the same parallel of latitude with Greece and yet there are deciduous trees growing up to as high as 11,000 ft., but precisely because of the elevation it did not seem anything like so high. From here we also had a beautiful view down to the village from where we had begun the climb, and beyond we could see the road snaking its way through the valley into not-so-distant China, or Tibet that was.

The mountain ponies are extraordinarily hardy as were the mountain men that accompanied us. They have dark brown, worn and cracked hard skin, like the rocks on which they walk barefoot.

During our return journey we stopped to look inside a watermill. About 5 or 6 dozen grains of what passed through the grindstone every minute, emitting only a few ounces of flour. Two men stood over and watched this painfully slow process. Another stop was made to see inside a Gujar's (or mountain man's) hut. These people were illiterate; they live high up in the mountains during summer, moving down with their flocks in winter. Theirs is a kill or cure existence, and the survivors live to a great age. I was horrified by what I saw inside this hut, which wasn't much, because having no window it was completely dark. Suddenly, I heard a cough and an old, withered hand emerged from the darkness. It turned out that the old lady on the floor was begging for an Aspirin as she suffered from fever and headache. Luckily, I had one in my camera case. Salama, our guide, told me these people often run after one for medicines.

We then wended our way back along a bumpy road beside the paddy fields, where men and women were wading through muddy water tending rice paddies; back at Nagin Bagh a shikara with a boat called "Crumpit – lovely big one" paddled us back to our houseboat.

Before we left, the Wangnoos invited us to their boat to a special meal, together with their children. The floor was decorated with rose petals laid out to spell "welcome". The meal was one we could eat with our fingers. We sat on the floor cross-legged, a position which came to us easily in those days.

It was time to move on and we left Kashmir with happy and enduring memories.

THAILAND, 1965

Flying in over the city of Bangkok I was struck by the wonderfully coloured pagoda roofs and, after landing, by everybody's colourful clothing.

In fact, the whole scene was an assault on my senses: the hustle and bustle of life, the outdoor cooking, the smells and the 'tuk tuk' taxis, or three-wheelers, with their noxious fumes.

Edward had arranged that we could live for six months in a house rented by an Australian couple, who had gone home on leave. We were to look after their dog Kilty as well.

It was a large airy place with a huge terrace leading off the bedroom and a long, highly polished wooden staircase, which Edward started to descend in his socks and promptly slid all the way down on his backside, clutching a briefcase.

Imagine my astonishment upon looking out of the window one morning to find a herd of buffalo making free in our garden. Later when the rains came the whole garden was under water, which was a delight for frogs that kept us awake at night with their amorous croaking.

We had to ask a servant to come and despatch a banded krait, which had sought refuge from the wet in one of the bushes. These are poisonous snakes, but this species is back-fanged meaning that they can almost never bite a person.

We had the visit of the Nestlé executive (who had stood in for my deceased father and given me away at our wedding) and to welcome him our driveway was illuminated with dozens of little candles in glasses, which looked very welcoming.

There was plenty of time for me to house-hunt. I found a place in a side street just a few hundred yards of the Company's office. As soon as I explored it I felt the presence of our, as yet unborn, children in that place, so I knew that this was where we were to come.

It was a two-storey house. On the ground floor were a living room, hall, small kitchen and toilet, and, on a slightly lower level, a dining room. Upstairs there was a large bedroom, and two smaller ones, one of which had an air conditioner, and a bathroom with basin and a cupboard with a shelf. The bath. which was of an unusual shape, was quite large and built into a corner. We could both get in!

When the time came, we settled into our new home with a cook and another girl for cleaning. This was a problem for me; I had been brought up to serve, rather than be served, and I found myself having to give orders to a lady who was old enough to be my mother. This was something I had to treat carefully.

We soon bought some beds and unpacked the few things we had brought from Europe, and I arranged to borrow a sewing machine from another English lady and made curtains for our bedroom.

At the back of the house was a concreted area with taps for washing, and, on the other side of this area in a separate building adjoining the garage, were rooms for three servants and the kitchen as there was no kitchen in the house.

The nights were almost impossibly sweaty and hot, so we bought a fan. The mosquitos were plentiful, despite the mesh panels at the windows to prevent them entering. Boy! Did they love my blood. Edward was not so plagued. Eventually when we could afford it, we bought an air conditioner for the bedroom.

When eventually I looked into the kitchen, I was amazed at what our cook had been able to produce, as it seemed the only oven was a tin box placed over one of three holes for charcoal. The temperature was regulated by adding and removing charcoal from the lid, and surprisingly good meals were produced.

Some months later we heard a very strange noise. Upon inspection we discovered a termite colony in the garage. There seemed to be millions and they were slowly destroying the wooden wall. The pest control people dealt with it efficiently, happily we had caught it early.

Before coming on leave Edward had bought a sturdy Standard Vanguard shooting brake from a departing English couple. This was well able to stand up to the thrusting Bangkok traffic. It had a compass over the glove compartment, which proved a great help as I learned my way around. To stop me sticking to the seat I bought a double-sided rattan square which I sat on allowing air to circulate! Traffic lights sometimes worked and sometimes didn't. This was fun! A traffic policeman would then eventually appear and try to sort out the mayhem.

At some point we realised that the pictures we put up were always at a slant and discovered that this was deliberate as the evil spirits might sit on one that was not askew, and so the maids made sure they were at a slant and thus slid off the picture!

As soon as I was able, I began work, typing letters to various companies in search of a job. Eventually, I was accepted at ECAFE, an Asian arm of the United Nations. This was on the other side of town and the compass proved a real friend.

I used to take a picnic and have this in the car during the lunch break. It was interesting to see how many young male typists there were at the UN. During the lunch hour they would fall asleep over their typewriters. On one occasion I returned from lunch and was rather startled to see the Indian gentleman, for whom I was working, was laid out on a bed snoring.

We had the local language all around us; during his first tour Edward had been obliged to take lessons in Thai and had eventually sat the exam offered by the British Chamber of Commerce, so he was able to communicate reasonably well. The servants had a few words of English and so we managed, but I'm ashamed to say that I never learned the language. I didn't need it at work.

Chinese dinners with 15 courses in Bangkok were never a problem. We had two or three business ones, and I never once had a stomach upset after these meals, partly because one had only a very little at a time and had long pauses between courses.

Edward was given three days of local leave to attend an international conservation conference in Khao Yai National Park (this I think was in 1966), and we had the pleasure of hosting two of the attendees at dinner in our Bangkok home. They were Sir Peter Scott from the Wildfowl Trust, now the Wildfowl & Wetlands Trust, and Dillon Ripley from the Smithsonian Institution in Washington D.C. Both were senior office bearers in WWF (the World Wide Fund for Nature) and it was lovely that their wives came too.

Looking around as he entered the dining room Sir Peter said, "Don't scare the 'chinchoks', they are your friends". He was referring to the little lizards that run up and down the walls and hide behind pictures: they are our friends because they help to keep the populations of mosquitoes and other small insects in check. We also had a "tokay" as an inhabitant, this is the onomatopoeic name given to the larger lizards.

I seem to have been blessed with fertility. Neither the French Cap nor the coil stopped me from becoming pregnant, and in January 1966, it was with great pleasure that I announced to Edward that we were expectant parents.

During my pregnancy I distributed business cards advertising secretarial help for anyone on holiday who needed it. Once it was a man who had fallen and broken his leg, another was an executive of an American company who had booked into a hotel and was clearly very busy as he sometimes kept me up late in the evening.

Our doctor was a British man married to a Thai wife, and I was happy to go to him once a month to check that all was progressing normally. There were no scans or photos, but we would not have wanted to know the sex in advance. Ignorance makes it all much more exciting when the time comes.

I was to give birth in the Bangkok Nursing Home, which was next door to the English church. The matron was an Australian lady. Each patient had a large, single room overlooking the tropical gardens. The bed was metal framed, which I found good to grab onto when the pains began.

Edward did not attend the birth, nor would I have wanted him to. Our son Philip came into the world, with some help from the ventouse or vacuum extraction method, at 21.14 on 1st. October weighing 8 lbs. 15 oz.

THAI WEEKENDS AWAY

It was important to get away from Bangkok from time to time. Some friends of ours, a British man and his Swedish wife, rented a large villa in Pattaya on the coast of the Gulf of Thailand, about a three-hour drive southeast. We were invited to join them several times and they had a young daughter which made company for Philip. So, we revelled in the sand and sunshine, and enjoyed snorkelling because the coral and fish were all visible quite near the shore. In those days there was just one hotel in Pattaya, and the nearby island was uninhabited.

Another escape was to the hills with cooler air and fewer mosquitos, typically we went to Khao Yai National Park, always with the hope of seeing elephants (which we did see) or tigers (which we only heard). On one drive in after the first climb to the plateau we saw the evidence of elephants having had fun pulling out the various poles or markers along the road.

Before I arrived in Thailand, and while Edward was visiting the park over a long Easter weekend, he and the Cumberledges drove up on Thursday evening in separate vehicles as usual. But the Saturday was a working half-day for Edward, so that he had to drive down to Bangkok on Friday evening and then back up on Saturday afternoon.

Next morning Edward woke early, but apparently pleaded a need for more sleep, and going out the Cumberledges saw a tiger attacking and killing a gaur (which is a large Asian bison); they teased Edward about this for years!

We were usually awakened at dawn by the joyous whoops of the gibbons, first when they called to each other early in the morning, and later as they moved through the jungle leaping from tree to tree.

Colourful birds were everywhere and a lasting memory of mine is watching a pair of hornbills flying over the golf course – the Thais originally saw the park in the light of an Indian Hill Station, providing rest and recreation despite the potential danger from elephants, tigers and other large game; but this changed as about this time conservation began to be promoted strongly.

Before coming on leave and our marriage Edward had been much involved in compiling a first rough list of the bird species known from the park, while the friends he went with compiled data on the many orchids, while also enjoying birdwatching. This had led to quite useful contacts with key people in the Forest Department.

The park provided small bungalows for rent and there was a central cafeteria, but it was noisy and the menu was limited so we used the small kitchen in the bungalow and took our cook with us – as we did when we went to Pattaya.

After the birth of Philip, I secured a half-day job working for an Israeli gentleman, who imported goods such as swimming costumes. I drove to work, which was not far away, and, near his premises, I was always amused to see the sign "Antique goods and artful things" over a nearby shop. My boss was delighted to know that I spoke French and he often dictated a dozen or more letters a morning to be typed in French, which I had rattled off quickly to the surprise of a Chinese girl who he employed as his accountant.

It was quite satisfying work, and I came home in time to enjoy Philip for the rest of the day. He was looked after by a cheerful new servant we employed called Narlee, who stayed with us until we left the country. She became pregnant whilst working for us and had thought she would just have the baby in the back room with her mother's help. I forbade this and insisted she go to the hospital. It was fortunate that I did because a Caesarean section was necessary. The Women's Hospital had a notice in the hall reading "If you want an ambulance to fetch you to the hospital, order it two weeks before"!

ANGKOR WAT, CAMBODIA, 1967

One of our first visitors in Bangkok was our Scottish friend Averyl, who had taken me on that unforgettable mountain walk. Because she was very thin and felt the cold, she flew into Bangkok wearing a thermal vest! I had stopped working at this point, so I had fun showing her the sights.

Averyl had told us she wanted to visit Angkor Wat, the temple in Siem Reap, Cambodia and wanted to pay for us to go with her.

Marvellous! This sounded like an opportunity not to be missed. However, we could not take Philip with us. Just at this time, very unfortunately, poor Narlee came down with dengue fever, which is spread by mosquitoes and can cause bleeding in strange places. It is usually not very serious, but we would have to look after Philip and thus miss the trip with Averyl; so, she set off on her own.

Later, after Averyl had gone home, Edward and I were able to take the trip to Angkor Wat, and this we did by bus overland through dry dusty country. We took a Thai bus to the Cambodian border and then crossed the border stream on foot, as the railway connection had been severed and no vehicle crossings were allowed. But a Cambodian school bus was there to meet us and take us to Siem Reap. The seats were so cramped that Edward was hardly able to fit his long legs in. The hotel was used to tourists, but the French they spoke was very strange!

The magnificent and mysterious ruins of Angkor Wat lie about fifty miles north-west of Phnom Penh, Cambodia's capital city. They are monuments from the Khmer civilisation between the ninth and thirteenth centuries.

The Thais sacked Angkor in 1431 and the Khmers abandoned it the following year. Nature then took over and the place soon disappeared into the jungle. Rumours about a hidden city circulated amongst travellers, but it wasn't until France assumed Imperial responsibilities and a wandering naturalist called Henri Mouhot, spied the grey towers of Angkor through gaps in the greenery and brought the finding to world attention.

He was astonished, as were we. The tree roots have wrapped themselves around masonry before plunging into the earth. The bas-reliefs are intricately carved and are proof of a sophisticated civilisation. The vastness of the place is intimidating. I remember starting to climb some steep steps which seemed endless and suddenly becoming quite dizzy, so that I had to carefully descend.

We stayed in the one hotel there and in the evening joined a group to be entertained by a group of dancers against the floodlit backdrop of the ruins.

Several weeks there would be insufficient to see everything, but we appreciated the little we did see and were very grateful to have had the opportunity to travel there.

OUR FIRST JOINT HOME LEAVE

We were coming to the end of our first tour together (Edward's second) and this meant a few months leave.

The doctor had given me the coil as a contraceptive, but I felt sure I was pregnant again and asked for it to be removed; another doctor assured me it would be fine and not to worry.

Edward had been offered the opportunity to study bird skins in the natural history museums in Chicago, Pittsburgh, Washington DC and New York, because he was in the process of writing a Field Guide to the Birds of South-east Asia, which had been agreed with the Managing Director of Collins, who had stopped in Bangkok to discuss this project on his way to Australia.

It was winter in Europe, and I set off on my own with Philip, having knitted him various woollen garments. We were going to stay over in Switzerland for a night or two with friend Averyl, but Philip picked up a cold, and I had to wake Averyl in the night because I felt I was having a miscarriage. So, we bundled Philip in a blanket, and she drove me to the hospital.

This was an unpleasant time, but after waiting and feeling very chilled and shaky, a lady doctor

arrived and took me in hand immediately for a
D and C. I lost a lot of blood, and in fact it was
concluded that the coil, or the removing of it, had
given me a blood infection.

A kind Dutch lady, the wife of another Nestlé
employee, and known to me through the church in
Vevey, took Philip to stay with her and her three
boys while I recovered in hospital.

When I arrived in the UK mother apparently nearly
fainted when she caught sight of me looking pale
and ill, as I had not told her about any of these
problems.

Edward flew back from the USA and joined us in a
freezing flat in Southwold on the Suffolk coast,
where we stayed for a few weeks.

MY SECOND TOUR IN THAILAND

Tours were now 2 years long instead of 3. In a way this was more difficult as we had less time to get stuck into something before it was time to prepare to leave again.

But we picked up the threads of our life easily enough. Edward's role had changed and now he often had to make business trips around the country and eventually we noticed that he had managed to visit nearly all the Thai provinces. Philip now attended a little school run by an American lady that was not far from our house. He looked so smart in his pale blue shirt and shorts, white socks and black patent leather shoes!

At home he played happily with Nongying, Narlee's little daughter. We had a plastic paddling pool in the garden to help them keep cool. One afternoon we discovered they had been quite mischievous and emptied an entire bottle of talcum powder all- round the patio and garden.

After my recent medical problems, I was afraid that I would be unable to conceive again, and I prayed hard that Philip would not be an only child, like Edward and me. So, you can imagine, it was with delight that I learned that another baby was on the way, and the expected date was due about the time of Philip's third birthday.

As before, I felt fighting fit and well the whole nine months. When the time came, I was just trying to ice a birthday cake for Philip and had to say "Sorry, but Mummy has to go to hospital now, enjoy your birthday".

Serious labour pains started about 11 p.m. and I told Edward to go home to bed, which he did. Nurses came and went to examine me, which was very painful. At one point I said to one of them "How many children do you have?". She replied "Oh, I don't have any, I'm not married". At 2 a.m. I was taken to the delivery ward and the doctor finally arrived. Once again, at about 5.30 a.m., it was a birth aided by the ventouse or suction method, without which it might have taken three days.

Melanie weighed in at 10 lbs 8 oz and looked like a three-month-old at birth. She was beautiful, of course. After her birth I was given a pill, and a much-needed cup of tea, and then I slept for 24 hours. When I awoke Melanie was beside me all wrapped in pink and looking gorgeous.

Back at home, I leant out of the bedroom window and said to Philip "Come and see your baby sister". But he didn't come! He wasn't in the slightest bit interested; he was far too busy playing with Nongying!

So, life went on and we continued to spend a weekend a month away, either at the beach or at the National Park.

I had bought an upright piano, which I enjoyed playing, although it was rather trying in that it was short, with only six octaves. However, the sounding board was very good and so the tone was a good quality. This gave it a healthy sale value when we came to leave.

Thai silk is lovely, it was very hard not to spend a lot of money on it. It came in various weights, and I had a dress made that I loved dearly, which I would give anything to still have. It was eventually burnt in our house fire in the Philippines.

Jim Thompson was an American who was known as the Thai Silk King. He was a businessman and architect and had come to Thailand just before the war (and the Japanese did not in fact occupy Thailand). He became known as the father of the Thai silk industry after World War 2, having fallen in love with the country and settled there permanently. Thai silk products were then considered old-fashioned, but Jim decided to revive the industry and founded the Thai Silk Company in 1948.

In the USA, the musical "The King and I" the

actors used Thompson's Thai silk for all their costumes. Country folk began weaving silk at home for an income and so avoided coming to live in an expensive Bangkok.

His home is now a museum containing all the best examples of traditional furniture and art, and it is surrounded by lush tropical gardens, and is situated next to a canal. The house was built from teak, obtained from various others houses that had been dismantled.

Thompson was unlike other expats. He was a retired army officer, an ex-architect, an antique collector and, reputedly, in the American CIA. Maybe this last activity had something to do with his mysterious disappearance from the hotel in the Cameron Highlands in Malaysia which is a hill station surrounded by jungle. When his absence was noticed people (Malaysian police, and American and British officers) carried out searches in the jungle for eleven days, but apparently no meaningful clue was ever found. Some said he might have been eaten by a tiger, but there was also a report of two black saloon cars descending from the mountain. For a period, there were rumours that he was alive and well and living in China. His legacy is the silk industry.

BACK TO SWITZERLAND, 1970

We arrived in Vevey at the end of 1970. Philip was four years old and Melanie one. After staying a few weeks in a chalet in Blonay, we found the perfect flat by the lakeside in Clarens. Mother was now living in Switzerland, having been offered the flat that Averyl was leaving. So this became a very special period for her as the flat we found was just a short walk away from her.

Philip was enrolled in a little local school in Montreux market-place, run by a kind and warm-hearted lady, and he began to learnt French. Melanie soon wondered where he went and wondered why she was being left out. She would ambush him when he returned home!

We were in a large house divided into flats, one on each floor. Ours was level with the main road. It had a long hallway, a sitting room, three bedrooms, a tiny kitchen and a bathroom. There was an enormous balcony overlooking the lake, which could be accessed from the sitting room and from two of the bedrooms (ours and the guest room). There were beautiful parquet floors throughout. The reflected sunlight from the lake made patterns chasing across our bedroom ceiling.

There was a large garden with a mature oak tree and another tree, from which we could hang a swing. It also had a small 'harbour' where a boat could have been kept, but we saw a large leach in the water, which put us off swimming there.

The gardener befriended the children, and they had great fun in the autumn leaping into the enormous piles of leaves he had gathered. We had a birthday party mainly in the garden, but we had to remove a grass snake before the invited children came. There was a fisherman living just over the garden wall where the harbour began, and he had three daughters who we invited to the party.

Mother was always happy to walk round and babysit for us and enjoy the grandchildren, having been deprived of this for most of their early years.

Our first Christmas in the flat I had put the children to bed and Edward, mother and I were about to enjoy our dinner when there were wails from the bedroom; "Mummy I don't feel well". It proved to be measles and both children came down with this.

OUR FIRST HOLIDAY WITHOUT THE CHILDREN

This was possible because Granny agreed to look after Melanie, and the mother of a school friend took Philip.

Edward and I set off to France in our little Ford Taunus stopping at places I had pre-booked. The ultimate destination was the Camargue, which is a National Park where you can see flamingos. We went there via Avignon – to see its famous incomplete bridge – and made sure we visited Arles and Les Baux. We also went to see the Pont du Gard aqueduct. Every morning we stopped at outdoor markets and bought food for our picnic -lunches.

The weather was fine all the way, and it was a great holiday! However, we did have minor issues to deal with! Deep in the Camargue our car became stuck in the mud, but we remembered that we had our snow chains in the boot, and we managed to put them on to get ourselves free! Soon afterward the car radiator boiled over, but we managed to fill it with water from a roadside ditch. We saw some of the famous Camargue white horses close to Les Saintes Marie de la Mer, where we ate our picnic that day on the Mediterranean beach.

A STRANGE INCIDENT

Back home in Clarens at 147 (the number of the house with our flat in it) we were wakened one night by a loud splitting and cracking sound, followed by a loud bang and a crash. It did not sound as if the noise come from the road in front of the building, and when we looked out there was nothing to see. But at the top of the long flight of steps from the garden we were met by a young man staggering up. "What happened" we asked, "Are you alright?".

He mumbled something and disappeared along the road towards Vevey. We then went to look from the balcony into the garden below and were amazed to see a car on its back and a half-split tree. This event never made the news, and we heard later that the driver was the son of a local politician.

One day as I walked back home beside the lake from Montreux, with Melanie in her pushchair complaining madly about something, we met a lady coming towards us with a young boy, who was also complaining. We smiled and stopped, and thus began a friendship which has lasted all our lives. She was German, called Ada, and was married to a Swiss whose family owned a market garden. Ada has been like a sister to me ever since.

Three years passed quickly and happily, and we heard about our next posting which was to be to the Philippines.

AT SEA EN ROUTE TO AUSTRALIA, 1970

Edward had been appointed Marketing Manager at the Manila office of Nestlé, which at this time was named Filipro. It was agreed that he should spend an initial month or so to see the country and understand the job and that took him to the major cities in the country, which is comprised of several large islands and thousands of small ones.

This sounded sensible, but, whilst Edward was travelling, what would the children and I do – newly arrived in a strange place and not knowing anyone? I enquired if it would be possible for the children and I to go most of the way by ship instead of by plane. The Company agreed and so it was that we caught the R.H.M.S. Ellinis, belonging to the Greek Chandris Shipping Line well known for transporting migrants from Southampton to Australia.

Our good friends from our days in Thailand when we visited their beach house, had moved to Australia, and, when they heard of my plans, they invited the children and me to come and stay with them near Melbourne. The voyage journey took a month and a day, because the Suez Canal was still closed with ships blocked in it since the start of the Six-Day-War in 1967 between Israel and Egypt. That meant that we had to sail down to the Cape of Good Hope and then across to Freemantle, where we had a quick visit to Perth, before continuing to Melbourne.

Philip suffered with sea sickness for the first three days, but after that he was fine.

We had a cabin next to a young Australian with her two boys.

Our first brief stop was the Canary Isles. We were allowed off the boat and took a short walk.

We accustomed ourselves to life on board and the hours for meals. This was a "£10 Pom voyage" (as such sailings came to be known). There were many families with children, who had brought all their furniture and worldly goods. Someone even brought an organ we learnt. After the parents had accompanied their children to a meal, and at the beginning we watched them pour ketchup all over the place, we didn't feel much like eating anything ourselves.

There was a sort of school organised, but I don't recall it every being popular with Philip and Melanie. They preferred dashing about on the deck and throwing quoits over the side into the sea.

It was fun watching flying fish following the boat and different birds overhead as we headed south down the coast of Africa. There was the usual ritual associated with crossing the Equator; people seemed to go mad, spaghetti was flung around and those with it wound around them jumped into the swimming pool. There was an on-board daily newspaper, and shows and films for our entertainment, and if one wanted to play cards there were always groups of people playing various games.

Our second stop was Cape Town, and we were only in port for a day, but my aunt Ando, who was working for the Red Cross in Swaziland, came all the way by train to meet us and take us out. A taxi was hired, and we went part way up Table Mountain together, telling Ando all about our adventures on board. It was wonderful to see her.

The next leg of the journey was the longest without seeing land, taking us across the Indian Ocean towards Perth. Whilst we were on board Christmas Day arrived, which necessarily meant there were many different settings for mealtimes. The children were fed separately, after which the parents ate. I seem to remember eating lunch at about 3 p.m.

Whilst on board I asked if there was anybody who would be willing to teach me some Greek as I was keen to improve on what I had picked up when living in Athens. One of the crew was a little too keen, which meant I always had to have the children in tow. He bought the children presents, which I'm sure was a stretch for his finances. I felt sorry for the crew who missed their families and were away from home for long stretches at a time.

There was just time in Perth for some shopping for summer clothes for all of us. It was incredibly hot and dry when we were there, but we managed to find what we needed.

Then it was countdown to Melbourne, where we disembarked and were met by the friends who had invited us to stay. They, and their two daughters, made us very welcome and took us on an outing to Phillip Island to see the unforgettable sight of the tiny Fairy Penguins coming on land to reach their breeding burrows. It was not a very touristy attraction in those days, so we were able to sit on the sand quite near them and enjoy it all from close by.

Then we were delighted to see live koalas. How adorable they are, and just like the ones in the toy shops.

Insects are a problem, especially redback spiders which have a venomous bite and can be dangerous. I was not sure I would like to live in Australia, but our friends seemed to have adapted quite well.

We had been in touch with Edward and now we had to fly up to Manila to meet him.

THE PHILIPPINES, 1971-1979

Edward had been working here for about two months when we arrived. "Hello Far East" I thought, it will be reasonably familiar. How wrong I was!

The Philippines is composed of over seven thousand, six hundred islands of which about two thousand are inhabited. Manila, the capital, is situated in the most northern main island, Luzon. There are several active volcanos in Luzon, of which two were quite active.

In Luzon the dominant language is the local Tagalog, but other local languages are favoured too, like Ilocano in the northwest of the island; most people speak English.

A small percentage of the population still speak Spanish, the Spanish claimed the islands following their discovery by Magellan in 1521. In 1898 the Treaty of Paris was signed, ending the Spanish-American War and selling the Philippines to the US for $20 million. Then Spanish rule formally ended, but the established upper class was clearly Spanish by descent.

When I spoke in the shops, I was told "you speak a very strange English, where are you from"?

Schools had to be found for the children. Philip, before starting boarding school in England, attended one which had several thousand pupils. Melanie went to a Montessori school, where she was tested and told she had an IQ way above her age.

We lived in one of the guarded villages in the Makati area of Manila, which was called Dasmariñas. The house was a two-storey building with a large sitting room, a kitchen, servants' quarters and an office downstairs. Upstairs there was a master bedroom and two smaller bedrooms with bathrooms. The master bedroom had a large clothes storage area with many wooden cupboards and shelves. All the windows had bars for security reasons. The garden, mostly at the back, ran the length of the house. There was a park a short walk away which had play equipment for children.

We made a few trips to acquaint ourselves with our new surroundings. One such trip was to the famous Pagsanjan waterfalls in the province of Laguna. They were reached by a river trip upstream in a dugout canoe, which had to be carefully manoeuvred over the shallow rapids. The falls were certainly impressive, and it was possible to take a raft and go round the back of the waterfall, something that Philip wanted to do. Thankfully the raft was a hired one with its own punter.

Another trip, also south from Manila, was to Mt. Makiling, which is a dormant volcano. Our walk uphill led us beside hot springs, mainly consisting of bubbling mud making sucking and plopping noises. We climbed some way up the mountain but stopped when we reached an area where leaches were numerous. The children were always running noisily ahead and disturbing birds Edward wanted to see.

The Filipinos loved music and it seemed that just about everybody had a guitar. This was a complete contrast to Thailand, and the music was European in style.

As I was not allowed to work, I thought I would take some guitar lessons. The teacher turned up at 7 a.m. and, if we were still breakfasting, he waited in the garden. It wasn't long before I met a group of foreigners who had formed a group and called themselves the Asia Minors.

ASIA MINORS

The founder of the group was an American and the group included an Irish lady with a beautiful singing voice, an English friend of mine, a Canadian, a Filipina and a Japanese lady. The American lady was married to an Irishman called Kelly, and each year when St. Patrick's Day came round, they had an open house with green beer to drink! They were humorous friends, and behind the bar they had a sign saying: "BE ALERT THE WORLD NEEDS MORE LERTS".

My singing voice wasn't marvellous, just the average soprano, and my guitar strumming was pretty basic, like some of the others, but I was welcomed into the group, and we practised twice a week. Our repertoire was large, and we sang in: Tagalog, Spanish, English and French. Many of the popular songs were those of John Denver.

We had two uniforms, one of which was a long dress, and the idea was to hire ourselves out to Embassy mornings; the other was informal and appropriate for coffee gatherings arranged to earn money for a special school, catering for children who could not go into mainstream schools.

SCOTTISH DANCING

Edward had danced in the White City Searchlight Tattoo, two years running, and knew many of the traditional dances and we had had some Scottish dancing in Bangkok at the British Club, where Edward had acted as instructor.

In Manila, those who were interested, gathered at the Golf Club (of which we were members). There was a very large hall with doors on either side that opened to the outside, and a sprung floor. We had some practices and got ready for some demonstration dances for St. Andrew's Day when haggis was flown in specially by British Airways. I particularly enjoyed the Eightsome Reel, the Gay Gordons, and the Dashing White Sergeant.

IMELDA MARCOS

The President's wife was famous for her collection of shoes, which reportedly numbered several hundred. Her staff went to the stores and brought pairs back on approval.

Like her husband she was keen to see the Philippines on the world map. One day we heard that she was thinking of having the country buying a Concord jet plane and that one was on its way to Manila for her to inspect. This interested quite a few of us amongst the British, so when the plane was at the airport the British Embassy made it possible for us to go and have a look.

We found the seats very small and cramped, and the interior quite disappointing. Mrs Marcos decided not to have one.

BACK TO SCHOOL IN ENGLAND FOR PHILIP

The time came for Philip to return to the UK and continue his education at an English preparatory school. Unfortunately, at this time there were no direct flights from Manila to London, so I had to accompany Philip to Hong Kong for a connecting flight, off which he would be met in London.

We planned to stay overnight. This meant Philip and I could explore the streets and absorb some of the atmosphere of the British Colony, which felt very Chinese and very different from Manila.

A horror show was advertised, and Philip and I thought this might be fun! A guy with biceps like tree trunks appeared on stage with a large black inner tube from some wheel which he proceeded to blow into. He kept blowing and blowing, and gradually we slipped down into our seats as the thing began to look as though it might burst. It did! What a pair of lungs! Then there were men who pushed swords and knives right through one side of their mouth and out the other side, and there were fire-eaters, of course!

Next day, all too soon, it was time to head for the airport where Philip had a special unaccompanied label tied round his neck and was put in the care of a British Airways stewardess, who had been previously alerted. This was not easy for me, and not for Philip either. He was met in London by my aunt Ando, who dealt with the next phase of his journey.

In due course Philip came out for the long summer holidays to join us, and we enjoyed endless trips to swimming pools to keep cool. Perhaps the most favourite pool was at the Makati Sports Club. One day we went there, and I went off to an exercise class while Philip and Melanie went swimming. They were very good swimmers, and I was quite comfortable about them being there together without me. However, what I had forgotten was how Melanie loved to copy everything her brother did, and when he leapt from a concrete block in the centre of the pool to the side, Melanie tried to do the same and didn't quite make it! Instead, she hit the side and nearly bit her tongue in two. Ouch! Blood everywhere. I was hastily summoned, and we rushed off to the local hospital, where Philip turned a ghostly shade of white as he watched Melanie's tongue being stitched back together with the use of a curved needle. We then discovered that in addition two of her teeth were broken.

ILL HEALTH IN MANILA

One evening we were invited to a well-known chic Spanish restaurant. The waiters wore white gloves, and the meal was excellent; or maybe not so excellent, because very soon I felt very ill. The doctor, Dr. Varvik, a German, suspected typhoid and after a few tests this proved to be the case. So, I was hospitalised for a while and gradually recovered at home.

Melanie had problems with viral warts on the knee and legs. This was a problem when we went swimming and caused her embarrassment. The various treatments the doctor recommended did not help, so eventually it was decided to excise them under anaesthetic. When Melanie eventually came round, she was very groggy, and a hot black coffee was brought. After drinking it she was very sick, and she has never drunk coffee since. The warts returned and eventually, as a last resort, a special tree bark was tried, taped to her leg and after the inflammation died down, we found that the warts had finally disappeared.

One afternoon I discovered a large blister on the roof of my mouth. This soon developed into full-blown Erythema Multiforme, which meant that swallowing or eating anything was a problem. I was in bed in the air-conditioned bedroom, hallucinating on the medication and feeling utterly wretched. In fact, the whole lining of my mouth and throat slewed off, leaving it so tender that it was several weeks before it was possible to drink a lemonade.

At the same time Philip and Melanie had bronchial pneumonia, so Edward was obliged to hire a nurse to come and administer medication.

After that episode, I awoke one morning to find my right leg was completely numb! Yet again our doctor was called, and he felt my heart was not pumping properly so he prescribed me a tiny booster pill. At least it didn't seem to have been a stroke.

One of our maids needed a hysterectomy; and finally, Edward and Philip both contracted mumps!

Much later, on reflexion, I wondered if the electricity sub-station just over the road had anything to do with our ill health.

GETTING AROUND IN LUZON

So, the overall picture of our life in this country seemed to be one of dark and light. There were plenty of light times, like when we went to the beach at Wawa near Liloan in southwestern Luzon. We made this trip, well away from the crowded capital, about once a month to get some sea air. Sometimes I drove ahead with the children, or with Melanie alone if Philip was yet not with us for his holidays. Edward had to work on Saturdays, but we would leave on Friday together with a maid, and some of the ready meals we would need when there.

It was a journey of about three hours on reasonably good roads and we passed the huge crater lake of Taal volcano. This is an active volcano and an island in the lake held the remains of the last minor eruption.

Because travellers would stop in the hope of seeing some smoke from the volcano this was a place for the farmers to sell their produce. The roadside vendors were waiting to sell us whatever they had grown, and the volcanic soil is an excellent fertiliser and there were several varieties of banana (in fact botanists told us there were about 40 species in the Philippines).

We usually bought the little Princess bananas; we bought generously knowing Melanie would have scoffed half of them before we even got to the beach.

When we arrived in Wawa there was a small creek to cross by boat with our luggage. Once across the creek the luggage was transported by a water buffalo called Rosemary, and sometimes the children – ours or those of friends who came with us – rode on her back.

A German gentleman, Mr. Redinger, who had worked for the tobacco factory Tabacalera, as national sales manager owned some land and three houses in this extension of Wawa village and he let out two of them to foreigners like us. They were perfect for Wawa beach having slatted wooded floors through which the sand could be swept. The house was about two feet above ground and there were two bedrooms, a toilet, and a sitting room with a covered veranda. Outside was the kitchen, a maid's room and an outdoor tap. Usually, we booked the second house and invited another family with children to join us, so we all gathered for the evening meal and games afterwards.

There was a generator providing electricity; this was turned off at 9 p.m., after which we used lamps or candles. The insects swarmed to the light, and this brought the geckos peering round the wall.

Before going to bed, it was as well to check there were no snakes around. Then as we lay down, we saw palm rats racing across the beams. They didn't cause us any problems, but they were why snakes went into the roof. Fireflies were a delight to watch as we became drowsy and listened to the gentle lapping of the sea just a few hundred yards away.

After breakfast, we couldn't wait to go across the one field between us and the sea. On our last leave in the UK, we had bought good fitting masks for each of us and, together with the snorkel, we were straight away able to marvel at the wonders just below the surface.

It was not necessary to swim more than a few yards to see coral and exquisite fish of all colours. One animal we had to watch out for was the stone fish; this is said by some to be the world's most venomous fish. It is disguised to look like a stone and lies on the sea floor, and woe betide anyone who comes into contact with the thirteen poisonous spines on its back.

There were also poisonous sea snakes there and one did swim not far below me once. They weren't interested in us, and sea snakes are probably all back-fanged.

Once we came with Filipino friends, a rotund father with infectious laugh, a wife and three children, good company for our two. Another time it was an English family with two girls, and so on.

Even Edward, who does not enjoy swimming, was captivated by everything we saw, and there were some good birds as well. I remember the oriole, a yellow bird with a melodious song. Yes, these were good times.

One Saturday we decided to get to the east coast on the other side of the large lake called Laguna de Bay. We took a company Land Rover because we had been warned that the road would be rough, and Edward's driver called Mandy drove. We turned left as soon as we could see the lake and headed over the low hills on the far side to Siniloan, and beyond that to the sea. I had my guitar with me and when we reached the end of the road, with nothing but a few fishermen's huts, I started to strum Dahil Sayo, the song supposedly composed by Imelda Marcos, which attracted a small audience. The only way back was the way we had come.

Some weeks later we joined our friends, called Roberts, who had been invited to spend the long Easter holiday on the island of Mindoro, which lies south-west of central Luzon. The invitation had come from a Filipino, who had a house on

Mindoro, in the northern hills close to a mine that he owned. He arranged a boat from Batangas which seemed rather like a wartime landing craft! When we had disembarked, we travelled up to his house in jeeps, and we stayed one night there before riding down to sleep on the beach for two nights with palm leaves on the sand and food ferried down from the house.

The strait between Batangas and Mindoro is known for the fast current that runs through it, and there have been ferry disasters there a couple of times. When we swam off the beach the current carried us quite rapidly eastwards, so we kept close to shore, and landed and walked back. Just along the beach that way there was a small bay with a narrow entrance and lovely coral on its floor: here we floated quietly, unaffected by the current.

Having had the visit of Concorde to the country, it was the turn of Queen Elizabeth II. Well, not her actually, but the luxury cruise liner of that name which was visiting. Of course, it was impressive and naturally, friends and I asked if we could go on board, and we were shown round by a friendly gay man, who looked after the costumes for the variety shows. Amusingly as I looked down onto a lower deck, I spied one of the cooks below me and in the top of his cook's hat was a packet of cigarettes!

One Christmas we decided to go north to Baguio the "City of Pines" and home to some universities. The cooler weather is also a draw. An Australian family with three daughters joined us for the 250 kms. trip. The husband was of Russian extraction. The turkey dinner came with us. The bustling market seemed to be awash with strawberries.

The whole city was one big Christmas decoration, even to Santa crawling up a ladder into a house. So, it was possible to appreciate a roaring log fire, which added to the atmosphere. Unfortunately, a church service was not part of the scene.

From Baguio we drove a couple of hours further north and spent a night in a hotel built at a place where one could look down from the ridge to see the rice terraces, which stretch down the hillside to the broad valley with the Sierra Madre beyond, with the ocean on the other side of that, which we could not see.

After returning to Baguio and heading back down to the lowlands, we decided to head further west to the coast, just to see what the beach looked like in an area called the Thousand Islands before the long drive back to Manila.

THE ENGLISH CHURCH

The vicar was Belgian with the rather apt name of Father Dimanche. His wife was Filipina.

It was one of the first non-Catholic churches in the Philippines. I discovered that quite a few foreigners with some nursing experience had offered their services to a clinic on the church premises that offered advice about contraceptives, and examined internally those who came, if they wished it. As I had no nursing experience, I ended up keeping records and helping to man the autoclave.

Melanie and I attended the Sunday service and Melanie joined the choir along with friends.

One of my favourite places for a quiet walk was in the American Cemetery and Memorial Garden. This covers 152 acres and is set on a plateau not far from the golf club, and it is visible at quite a distance from the east, south and west. It was also home to a few bird species that we did not see elsewhere.

It contains the gravestones of nearly 17,100 war dead and nearly 36,300 names on the Walls of the Missing. In addition, these walls display mosaic maps of the various stages and battles of the Pacific War. The headstones are made of marble and are set in a generally circular pattern, among tropical trees and shrubbery. The atmosphere is very restful and reverential.

Philip continued his travels to and from boarding school in England and eventually made the journey without my accompanying him to Hong Kong. On one famous occasion the onward flight to London was delayed a day, and this meant that Philip had to share a hotel room with a stewardess as he was still an unaccompanied minor. This was a story he was able to boast of at school!

THE CHILDREN AT SCHOOL, INCLUDING BOARDING SCHOOL

Philip was physically quite small and did not have a real growth spurt until his mid-teens. He was always very agile and quite daring. He had quite prominent teeth which were corrected in later years by removing several molars, after which braces were fitted. These had to be constantly adjusted which meant trips to the dentist needed to be organised. He was usually quite pale in complexion with very fair hair. Edward's company driver always said that Philip should have been the girl of the family, and Melanie the boy.

He was an affectionate, sensitive child, who unknown to us probably took many knocks at school. In later years he appreciated the fact that we had had to send him away to boarding school, and although he had a mixed experience, he was nevertheless grateful to have had the opportunity of a good British education, rather than stay with us and have an interrupted education at various schools – potentially in other languages. After several terms in a Swiss school, he learned neat writing and was able to converse in French.

Melanie, although she had the exact same start in life regarding food, was of a completely different build, with heavier bones and with a darker complexion. Initially she was quite a wilful child, very intelligent and determined to have her own way. A New Zealand lady came to my rescue in the Philippines and suggested Melanie start clarinet lessons with her. This was a success as she was musical. We had a piano and for a while I took Melanie for piano lessons with a rather strange lady and her dog.

When she was quite young, she used to have screaming fits, for example when I tried to wash her hair during the ocean voyage the neighbours in the next cabin thought I was murdering her!

Overall, we were all friends most of the time, and Edward was always there to back me up on major issues.

BURGLARIES

These were not uncommon, and we had already suffered them when we lived in Thailand. There it happened whilst we were sleeping and later it didn't bear thinking about that strangers were wandering around where Philip was lying in his cot.

Some wedding gifts of silver were taken, and also some blankets. The Thai police were never very interested, but Edward hoped to bolster their interest by going to the local police station when asked to play a game of Scrabble with the officers. The police won, naturally, as they had learned every two-letter word allowable! It did not lead to any further action as far as we could tell.

In the Philippines I lost my cine camera amongst other things. Police came and took fingerprints from the doors, but we never heard any more.

OUR DOG SALLY

Our dog Sally was a Heinz 57 variety bitch which had belonged to Australian neighbours, who were returning home and needed to find a home for her. We knew her because our children and theirs had played together, and with the dog.

Sally was an amusing dog, full of beans, leaping over the sofa and chasing the children over the polished concrete floors, trying to gain momentum as it was so slippery, and then disappearing into the garden. When she came with us to the park she would dash ahead and then peer round the next block to see if we were coming.

We had been told she was infertile. However, one day the children and I were faced with a sex lesson on the front doorstep, thanks to the visit of a Red Setter from somewhere in the village.

Soon it was obvious that Sally was pregnant. A wooden shelter was made for her in the garden; I thought it would be good, when the time came, for her to have her pups there, and I made a loose leash to attach her to it. However, I was awakened by her crying and came down and released her. She immediately went over to a flowerbed and started digging a shallow hollow under a little Kalamansi bush. Kalamansi is a citrus tree, and it has delicious little tangerine-like fruits, green outside, orange inside. Dozens of them were needed to make a very pleasant drink, which needed a little sugar and some ice. We drank it often.

Upon checking in the morning, we discovered Sally with four pups, and she gave a little growl when we approached. There were three males and one female in the litter. We kept one of the males and called him Prince. Another male went to our New Zealand friends, and they called him Barnaby. A third male went to a Scottish friend who, together with her cook, spoiled him rotten and he grew too fat; one Christmas Day after a huge feast he lay down and died!

The female was given to Filipino friends. Sadly, she came to grief when in a gale a screen door slammed on her and killed her.

Sally had a habit of rushing out of the gate to chase any passing vehicle from houses further up the road. This was her downfall, as she fell under a car and was badly injured. We took her to the vet immediately, but he was unable to save her. We all cried – the maids included.

As for Prince, I tried to teach him to fetch the morning paper, but he was clueless. Quite unteachable in fact. One morning he was discovered dead in the garden, and we thought the cause was probably a snake bite.

I must tell you more about long-lived Barnaby. Our New Zealand friends were soon posted to Indonesia, so Barnaby was crated up and emplaned for Djakarta. Their next posting some years later was to Pakistan. Apparently, Barnaby arrived by air in a crate again, but the crate fell off an airport trolley and broke open allowing Barnaby to rush off. Efforts to recapture him resulted in delayed departures for several international flights before he was caught. In due course, he went on to their next posting in Istanbul, and visiting our friends there we caught up with him again. Sadly, making one of his usual daily expeditions into the surrounding town he never came back.

FLIGHTS

By now we all felt like seasoned flyers. I had to take many flights with one or two children, without Edward. Some were indeed memorable. One early one was when Melanie was still a baby, a cot was assigned to her attached to the bulkhead of the cabin. This meant that she was able to sit up in it and jump out at stewardesses as they passed with trays of food!

One flight with Japanese Airlines had very few passengers and the captain mentioned that we had to go much further south to avoid Vietnamese airspace due to the war, making the flight more expensive. The stewardesses, with few to serve, had plenty of time and were able to sit and entertain Philip and Melanie. We were invited into the cockpit to admire the view and all the instruments.

Sometimes, if the flight was overnight, I took the doctor's advice and gave the children a syrup hoping to help them to sleep. Usually, it had the opposite effect, and they were jumping all over the place.

One of our very best flights was in First Class with Singapore Airlines. Melanie had a large seat to herself and so did her large Teddy Bear. We were offered roast beef from a silver salver and other culinary delights. We had the company of a delightful, good-looking businessman who chatted amiably to us, and we were sad to see him deplane when the flight landed in India.

A new route to England via Copenhagen was advertised in Manila, the flight landed in Tashkent to refuel, but made good time. I opted for this, and the children and I were rewarded with a penthouse suite in a five-star hotel in Copenhagen overlooking the Tivoli Gardens. We were met by a taxi with white, fur-covered seats and it was wonderful to breathe cool air again. A very charming Thai maid was part of the service, and we had our meal in the room, and then luxuriated in all that the bathroom and the huge sitting room had to offer. That afternoon a trip to Tivoli gardens was a must. There was so much to see and to do. For starters we took a ride on the big wheel.

Sadly, next morning time came to leave and head for the airport. For some reason we were late, and the plane was just about to close its doors, so we had to run across the tarmac to the manoeuvrable access stairs.

HOME LEAVES

Early in Edward's career there were sometimes problems because we had no fixed address in the UK. Edward's mother did her best to find us places near where she and Charles were living. One of these was in the village of Lower Benefield in Northamptonshire. This was owned by a teacher at Oundle School who, as a house master, had accommodation at the school.

We loved it and, in fact, were able to rent it more than once. The first time was during the Easter holidays, and it snowed! Almost opposite lived the village blacksmith with his forge where the flying sparks proved a big draw for the children. He was always friendly and willing to explain what he was doing. The rooms in the house were sunny and airy, and we were happy to be able to welcome my mother, who enjoyed these visits very much and loved the surrounding countryside. Aunt Ando also came to stay.

Melanie started to attend a little school, which was a short walk away across a couple of fields. I did not give her permission to say "no" to the rice pudding for lunch. She was obliged to stay and finish it, and for this I definitely got a black mark!

During our first stay here, I remember being busy sewing name tapes onto all the clothes Philip would need at his public school in the Autumn.

One "leave" was not really leave, because Edward had been asked to attend a Management Training Course at IMEDE, the International Business School in Lausanne.

LAUSANNE AND IMEDE

We needed to live here for about six months. We rented an apartment, which overlooked the main railway line from Geneva to Lausanne and on to the Rhone valley. The rooms were large and there was a piano.

Melanie needed to be enrolled at a school, so she attended an American school for a few months and took the skating lessons it organised. Over Easter Ando came to stay and so enjoyed herself making birds' nests in the garden shrubbery and filling them with Easter eggs for the children to find.

Edward worked very hard on his course and remembers waking up in the bath one evening with all the papers he was meant to read floating around him.

Whilst we were there, there was thought to be a scandal. Cats went missing. It was rumoured that certain oriental restaurants were being sold what was said to be chicken meat. We never heard whether there was any truth in that.

The cat rumour was mirrored by rumours about the "White Slave Trade" in Lausanne and to be wary about it. Being rather naïve, I thought it entirely possible that white, European girls had indeed been known to disappear. Supposedly, they entered changing rooms in stores to try on a garment for size and never re-appeared. It was said that they were shipped off to Middle Easterners who fancied a white girl in their hareem. We were never able to ignore the rumour despite it seeming most unlikely to happen in Switzerland.

After returning to Manila, Edward's role expanded to make him responsible for both Marketing and Sales because the Filipino who had been Sales Manager was simultaneously sent to IMEDE to attend the same course.

Melanie and I once again picked up the threads of life there. Melanie decided to take macrame lessons. Macrame had become quite popular; it is the art of using several knots, for example the reef knot and several different forms of tying the knots, to create plant hangers, wall hangings, belts and so forth.

BACK IN THE PHILIPPINES, AND THE BRITISH SCHOOL, 1976

There was an American School in Manila, but no English School and we now found that there was a widespread desire for there to be one.

A Scottish lady, married I think to an international banker, was identified by some of the British community as the founder of such a school in the Middle East; and discussions soon began about the potential launch of one in Manila when she indicated that she might be available.

Over the next few weeks several evening meetings took place in our house to discuss the availability of teachers, and happily there were some interested candidates in the community. Questions of location, uniforms and many other things also needed decisions. Premises were found for rent and all the expats were asked whether they would be prepared to send their children to this school. Enough children were enrolled, a uniform was chosen and finally the day came to start. The uniform was a blue and white chequered dress for girls and shirt of similar material for boys. A special T-shirt in red, white and blue was sourced for sporting events: it was very easily recognisable as British!

A first Sports Day was organised, and each event

was available for junior and senior pupils. There must have been at least 60 competitors on what was a very hot and sticky morning: running, a sack race, a wheelbarrow race and, of course, mums and dads' races. Prizes were presented by the new headmistress, and Edward and I were proud to see Melanie receive two different awards and a cup. I was pipped to the post in the running race by a bare-footed Indian mother.

Involvement in the founding of the school was an altogether satisfying experience and, some years later, we learned that the school had three hundred pupils and custom-built premises.

Today, research tells us that it is a non-for-profit private International British School for pupils aged 3-18 with 950 students from 51 countries offering the English National Curriculum for English, Mathematics and Science, ICT, and International Baccalaureate. There are three houses named after different Philippine islands.

Looking back on all this we can't but help feel a warm glow.

The next event in our lives was a very unfortunate one.

THE HOUSE FIRE, 1976, AND THE NEW HOUSE

House fires were not uncommon. Much wood was used in the buildings. We had been told that the electrical current fluctuated quite significantly, and apparently dangerously. Also, it was rumoured that re-cycled copper wiring was used in the electrical fittings.

In late January, after lunch Melanie and I had taken a rest in the air-conditioning, as was sometimes our habit. Melanie was due to go to a macrame class afterwards, whilst I went to the Golf Club to discuss plans for a rehearsal of the chosen Scottish dances in preparation for the St. Andrew's Day celebrations the following day.

Whilst there I heard through the grapevine that there was a fire in Makati village, and I immediately tried to 'phone and find out if all was well. There was no answer.

So, I jumped in the car and returned home to be greeted by the Fire Brigade and flames leaping out of our house upstairs. Edward returned from his office almost at the same time, alerted by the plume of smoke. I wanted to run in and save my guitar, but that was not possible. Soon colleagues from the office came to see what they could do to help.

I'm afraid I was somewhat incoherent when

quizzed by the fire crew about my husband's date of birth and other seemingly unimportant questions. I guess I must have got back before he did.

The maids had been in the kitchen and had heard a bang from upstairs. They thought it was Sally and went to check, and when they opened the bedroom door were met with a wall of flame. Sally was not upstairs and was fine, but the bowl of rising dough the maids had begun in the kitchen was abandoned.

We had recently had work done on our bathroom to install a bath. All the wonderful cupboards and drawers upstairs including a large glass-fronted wardrobe were incinerated. The entire top floor and roof were in ruins.

We had electric light bulbs in some of the cupboards which were intended to keep the humidity down; could the problem started here? Perhaps a bulb was too close to the plastic bag where my photos were stored. We had always been a bit suspicious of a fan which sometimes slowed down because of electrical surges. Was it due to the irregular current? We shall never know, but the insurance inspectors – agents for Lloyds of London, with whom Nestlé had arranged our cover, thought the fan most likely.

What was salvageable downstairs was completely

soaked and many of Edward's precious bird books were sodden. The insurers organised for those books with damp pages to be taken several thousand feet up in a local aircraft, which apparently helped them to largely dry off. Some ironing followed!

Edward has reminded me that he was allowed to climb into the bathroom through a window from which the firemen had removed the bars and he did so and reached in to rescue important documents like passports from the safe which was in the bathroom.

So, there we were. No clean underwear; no change of clothes, no toothbrush. But we were SAFE, thank God. Had it happened the following night, Edward and I would have been at the St. Andrew's Ball and Melanie would have been asleep upstairs. Would she have got out in time?

Neighbours were amazing, offering us a bed for the night and clothes to wear.

As soon as we could think clearly, we had to deal with the insurers. We had to record our best memory of the cost and the date we had bought each item; and, as we had lived in three countries, in what country and in what currency!

You try thinking back to recall where your hankies, or your hat, or your cinecamera came from! As you may imagine this was a bit of a nightmare, and it took us at least six weeks going through our collective memory drawer by drawer, cupboard by cupboard.

Thanks to the insurance, and we knew how much we would get when we had been refunded, it seemed likely that we might be able to buy a property in England. This, of course, would mean that, if we did not let the property each home leave, we would have a base and appropriate clothes and belongings could be stored there. This, of course, implied we would need to find someone living nearby to keep an eye on things.

So, you could say that the fire was a blessing in disguise. Of course, we had to tell our mothers, and this was a terrible shock to them.

Philip was due to fly home to us for the holidays, and it wasn't until he had arrived at the airport that we explained that we would be going to a different house, and that we were very sorry to say that his entire Lego collection was gone. He took it all very well, what else could he do, poor chap!

The house we moved into after the fire was in a different gated village, called Forbes Park, sometimes referred to as the "Beverly Hills" of Manila. Here are the mansions of the wealthy, the celebrities, the successful businessmen and a few expats. There was little immediate choice, and it was a large, not very attractive and rather dark bungalow. There was a very large fish tank in the dining room, sitting empty. Off the main bedroom was a circular dressing room with mirrors all round, and a sunken area in the shower.

We decided to enjoy the fish tank, so we carefully measured out the necessary quantity of sea salt, and eventually bought some attractive tropical fish including the Neon Tetra and even a fascinating seahorse. All seemed to go well, and the tank lit up the dark room. However, when we had to go on leave and ask a pet shop to take over the responsibility in our absence, the pH of the water became imbalanced and, on our return, it seemed every morning we came down to find yet another fish had died. End of fish tank!

Edward and I were invited to the annual dinner of the Philippine Paediatric Association, Edward having arranged to be invited to give a speech in return for sponsorship of the meal. I remember sitting between two lady doctors, one of whom had eleven children and the other thirteen. Obviously, I couldn't compete and when I mentioned having just two children, they probably thought I had a physical disability, or hadn't done my duty; at least that was the feeling I came away with.

Overall, we found Filipino food rather bland compared to the Thai diet we had enjoyed for years.

A VISIT TO BANGKOK

On one occasion, instead of returning direct to Manila, I decided to stop off in Bangkok and to show the children where they had been born.

We stayed at the Oriental Hotel, on the banks of the Chao Phraya River. At the time a large skyscraper extension to the hotel was being built, and because of this, on leaving, we were given a voucher for a one-night free stay, because of the imagined inconvenience or noise. To this day, I still have this voucher and often wonder if it would still be honoured all these years later.

Here Nestlé went under the name Pronesiam and we had managed to contact an employee called Nanthana, who met us and who forewarned, had managed to locate and contact Narlee, our previous maid, so that she agreed to come and meet us with her daughter Nongying, Philip's first playmate, not that he remembered that. I had bought an embroidered denim bag for Nongying from the Philippines and gave Narlee a present too.

Next day we visited the crocodile farm where we saw a man do battle with one of these creatures by pulling it out of the water, and then, once it opened its mouth, propping that open for us to throw money into. All very gruesome really. There was a young elephant here, which both children rode a short way.

We took a taxi to see the English doctor who had delivered the children, and then the Nursing Home where they had been born. Upon arrival at our old home, I was delighted to see a sign over the doorway which said, "Pearl Buck Foundation". I had read all Pearl Buck's books from British Library when we lived there. This Foundation was created to help provide for children who had been born of Asian mothers and U.S. fathers, who had then returned to the States after the Vietnam War and may not even have known of their existence. I found it very pleasing that their office was in what used to be our dining room. We explained that we had lived there, and we were made welcome and offered drinks.

The Oriental Hotel put on a show of Thai dancing in the garden during the evening. The Thais use their fingers and especially long nails to accentuate their hand movements, and the dances are always a delight to see, especially because of the dancers' wonderful colourful silk garments. After our busy day, the children went to bed, and I enjoyed the best prawn soup before turning in for our last night and next day's return journey to Manila.

A HOME OF OUR OWN, 1977

Thanks to Edward's solicitor cousin in Banbury (Mike Barlow), who felt sure his contacts would be a help, and the money paid us for the fire in the Philippines, and having in mind 'public schools' for the children, we began to decide where we wanted our home to be. We expected to send Philip to Oundle which I had visited, this is between Thrapston and Peterborough, and we had agreed to send Melanie to the Godolphin School in Salisbury, which was my old school. We were able to count on Nestlé for the school fees.

Philip was at prep school at Dunchurch, just south of Rugby, recommended by Peter Cumberlege; however, from here to Portsmouth – where we took the ferry when returning to Switzerland – the route was almost directly south. Oundle seemed likely to add significantly to the effort of getting him to and from school. Marlborough was an alternative also recommended by the Cumberledges and was potentially appealing because we could pass through Marlborough on our regular travel between Switzerland and England. So, we drove down to see if it was as promising a choice as Oundle. Edward had not visited Oundle and so the decision was really down to me, and I felt that the two schools seemed equally good, so we agreed that the travel advantage gave Marlborough the edge. After

Edward and I had agreed on Marlborough we were able to focus on where to buy a house.

Somehow, we discovered that an attractive property in Aston Magna, near Moreton in Marsh – where there was a railway station – was on the market and, after a visit when we met the lady who owned it, we offered to buy it. We were prepared to make a down payment and had help from Mike in arranging to take out 15-year mortgage. which we would pay off in due course. The property was called Norman Chapel; it had once been and much of the structure was original. It is a listed grade 2* building. We needed a UK bank account, in joint names, and arranged for that at the Midland Bank in Moreton in Marsh. Once the documents were exchanged, and we had permission to occupy the cottage we bought some new or second-hand furniture. The children and I spent a night in a dire hotel in Chipping Campden, where we heard sounds of chairs being thrown and the owners arguing. The place was dirty, including the bath, and should have been shut down!

Norman Chapel had been a small chapel. As one entered the covered front door, one could walk straight into a room that we called the dining room, but just inside the front door and to the left was a door into the sitting room. In the dining room there was a huge fireplace and chimney, which had had a built-in bread oven; the original wooden door of that had been removed and was displayed as a curiosity; as was an interesting bone needle, framed and hanging on the wall.

There had been a Norman arch, but it had been blocked-in and plastered over on the dining room side where the stairs had been installed, and this made clear that the nave in the tiny church had comprised the two rooms.

I felt quite strongly an atmosphere in this property which can only have come from its ancient Christian past. I used to go for my "quiet times" into an upstairs bedroom which had a niche in the wall into which I placed a wooden statue of Christ brought from the Philippines.

The property was surrounded by a garden with a pear tree in the front, a flowering cherry on one side and at the back a few apple trees and a plum tree. This beautiful plum tree produced a large quantity of fruit, but sadly, we may have caused its demise by pruning it at the wrong time of year or with unsterilised secateurs. One of the apple trees was a bramley, which gave us magnificent crops. We were novice gardeners, and not only did we have to learn as we went along, but we could only do the work when we came over from Switzerland, which was basically during the spring and summer school holidays when I was able to spend much more time than Edward, whose annual leave was only four weeks a year.

We furnished the property gradually, some I collected from Eastbourne where mother had had it in store at one of her friends' homes. We bought six raffia seated chairs in Cheltenham for the dining room and the sofa and a reclining chair for the sitting room came later.

Philip had become interested in woodwork and was happy to practice this in the sizeable garden shed. Against the back of this shed grew a pretty rose bush and a mahonia. When we returned to the cottage, we often found birds' nests and were careful to avoid disturbing them until the young fledged. Because wooded areas were not far away, over the years we were blessed with visits of between 60 and 70 different birds in the garden.

When we first arrived in the village, some locals came to inspect us! These were the people who lived in the social housing, many of them Poles who had stayed on after WW2. We invited them into the garden for a ball game and did our best to be friendly, although some of the younger generation were decidedly not, and it clearly became a class issue. However, we were very happy to have help with house and garden from a very English local couple living in the social housing.

Our other neighbours included a semi-retired Colonel and his wife. They were most welcoming, and we were soon invited to meet the family, which included two daughters and their husbands, and a son who lived in a house in their grounds with his wife.

The road from Moreton-in-Marsh (our shopping town and railway station) turned off the main road north out of town, passing some municipal tennis courts where we sometimes played. The road led to Batsford, where there was an arboretum. The retired gardener of the arboretum and his wife lived in a cottage along this road. Here I must mention this dear Christian couple who were kind enough to take young Philip and Melanie for the day whilst I went shopping in a far- off town. They gave them some little woodworking tasks, presents to make and colour, and they fed them lunch How wonderful it would be if all neighbours were like them!

Our neighbour Ben, living directly opposite our front gate was a charming old man who kept bees and invited us to see him collect the honey.

There had been a brick works in the village of

Aston Magna in the past, which was a major source of employment for years, but was now disused and somewhat overgrown. It was a major loss to the village and because of this, the shop disappeared which was another blow for the inhabitants.

From the back of Norman Chapel, we looked out onto the village church, sadly deconsecrated. Whilst we were there it was bought and turned into a family home. Church has always been important to me and wherever we have travelled I have been lucky enough to find an Anglican, or episcopalian one as in the Philippines. It is good to worship with fellow Christians. One does not go to church because one is good but because one needs to become better!

REFLECTIONS OF A GARDENER ON LIFE

Gardening can teach one quite a lot about life and these are my thoughts.

As all plants search out the light and turn to it, so must we ever search out the True Light. Our lives are spent turning and twisting towards it as it draws us.

The frustrations of a gardener trying to eradicate stubborn weeds with ever-spreading roots and seeds could be matched by a doctor trying to quash cancer.

When a rose withers, its beauty gone, it can nevertheless be appreciated in a different way: a potpourri. So can old folk, no longer so lovely to look at perhaps, be cherished for other things like wisdom or calmncss.

A young plant or shrub is left to grow and shoot out vigorously, but then time comes for it to be tied, clipped and trained. When we are young and carefree we can grow wildly, then God gets out the secateurs and string. The result will be a thing of beauty for everyone's benefit and His glory. (Gal.4 vv.3-5).

Life here on earth is but the seed which will crack

and disappear to produce the flower in life hereafter.

BACK IN SWITZERLAND, 1979

We needed to house hunt and to facilitate that we stayed briefly in a flat in the main road through Vevey where Edward's Head Office was just one or two hundred yards away. On the floor above there was someone who walked non-stop clack-clacking across her uncarpeted floor. After a short while we found a very suitable flat in Corseaux; it was to be our home for the next eight years. It had a superb view of Lake Geneva and the Savoy Alps. I loved this flat.

We were on the western edge of the village and there was contemporary block of similar flats a little below us. In the field just to the west there was a huge walnut tree. In the summer this field was alive with the chirping of crickets; and beyond it was a vineyard.

The flat consisted of an entrance hall with a long corridor leading to three bedrooms. As you entered, there was a small guest toilet on the left and a door into the narrow kitchen with a very high ceiling and a door to the balcony that was also in front of the large dining room. From there a staircase led to a half-width upper level at the back where there was an office, a fireplace and a further small room at the west end which served as an office. From the area by the fire, one looked down onto this dining room, in which there was a huge sliding door opening onto the balcony, which had a canopy that could be extended or retracted from the inside. The balcony was large enough for a table and chairs and between us and the flats lower down was a grass area in which there was a stone table tennis table.

At the very end of the corridor that led to the three bedrooms was the bathroom with an excellent deep bath and a bidet. The window opened wide onto the field with the walnut tree.

We needed to furnish it and to begin with we had the container load that we had shipped from the Philippines where, before leaving, we had bought a round table with a rattan base and six chairs with seat covers of a colour that went well with the parquet floors. Also, from Manila came glass fronted shelving with cupboards below in two or three parts, and this too went into the front room. Our shell collection from the Philippines was in this large piece of furniture.

Then Melanie and I had an adventure. We decided to bring many things out from England to help furnish our new home. Melanie's desk was strapped on top of the car. Inside the back seats were flattened to allow us to load two beds and mattresses, one under the other. On top of these came two boxes of fruits from the garden that I had carefully preserved in glass containers, two boxes of various apples, two large oil paintings from the Philippines and our luggage, including clothes. By now it was no longer possible to see out of the back window! When we got to the port in Southampton, the Customs Officer walked slowly right round the car, came to the window and asked, with tongue in cheek "Got yer old man nailed up in there?"

Once we reached France we drove as far as Rheims and then decided to pack it in. This meant finding a safe place for the car overnight, which meant it had to be parked in the basement of the hotel where we stayed. On the road again, we finally crossed the Jura mountains and came down into Switzerland. Edward met us at the door of No. 8 Chemin du Chano and was somewhat open-mouthed when he saw what was loaded in the car.

The desk was removed from the car roof and installed in Melanie's bedroom; pictures and curtains were hung, and fruit bottles stored. As they say in French "chaque chose a sa place et chaque place a sa chose".

Our neighbour on the same floor was welcoming. Her younger son missed having a father, argued with his mother and threw tantrums. One day when locked out of the flat he simply kicked a hole in the door. Over time we became more acquainted, and they joined us to enjoy a fondue supper. The neighbours directly below us were a lesbian couple. They also had arguments and we heard chairs being thrown. One of them was obsessive about tidiness and their garage was a model of perfection with tools hung in order of size etc.

On the other side, in the fourth flat of the building, was an overweight Vaudois gentleman of a certain age who took a shine to me and invited me downstairs, ostensibly to view a very old copy of the Bible. I went out of politeness and luckily escaped any further contact.

Philip was delighted that we were based in Switzerland again and was able to meet his friend Sebastian, who had first been at kindergarten with him. His German mother, Ada, by now had a daughter Rebecca, who was a year or two younger than Melanie.

Sebastien introduced Philip to a moped ('velo moteur'), the kind all the youngsters rode in Switzerland and the pair or them went off to France to buy some fireworks, which were unavailable in Switzerland. The idea was to harvest some of the gunpowder in them to use in a miniature cannon which Philip owned somehow, I know not how. Would it work? Some shot was found, and they tried it out in a field near the flats and the shot went into a side wall.

As they say, boys will be boys. Well, I came home from shopping with Melanie one day and found a note on the door which said, "Gone to hospital". Melanie said that I turned white as a sheet; I guess that was hardly surprising. Had they blown off a hand, or had the cannon backfired into their faces? Mamma mia. However, it turned out that they had visited the hospital for a bad cut from a barbed wire fence, so nothing at all to do with the cannon. Phew!

Melanie had to attend the nearest local school, which was a ten-minute walk away in quite an imposing building. It was her misfortune that the year she started was the year the class began to learn German. This meant that all her tuition was in French, with added German classes. Poor girl. For the first three months she would come running home for lunch, crying. After that she managed very well, in fact so well she won the form prize at the end of term!

She enjoyed the walks to school and had to pass by James Mason's house, which was a little way up the hill. She confessed to having picked some fruit that was hanging over his wall.

During the Spring, Switzerland had a visit from our dear late Queen Elizabeth II. She was invited to a midday banquet in the Château de Chillon on the lakeside, and so we thought we must try to see her. Some of the Brits stood by the English church as she went by, but we decided to go and wait near the Château. We saw her cross the bridge from the chateau as she came out looking ravishing in a bright red coat and hat, and she waved graciously to us. Afterwards I was really annoyed with myself for not giving Melanie a bunch of lilies-of-the-valley, which were in season, that Melanie could easily have given to her as she stepped off the bridge before getting into the car and heading off to Bern.

Soon it was the summer holidays. Philip had to be fetched from Marlborough, a school uniform bought for Melanie, and Norman Chapel was due to receive a lot of TLC.

We hankered after the seaside and decided to visit north Devon, and we chose Ilfracombe where we found a hotel overlooking the sea and the three of us shared a room. It was here that we fell in love with Woolacombe Bay, a beautiful stretch of endless sandy beach where we swam and frolicked about until we returned exhausted, for an evening meal.

Towards the end of the holidays, after Philip had been returned to Marlborough, it was time for Melanie, aged eleven, to go to boarding school in

England. She was going to start at my old school in Salisbury. This could be the beginning of my trip back to Switzerland. When I dropped her off with her trunk and duvet. and all the other paraphernalia, I did not stick around, because drawn out goodbyes are never very comfortable. But I suspect Melanie has never forgiven me for leaving without a proper farewell – it wasn't easy for either of us.

Melanie did not enjoy boarding school, but it gave her friends for life and for this she has been grateful.

Mother often wanted to join us on these trips: she needed to replenish her dwindling stocks of medicines from Boots and to see friends. She was having increasing difficulties making the Swiss franc last as the English pounds that she was receiving from England bought less and less in exchange.

Once back in Switzerland I decided to look for a job and through an English friend landed one in Lausanne with a small publishing firm that produced travel books. This meant having lunch in Lausanne. The English-speaking team were a friendly crowd, and my job was to type the entire book on New Zealand.

This was over a few weeks, after which I became a

typist in the Company once again, but this time in a pool and it was a completely different atmosphere, and I missed the Advertising Department of the early Sixties!

A job offer came up at a school in Glion. This was a branch of a well-known school in London run by a Colonel who stood no nonsense. Two classes, each with about 12 boys, came out to Switzerland for a term. I was asked if I would teach English, to which I replied "Yes, but I would like to know what they are doing in London". No help was forthcoming. So, I made my own agenda. The boys were aged about 8 and already owned mobile phones which I insisted must be turned off. In addition to the lessons, I was asked to prepare lunch. There was a lady who came in every day to peel potatoes and do basic preparation of food, but I had to supervise the cooking. The meals were quite frugal. For example, dessert was half an orange! The boys had to walk down into Montreux and bring back the necessary groceries in their rucksacks! The Colonel's wife lived in the house and was bed-ridden. I was expected to go and make polite conversation with her, regardless of her mood at the time.

There was a young New Zealander, who took charge of the other class, and I was able to carry my woes to him. For the second term, I was asked to teach French, and I agreed as I felt reasonably confident about my capabilities there – at least at that level.

When the time came for me to fetch Philip from school in the UK and the dates didn't quite fit with the start of the Colonel's term in Glion, that was the end of my employment there.

FRENCH EXAMS, 1981-1982

Together with Margaret – an English friend, married to a Swiss – I decided to take a French exam which would provide us with a certificate of some kind to prove we could speak the language. Neither of us had taken the A-level certificate when at school.

We found a French lady who was willing to prepare us, and she obtained the necessary books that we had to read, and we went to her for lessons. One of the books was by Honore de Balzac, something I would never have chosen to read, but I really enjoyed it.

When the time came for the exams, we had to travel to Annemasse, a small town in France near Geneva. Margaret and I soon discovered that we were the "grannies" in the class! As we all sat waiting at our appointed desks, nothing seemed to happen, so we started chatting with our neighbours. But that was a mistake! Footsteps were heard approaching and the door was flung open to show a furious Napoleonic figure. We had no business to be talking before a serious exam. Who did we think we were?

We were given a dictation by this gentleman. Later, when we each had to go into a private room for conversation with an examiner, I was dismayed to see that I had been booked that with 'Napoleon'. But, in fact, I found him quite pleasant and was very pleased upon learning, much later of course, that I had passed with "mention très honorable".

The following year Margaret and I went to sit the Alliance Française Higher Certificate and were delighted to learn that we had passed that as well. We celebrated the results with the French lady, who had coached us, and we took her out for the day on a paddle steamer on the lake.

WINTER SCHOOL HOLIDAYS

These were fun and a draw for the children's friends, who wanted to come skiing. So, over time we entertained several friends, and at the weekends Edward joined us to go further up the Valley to some of the more popular resorts. Mother sometimes joined us to enjoy the mountain air. There is something quite magical about sun on sparkling snow, it really gives one a 'lift'. Luckily, we never suffered any broken bones.

In the flat in Switzerland the fire on the upper floor was a huge success, the wood was dry and there was never a problem of starting a blaze. There was nothing nicer than sitting in front of that fire and looking down to the big window and watching the snow falling.

Aunt Ando came to stay for Christmas more than once, and our dear Scottish friend Averyl. often joined us.

We returned to Normal Chapel only once for Christmas and this was partly to be with Edward's mother, who was now a widow and living in Moreton-in-Marsh. There were storage heaters in the cottage, these were rather unsightly radiators containing bricks which were heated by electricity at night when it was cheaper; they then radiated heat during the day. But it was never enough. So, we were endlessly trying to light fires, the wood was invariably damp, and we held newspapers against the wall to make a vacuum and hopefully encourage the flames.

SUMMER SCHOOL HOLIDAYS

These were spent at Norman Chapel, and we welcomed friends here too, including my aunt Ando and mother who dearly loved the place.

Because there were woodlands not far away, we were fortunate to be visited by many birds in the garden. Green Woodpeckers were always probing for ants' nests in the front lawn. Treecreepers and Nuthatches are both arboreal, treecreepers climb up the trunk and nuthatches climb down, and both liked the pear tree. Spotted Flycatchers darted between the apple trees in the back garden. Many starlings came to bathe in the birdbath after eating wild cherries and left the stones in the water. A Song Thrush amused me by whacking the snails on the path to crack the shell before extracting and swallowing it. Wrens used a bird box and raised a brood of young: when they were ready to fledge, we happened to be there as they began to tumble out through the small hole: we counted twelve of them. We had a gorgeous Goldcrest on the cotoneaster outside the kitchen window and it climbed up onto the windowsill. Other rarer visitors included a Bullfinch, two Lesser Spotted Woodpeckers and, one spring, a Hawfinch came to our bird table, on which on another occasion we had a Yellowhammer that was swept off by a Sparrowhawk. One morning, when we were leaving early to go and pick strawberries, we passed under the lower branch of a tree where 3 Little Owl fledglings were perched. Then a Swiss neighbour who lived a mile down the road brought us a Short-eared Owl, which she thought might have been hit by a car. We looked after it briefly until it recovered and flew off. Near her house we heard Nightingales, but they were just arriving in England and may not have taken up residence.

We did have some unwelcome visitors in the shape of wasps, which made a nest in our roof. One day I noticed some emerging from between the roof tiles and so I called the Pest Control brigade. A chap in white uniform came with a spray canister on his back and a long extension to it. He sprayed along the roof and declared that the poison would kill any that emerged.

The next day there seemed to be even more wasps around, so I called Pest Control again. He came again and sprayed a bit more, but it was still no good. So, eventually he admitted that he would have to go into the roof space. This was decidedly awkward, but eventually he was able to extract an entire nest, which was quite sizeable. After that, a few dead wasps needed removing from the cottage and all became peaceful again.

One summer Philip decided to go cycling around

Scotland with two friends. While he was away, Melanie and I thought we would explore Devon again. We did not always book ahead and once we were still driving as night was falling, so we entered a field and prepared to go to sleep in our roomy Opel with the back seats down. We did have sleeping bags. When we awoke it was a frosty morning and the car didn't want to start, so we had to wait awhile before the engine turned and we headed up the incline, hoping the farmer wouldn't appear. Our tour took us around Land's End and along the southern coast of Devon and Cornwall, before heading back home, with one more night in the car.

Ando was a champion at making bonfires, great big ones, which smouldered for days. We always had so much to burn; all the surrounding hedges that Edward had to cut and the tall cypress hedge. To cut that Edward had to begin by climbing onto the top and trim it with the electric shears: this was quite dangerous! Once back on the ground he would then trim all the face of the hedge. The apple trees needed pruning too. Edward climbed the pear tree in the front garden, knocked over the steps that he had climbed and almost at once fell out of it, landing on the fallen ladder. We had to drive back to Switzerland next day and, when he got there, he found he had cracked several ribs. This explained why the drive home had been rather uncomfortable.

SCOTTISH GETAWAYS

Peter and Shirleyanne Cumberledge, who Edward has known since he first went to Thailand, first retired to his own little olive plantation in France, where clearing the maquis Peter discovered a variety of ground orchids in the soil around his olive trees where we visited them once. Later they moved to Scotland where they took up residence in Evanton, where Shirleyanne's parents had been living on the left-hand side of the road up to Glen Glass in what had been a "hut" for a troop of scouts. Although Shirleyanne inherited this, it was not suitable for the two of them. Evanton is reached from Inverness by crossing the full length of the Black Isle on the A9 and, after the bridge, turning east with it until the first turning off which leads into the village. Just the other side of the village there is a turning on the left that leads up Glen Glass. Peter and Shirleyanne bought a large cottage a few hundred yards up from the old scout hut and to the right. Their garden was large and troubled by rabbits and moles! A circular bed had been cordoned off for protection and here grew some spectacular blooms. Peter soon arranged permission from a neighbour to fish further up the river. He loved fishing and made his own flies. Shirleyanne was keen to provide support for local artists and formed she called the Balavoulin Art Group ("the BAG" for short) inviting friends to join as members, and she arranged talks often with slide shows which she usually gave. The monthly meetings became very popular and soon there were more people than chairs! If we were lucky enough to be staying at the time, I much enjoyed joining the group.

Shirleyanne took paying short-term tenants for the old scout hut, mainly for the winter, but she also invited friends to stay there when there was a vacancy. I particularly recall the occasion when Edward and I drove all the way there from Aston Magna in the Cotswolds in southern England, only stopping briefly for refreshments. We left about 5 in the morning and travelled up to Glasgow and then worked our way across to the A9 arriving, exhausted in the early evening. The 'hut' was really a very comfortable small house with a large sitting room, a sunroom, two double bedrooms, a single bedroom, a bathroom and a kitchen. We usually bought our groceries in Alness. Every visit we would dine once with them, and they would dine once with us. We found we could bring two friends with us, and we did not feel cramped.

The garden was in front of the house, parallel to the road and alongside it; but separated from that by a stone wall. However, the grounds also stretched down to the river where it was possible to see dippers if one was patient. Further up the river was one of Peter's favourite fishing spots and Edward had a phone call from him asking for a lift back home because he had mislaid or lost his car key! Edward arrived there and helped him search without success. However, next day we managed to find it!

There were plenty of excellent walks nearby. Fyrish Monument required a 15-minute drive to the car park, from where you can make the 50-minute climb, which is easy with a steady gradient. Just short of the monument, but already at its height, there is a small boggy pool. The view from here looked across the Cromarty Firth, with the oilrigs awaiting repair, to the Black Isle, and off to the west, more distantly Ben Wyvis (1046 m.) could be seen. If one goes right to the top of the Glen Glass road, and, with the keeper's permission, through the gate of the Glen Glass estate, Edward was allowed to park the car and climb Ben Wyvis from the east. One day, Edward hoping to find dotterel and ptarmigan at the top, climbed up and back down. On another occasion we drove round to the west side of the mountain which offers the normal climb and we did that together, but we made the mistake of thinking we could take a direct line down the mountain to the car park only to discover the very difficult footing.

One year we visited Ullapool where a young aunt

Giz spent at least one summer holiday. I remembered having heard that my relatives on my paternal grandmother's side of the family used to visit a property of theirs in the Highlands regularly in summer before World War II. We decided to try and find exactly where this lodge was and we ended up on the south side of Loch Ness looking down on the western end of the loch; so, we drove around until we came to a property that matched our expectations and rang the doorbell! It was answered by a nice gentleman, who was interested to hear about my relatives and showed us around the house which had plenty of stags' antlers hanging from the walls.

Edward and I were eager to visit the Cairngorms. To reach them from Evanton the trip is about 50 miles each way – virtually all on the A9 – and having decided the weather was favourable we set off. On this first occasion we walked up to the level of the restaurant at the top of the funicular at about 2,658 ft. keeping well to the left of the funicular. We picnicked nearby and then walked down the broad path to the south that reaches the car park. This was just the first of six or more visits to the area; on three of these occasions Edward alone or both of us also climbed up to Carn Ban Mhor, where, at the top, Edward once saw dotterel on the ground near him and on another occasion heard them calling in the fog. I remember once dropping

Edward off where the track leaves the road and coming back to pick him up, but suffering a worrisome long wait because the fog had come down on the mountain and Edward was disoriented until a break in the clouds showed that he was facing the wrong way! The area was also good for seeing Golden Eagles. We also looked for dotterel above the top of the funicular and once we found deserted eggs, the desertion being caused by a late heavy snowstorm.

On our many visits to these parts over the years we usually flew from Gatwick to Inverness, where we hired a car. One time, when we had asked Richard and Anne Meade to go with us, we went with them to the airport and saw them off home on a midday flight and returned for our own at about 4 pm only to find, after we had returned the hire car, that our flight back to Gatwick had been cancelled. Easyjet had apparently needed to bring football fans back from a European championship so we were advised to hire another car and to drive back to Gatwick and that our expenses including an overnight stay along the way would be refunded, which it was. The bonus was that passing through southern Yorkshire or perhaps Lincolnshire Edward saw a bee-eater on the telephone wires. The trip with the Meades had included taking a boat from Ullapool to Stornaway, where, before finding our lodging for the night, Anne bought tartan material to make a skirt and I bought something too. From there we drove down to cross to Harris and then to North Uist where we had booked to stay, and we spent much of the night listening to the rasping call of a corncrake that sounded just outside (during an early morning walk Edward was able to see one). Edward & Richard also went to a small loch on Benbecula where they had exciting views of Red-necked Phalaropes. Next day we took a boat from North Uist to Skye and from there to the Cairngorms before returning to Evanton.

On the 10th of November 2017 we attended Shirleyanne's memorial service having flown up from Gatwick to Inverness the day before and after hiring a car to drive to Strathpeffer for the service in the English church. Peter had had a fall and died before her, while she was in a care home.

In July 2019 we were invited to stay with Edward's cousin Vanse, who is married to a Scot. They live on the Isle of Mull near Loch Don. Vanse is a nature lover and suggested that we should visit to see the puffins on the Isle of Lunga in the Treshnish Isles, a short boat trip west from the west coast of Mull. What a marvellous idea! They did not disappoint. Here these birds do not seem to be bothered by tourists and one can approach them really closely. What charmers they are! I was able to take photographs to my heart's content. With the same tour boat, we also visited the Isle of Staffa and climbed round into Fingal's Cave made famous musically thanks to Mendelssohn, who was inspired by the acoustics there. Staffa was given to the National Trust for Scotland by Jock Elliott Jnr., of New York, on 26th. April 1986 in honour of his wife. Here one can marvel at the incredible geological feature, the towering basalt columns. We were lucky with the weather as the sea was not too rough.

Since then, we have not returned to Scotland, but the memories live on.

SEEING EDWARD'S FATHER

Edward's father, Lionel but answering to Dickie, was a professional soldier with the Lincolnshire Regiment and not long before World War II he was seconded to the Bermuda Regiment as its adjutant, and Edward was born there. When war was declared Dickie was shipped home and spent most of the war in Africa. After the war he and Edward's mother divorced. However, he paid for Edward's schooling and Edward went to stay with him in his summer holidays.

On leaving the army Dickie married again and bought a house near Wimborne with a large garden. While they lived there, he was a passionate gardener and he won many annual prizes for his dahlias, so that in the end he was given the silver cup. He displayed and sold his surplus garden produce and flowers beside the road.

By the time we were married they had moved to Ferndown where their house had a peach tree against the sunny wall which dripped with fruit. Sadly, his second wife died and next time we visited he had moved again and married again! He and his new wife were very welcoming and had us to stay with them before this became impractical, when they reached their eighties. We went to the beach where he swam with us and took us to a wildlife park near Bournemouth.

Another of Dickie's passions was the game of Bridge. He was a social member at Ferndown Golf Club, where playing bridge he won enough each year to cover his annual subscription.

After his second wife died, we were rather astonished, but of course pleased, when we learned that he had married again. This lady had previously been married to the Managing Director of the Reserve Bank of India. She was charming and caring, and was also very hospitable, and after he went into a nursing home, she visited him regularly until the end.

A DIFFICULT SPRING JOURNEY TO THE U.K.

Mother wanted to join me on the journey to the UK. We had carefully packed Easter presents in the car along with the usual luggage.

The weather forecast wasn't too good, but we had tickets for the booked ferry crossing so it was time to go. As we set off towards the Jura mountains and the border between France and Switzerland it began to rain, and then to snow. At the French border we were stopped, and the officials wanted to see what we had in the boot of the car. It was a nuisance getting things out in the falling snow.

Once that was over, we gradually pressed on up the mountain, and the snow became thicker and more insistent. I told mother, that we must stop and put the snow chains on the wheels. This was not one of my favourite jobs. Mother did her best to hold an umbrella over me while I got down on my knees and tried with freezing hands to attach the chains. Eventually we managed and we were able to proceed more easily with the front wheels now getting a good grip.

It was not a pleasant drive, but we made it to the mountain top and then, as we came down on the other side, the snow turned to slush. On the main road it became necessary to remove the chains, so once again I was down on my knees in the slush muttering oaths. As the driving was now easier, I must have put my foot down rather heavily on the accelerator because before we knew it, we were stopped by French police who gave us a speeding fine! Just what we needed, and we had to pay up there and then!

It was a relief to arrive in the UK and go to Salisbury and Marlborough and pick up the children from school.

A CANARY

During one of the holidays in Aston Magna my neighbour in the church building – which was now converted into a home – asked me if I would mind taking her canary for a couple of weeks while she and her husband were away. No problem. It came in its cage and sat on the top of the glass-fronted bookcase by a window looking out onto the front garden.

I thought canaries were supposed to sing. This one did not, and it seemed rather scared every time I approached the cage to feed it or to change the sandpaper on the floor of its cage. So, I felt sorry for it and thought "if only it knew, it could come out of the cage, be free, fly round the house or garden and come back to its cage later". Then came what might be considered a spiritual revelation to me: I felt Jesus was saying the same to me: "spend the day with me, be free. You never sing to me!" So ever since that day I have played a hymn in the morning after my daily readings, and I remember the canary.

ISTANBUL, 1985

Our New Zealand friends Colin and Shirley, who we first met in Manila, had been posted to Turkey following a stint in Indonesia, and they invited us to go and stay with them in Istanbul. This was most kind and we accepted their invitation.

This was where we caught up with Sally's offspring Barnaby, whose arrival I have previously mentioned, was an elderly dog by this time. Sometime after we were back home in England, they told us that he used to wander off on his own and that one day he had simply never come back, and they wondered if he had been "put in a pot".

Istanbul or Constantinople as it was formerly known, where east and west meet, was absolutely fascinating for us and very different from the Buddhist and Catholic countries where we had lived before.

Our friends energetically showed us around. We saw the covered markets, the underground Basilica cistern (said to be one of many lying beneath the city) and the truly breathtaking Topkapi Palace Museum – full of exquisite jewellery and pottery.

Jane our English friend from Switzerland happened to be visiting the city with her brother and we all went for a cruise on the Bosphorus and marvelled at such sights as the Hagia Sophia which now has with its four minarets reaching to the sky, but had been built as a catholic cathedral and the seat of the Eastern Papacy, however it is now an active mosque and we were able to visit that too.

Then, of course, a trip to the Black Sea was a must. Colin drove us there and Shirley came for a swim with me.

The local food did not much appeal to us, but we remember eating a Greek baclava.

Some of the shops were strange in that they seemed to plunge away underground. Clothes were much cheaper than in Switzerland, so Edward bought a leather jacket, and I bought a mackintosh, a skirt and a shirt.

VENICE, 1985

Before leaving Switzerland again as we knew we soon would be, Edward and I decided to take the train to Venice as Edward had never been there. It was an overnight train, and we were rather disgusted to find the linen in the sleeping car was dirty including the pillow. Our night was not very comfortable either, the car had from top to bottom three beds on each side, and we arrived next morning feeling jaded and not in a very good mood to start the holiday – indeed Edward was grumpy! However, the sun shone and once we had crossed the Rialto bridge and we had an ice cream in hand, Edward's smile suddenly returned.

We were very fortunate to have a room in an hotel which overlooks the lagoon, while just around the corner was St. Mark's square. We soon took a boat (vaporetto) to the island of Murano to see the glass blowing and came away with a set of glass dessert dishes.

Clearly, the way to explore was on foot, around the confusing passageways and passing all the tempting shops. I fell for two carnival masks which we later wore to open the front door at Norman Chapel when we had trick or treat visitors! We visited the Peggy Guggenheim Museum, and this American art dealer and collector had lived in a house on the Grand Canal. It is reportedly one of the finest museums of modern art in the world. And, yes, of course we had a short trip in a gondola with the accompanying voice of the gondolier. Very memorable and well worth the trip.

OFF TO A JOINT-VENTURE IN THE U.S.A., 1985

We were to move to the U.S.A. for two or three years. A joint-venture company in Chicago was involved; Edward had been offered, and had accepted, the position of Vice President of Marketing and had agreed with Nestlé that, as they could not get him a US work visa, he would actually leave Nestlé and take ownership of his accumulated pension rights. So, in late November he flew over to see the area and the office and to meet the other senior staff and to house hunt if he could. The location proved to be well out in the northern outskirts of Chicago, not far from the lake. But he was booked to fly home for Christmas.

It was the year end, and the children were coming out to Corseaux for Christmas, so we decided to book a chalet in Champery that belonged to an English dentist who practiced in Fribourg. He had turned this chalet into something unusual and very special. It had a balcony, a fireplace, a trapdoor that one could use to get down to the lower floor quickly, a bathroom and separate shower room, a urinal and several bedrooms which would be suitable for either Philip or Melanie. By agreement Philip had invited a friend over from school.

A day or so after we arrived at the chalet Edward was to arrive back from Chicago, and I went to Geneva to meet him and take him to the chalet in

Champery. There was a very good butcher in the village, who provided us with the traditional turkey, and all the shops were just a short walk away. On Christmas Day we went to the local church in the evening, and we were all given oranges as we left the church.

Various friends who lived in the Vevey area, including Ada and her children Sebastian and Rebecca came over to ski with us. The snow was perfect, and on Christmas morning, after Philip and Melanie had each received their present of a guitar, they went skiing and said the slopes were empty and in glorious sunshine. What a fabulous farewell to the mountains.

Another farewell took place in Corseaux, where we rented the village hall and invited friends to a meal which was bought in from outside. Ada's two children offered to serve and wash up, bless them.

Soon after New Year and everything had been packed up, our flat had been cleared, and the children were about to go back to school, we stayed in the Hotel du Lac in Vevey before our farewells to mother.

THE UNITED STATES OF AMERICA, 1985

When it became news that we were going to the States, a few people said, "You want to be careful of the sects out there so choose your church carefully".

I discovered that there were three Episcopalian churches within a reasonable distance of our house, so I decided to try them out on Sundays. At the second visit to one of them, we stood up to sing the first hymn and to my astonishment, printed at the end was "Christopher Dearnley", previously the organist at Salisbury Cathedral whose wife had given me piano lessons! Of course, I took that as a sign that this was the church that God wished me to attend. Thank you, it all seemed very clear.

The vicar and congregation made me very welcome and I soon became involved in the Altar Guild which, over the Christmas period, saw me clearing up after the Communion service resulting in my not getting home until after 1 a.m

The plane carrying me across "the pond" in late January (Edward had left earlier) was a jumbo and I was interested to note that the bulge at the top was in fact a sitting room. Chicago's O'Hare Airport seemed intimidating, and I felt a bit panicky, but I can't recall any problem over immigration, and Edward came in a limousine to meet me and took me to a Marriott Courtyard Hotel in north Chicago which was to be our "home" for the next six weeks, while we waited for all our furniture and for the purchase of our house to complete.

Our hotel room held two enormous king-sized beds. Edward went off to the office and I was left wondering what on earth to do, but an enduring memory is the honking sound of the Canada Geese which were everywhere.

A charming company wife called Mary Condella took pity on my plight and arrived at the hotel one day with her young daughter in tow to take me out to lunch. As I write these words nearly forty years later, our friendship continues.

When we left the hotel, it was to move to live into a house we had bought in a gated community called Lake Barrington Shores, this is about an hour's drive north of Chicago, close to the town of Barrington and was about 35 minutes for Edward to get to the office. There was a guard at the gate to check who was coming and going. The lake was about a mile long and surrounded by cleverly designed houses so that neighbours did not overlook one another. Boating on the lake was enjoyable but there were snapping turtles in it so swimming was not a good idea!

The garage was large enough for two or three cars and had up and over electrically operated doors so one did not need to leave the car until you were in the garage which makes much sense in winter. From there one could go directly into the house. There was a basement room along with a toilet and shower and the heat and cooling system was controlled at that level. The first floor housed a kitchen, a sitting room and a dining room and gave access to the communal gardens at the rear. Upstairs there was an office, a master bedroom and bathroom, and a second guest bedroom opposite with a shower room and basin.

The house was heated in winter and cooled in summer by an ingenious system which is designed to be able to maintain the same indoor temperature throughout the year.

Our neighbours on one side were a middle-aged couple, and the wife soon invited me to join her bowling group, which I did. I had never played ten-pin bowling before, but I came to quite enjoy it. The son of our neighbours on the other side had been to Oxford and thought that the very worst thing in the whole of the UK was Marmite!

Our house was placed quite near the large community building which housed an indoor and outdoor swimming pool. The tennis courts were a short walk away and there was a golf course. All these facilities were covered by an annual membership fee. There was a very pleasant walk all round the lake amongst the trees where it was possible to see squirrels, racoons, cardinals and woodpeckers very easily.

The seasons were very clearly defined: the winter came with dry cold not like the English winter and plenty of snow, and an explosion of life in spring with the grass turning rapidly from brown to green and birds often nesting in bushes where it was easy to see them. Summer could be almost unbearably hot, in fact we had a whole month when the temperature was 100 F. or more, when by 10 a.m. it was too hot to go to the swimming pool. The change to autumn was rapid and brought fabulous colours for a relatively short period and fruits to be picked at a nearby pick-your-own farm.

A RE-UNION WITH FRIENDS IN CANADA, 1985

Our friends Christopher and Carole had been living near Hamilton in Canada since their marriage and two daughters had been born there; they were now about 2 and 5 years old and quite entertaining. Carole confessed that it was extremely difficult in winter and unsafe to take babies out into temperatures that dropped to minus 40 degrees. The had bought quite a large home and when we were living in Chicago they invited us to come and stay. Christopher was a Professor at McMaster University in Hamilton and enjoying his role.

We flew to Toronto where they met us and drove us to their home, which was about a 40-minute drive. Their property was quite extensive and included a barn where Carole kept chickens. Christopher farmed the property in a small way and enjoyed hiring diggers and other machinery which he also used to enhance the surroundings.

Our first excursion was to Niagara Falls which was quite close to them. This was a damp experience as it was raining and blowing a gale by the time we got there. However, we were glad to have been there, and more than happy to have seen our friends again.

Eventually as we were heading home, we stayed a night in Toronto and we admired the famous

Toronto Tower which we ascended in a fast-moving lift. From the high point we could see a dizzying view of the various others tall buildings and I was pleased to be able to take photographs, a particularly pleasing one was of the reflection of one in the tall windows of another. We had arranged to meet and have dinner with a friend of Edward from Blackheath in England in the 1960s: Ian, who styled himself, "Ian kidney-wiper Sanderson" had trained as a surgeon in London. Ian also lived in Vancouver for some years, but I think that was before he came to Toronto.

A VISIT TO YELLOWSTONE NATIONAL PARK

The trip lasted for 12 days, and we covered 3,200 miles. We had both Philip and Melanie with us, and we hired a Winnebago campervan. Philip was very disappointed not to be allowed to drive it, but the required age was 21.

On the way west on a major Interstate Highway we left Illinois and passed through Wisconsin (the dairy land of America), Minnesota and South Dakota to reach the park which is almost entirely in Wyoming. Our first night was spent at a signalled camping ground close to the highway.

The park is 63 miles (101 kms.) across from north to south, and 54 miles (87 kms.) across from east to west by air. Here we parked in a large camping ground looking out onto a sizeable lake.

The Americans are very organised over camping, and this means is that one can plug into electricity, water and main drainage. One can then light the gas (carried on board) to heat the water and hey presto, you have a lovely hot shower available. The T.V. was a bit of a waste of time as once we were up in the mountains we couldn't receive the signals. We observed some vans with enormous dish antennas on top, obviously belonging to people determined not to miss their favourite programmes.

As we climbed up to the park, we saw other camper vans towing small cars and it was then we realised that such families were experienced visitors and were unhooking their small cars so that they could use them to explore the park. We did not have that choice and had to make our exploration in the Winnebago, but I think we were able to retain our spot in the camping ground car park for the several nights we were there. Winnebagos are large vehicles and we each had our own beds in the van, a queen sized one above the cab which Edward had; Philip had a nice wide one across the "dining area" and Melanie and I each had a single bed at the back. There was a gas stove, a fridge/freezer and a bathroom with shower, basin and loo. A big vehicle!

Most of the drive west was through a monotonous landscape of fields of 'corn' (which we call maize) and we used cruise control almost the whole time until we began to climb up to the park. But before reaching the park we noticed advertising for a shop called Wall Drug all along the highway for 500 miles; this apparently became famous for offering iced water to travellers. We also saw a circular construction of sleek long-bodied cars planted upright with the rear on the ground and head in the air, with other cars horizontally arranged on top designed to look like Stonehenge.

Then we passed through the very colourful Badlands in South Dakota, an interesting and very unusual geological feature exposing sharp colourful ridges that had been formed deep under the sea to eventually emerge when the land rose to appear as a forbidding arid range.

As we began to climb, we passed not far from the site of the battle of the Little Bighorn where the Sioux Indians surrounded the US Cavalry troop led by Colonel Custer. Soon after that we drove past Mt. Rushmore National Monument where the huge faces of Presidents Washington, Jefferson, Roosevelt and Lincoln have been carved into the granite mountain; this was done over a 14-year period (1927-1941).

On the way home, coming back across to Barrington on the next Interstate Highway to the south, running more or less parallel to our journey west, we added Nebraska and Iowa to our list of states visited. All these States, except for Wyoming and parts of South Dakota, are flat, flat countryside and in the prairie in the drier areas we saw prairie dogs looking as though they were sitting up and begging, and an occasional elk. The prairie dogs are, in fact, watching out for birds of prey looking for them.

On some days we covered 300-500 miles, but 65

mph was the maximum allowed on the highways. Roads stretched away to a seemingly infinite horizon – we called these roads "walkers' despair" and wondered how on earth people could actually walk across the U.S. Imagine driving for seven hours with the scenery looking the same all the way, and perhaps almost all in the same State. We crossed one time zone going, so we gained an hour.

The Mississippi looked more interesting on the outward trip than on our way back. We crossed it at a point where it looked like a huge lake with many wooded islands.

We did have a couple of problems with the Winnebago. The first was the cruise control cable which burned out. Apparently, this is a fairly common problem with this kind of vehicle when the cable is placed too near the exhaust pipe. Cruise control (rare in England at that time) is a great help on long journeys. You choose a speed and then you "set" it, allowing you to remove your foot from the accelerator. As the van is an automatic with no clutch, this means all one has to do is steer, and there's not too much of that on these straight roads. Stories are told of people who walk back in the moving vehicle to sit down to a meal, imagining that the car will find out how to manage the curves! The burn out only made our use of cruise control impossible, so we drove on.

The other problem we had was dirty fuel, and this clogged up both filters and eventually caused us to come to a grinding halt after struggling along at slower and slower speeds. This occurred at 11.30 p.m.at night just 4 miles short of our destination! Luckily, we had the emergency phone number of the company in Chicago from which we had rented the vehicle, and they contacted a local Ford garage, which sent a truck to tow us into town. There was a Motel next door, and we booked a room for the night leaving Philip and Melanie to sleep there while Edward and I stayed in the van outside the garage!

Yellowstone Park is set in the 'Rockies', a range of mountains ranging in height from about 7,000 to 10,000 ft., and it covers about 2 million acres including a very large lake. The trees in the valley are mainly lodge pole pines. While we were there the weather was beautiful and the vistas in the clear air were spectacular. It was very hot in the day and very cold at night, but a dry cold and a dry heat so we had to keep putting cream on our lips.

There were many animals about. The numerous elk we saw were mainly females. There were plenty of bison (and we were told to be very wary of them), and some handsome moose were quietly minding their own business at the edge of the forest. It was possible to photograph some of these animals from the roadway quite nearby, where masses of other curious campers had spilled out like us. We saw no bears, which was a big disappointment; but we were told they were fairly plentiful. Some years ago, the tourists got the bears hooked on peanut butter sandwiches, and they became a menace, and some tourists were injured due to their lack of caution.

Edward saw plenty of birds including Bald Eagle and Pelican., 105 species altogether on the trip as a whole, a good number of which were in the park, which sits on top of a huge dormant volcano. Evidence of this could be seen in the pools and geysers – some mysterious, some startling in colour, some quite beautiful; but it is essential to be alert to avoid their sudden spouting, which in some cases is quite prolonged. This is claimed to be the largest concentration of geysers in the world. Perhaps Old Faithful is the best known. This sends boiling water several hundred feet into the air every 90 minutes.

Some pools are like boiling vats of grey porridge, others a broad area of steam through which one can glimpse piercingly blue central water which appears when the wind blows away the steam for a minute. Some vents have built up calcareous and mineral deposits into curious castle-like formations, the tops of which yield a steam blow off every so often, while others pour their turbulent water into icy rivers nearby.

There are also deep quiescent pools with orange and ochre colours at the side, turning to green, blue and turquoise towards the centre, all controlled by the temperature of the water and the type of algae that grow around it. On the surface of some of the rivulets we saw a rare spider, which had a silvery aspect making it look like a diamond-studded broach.

Naturally, no bathing is allowed.

One afternoon during a walk through a section of geysers on the specially constructed boardwalks, Philip and Melanie were greatly entertained by the appearance and amusing antics of a number of Woodchucks. Philip said they looked like Russians wearing enormously long fur coats as they sat up and scanned the strange world around them. Their burrows must be very cosy in winter being constructed around the geysers.

There is a quaint and unusual old hotel named after the Old Faithful geyser. It was built entirely of lodge pole pine in 1903. It is vast and offers over 300 rooms.

On leaving the park we drove south into the Grand

Tetons, where there is a ski resort and there was a lift that we went up. But soon we had turned east for home and were driving back east, making one overnight stop at a camp site where we were entertained by a major thunderstorm.

We enjoyed the holiday and the camping experience, but agreed we would not do it like again; it would be better to fly to the nearest airport and rent a car.

YOSEMITE NATIONAL PARK, 1987

My friend Jane came over from Switzerland to stay, and she had a friend who had worked with her as a physiotherapist, and now she lives in San Francisco and was happy to loan us camping equipment, and Jane was keen to visit Yosemite, so we flew down there.

A short walk from her friend's house was a seashore walk that led along a winding path covered with colourful red poppies to where seals were basking.

At the hotel where we stayed a night, someone tried to access our room after we had gone to bed, but luckily, we had put the chain on the door which stopped anyone entering. But as two vulnerable ladies on our own it sent a chill down our spines.

We took a tour of San Francisco and saw Lombard Street with its famous steep eight hairpin bends, and from Fisherman's wharf we could see Alcatraz Island with its prison.

Jane rented a car and we drove to Yosemite National Park in the Sierra Nevada mountains. The redwoods are the stars here, and we felt like little ants at the foot of their grandeur. A particularly notable redwood is called Grizzly Giant, which is said to be 2,700 years old. The base of another one had had a square passage cut out so that one could drive a car through it. The two huge granite cliffs worth special mention are El Capitan and Half Dome.

We made good use of the camping equipment lent by Jane's friend. The first night I had to get out for a call of nature, and I thought I would find a spot a little away from the tent. There was a bright moon, and everything looked very different at night, so quite quickly I was confused. Boulders looked like bears. Bears were about, and everyone was told never to leave anything around which might entice them. Trying to find our tent again, I panicked briefly, but found the tent again with no harm done! We did eventually see a couple of grizzlies at a distance.

We were impressed by other campers, including a neighbour who had converted his van into a perfect kitchen/dining area. We did actually manage to light a fire and to cook some eggs. After breakfast Jane and I headed back towards San Francisco. On the way we passed a very pleasant-looking golf club hotel and decided, rather naughtily, to sneak into their changing rooms for a much-needed shower! In the garden there were some beautiful bluebirds, which were busy eating red berries.

We explored northwards across the Golden Gate

Bridge, one of the most internationally recognized symbols of San Francisco and California. This suspension bridge connects San Francisco Bay and the Pacific Ocean coast.

This was all we had time for before heading back to Chicago.

ALASKA, 1987

May-June. The 49th State or "The Last Frontier".

The Russian Empire agreed to sell Alaska to the United States in 1867 for the sum of $7.2 million (equivalent to $129 million in 2023).

This state is three times the size of Texas and is said to have a coastline longer than the whole of the coastline of the rest of the USA.

We were still living in Chicagoland, but Edward, who had been entitled to a trip to Europe, was invited to participate in a Clintec company visit to a raw material supplier in Sweden.

While Edward went to Stockholm I went straight to England, where I saw family, and Edward flew there to meet me. He had planned and booked the main elements for our visit to Alaska.

Before leaving the States Edward explained that we planned to fly back over the pole to Alaska, and that naturally he would repay the extent of any flight costs above the simple return tickets to Sweden/England. The Polar route only took about 9 hours, and in terms of local time we arrived in Anchorage just before we left London! It took us a few days for our biological clocks to readjust. I also remember that my feet swelled up and at the end of the flight I couldn't get my shoes on; apparently the pilot had the same problem.

After a night in an Anchorage B & B we set off north into the interior on a huge train headed for Fairbanks. It was pulled by 3 diesel engines on a single track travelling quite slowly uphill almost all the way. The journey of about 150 miles took about 7 hours. Some of the cars had domed glass tops to provide better views of the increasingly spectacular scenery. Of course we kept our eyes skinned for wildlife such as moose, caribou or bear.

Denali National Park. This was a goal we had chosen; it covers 6 million acres of land embracing the mountains where Mt. McKinley towers up to a 20,000 ft. peak. Due to fog and low clouds our best view of Mt. McKinley was later, on our way back down by train. This was the rainy season, and fog and low clouds were quite normal. There was a nice hotel close to the train stop for the park, with a view across the road into a deep bowl on the other side where, when we went back across the road, we saw a beaver. Our hotel room faced that way and outside the window was a big hot-tub welcome which we enjoyed!

The wilderness tour arranged by Park Service started with a bus from the hotel leaving at 5.30 a.m. (luckily, we were still on European time) and hotel breakfasts were already being served at 5.00 a.m. Lori, the guide-cum-bus driver was very knowledgeable and sharp eyed; and he pointed out how many trees to the left of the road were slipping down the hillside while still staying more or less upright

Passengers were encouraged to call for the bus to stop if they spotted something of interest to view or to photograph. For the animals' sake, it is good that traffic within the Park is restricted in speed and as to its route by fog and low clouds.

A sharp-eyed boy in the bus soon shouted "bear", upon which all the bus windows were lowered, and cameras clicked. It is marvellous to see these creatures in their natural state. The first ones we saw were a mother and a yearling cub, apparently digging for ground squirrels.

As the bus wound its way upwards through a pass it became colder and the vegetation less tall, until finally we reached the snowline. From one pass called 'Polychrome', on account of the many hues of rock, there were views stretching across the tundra, which is quite surprisingly beautiful and not unlike the Scottish Highlands. A water-colour artist's dream!

During this 7-hour trip we sighted bears several

times, moose with young, caribou herds, Dall sheep high up on the hillside and a lone wolf. The folk in a bus ahead of us witnessed a bear make off with a young moose only for it to be chased by the mother moose.

Back at the hotel we enjoyed an evening lecture by a ranger, who like the guide on the bus, told us what to do if we met a moose or a bear when we were on foot. Apparently, one should run from a moose, but never from a bear. In the case of a bear, you should always stand your ground and talk to the bear. Bears have poor eyesight and need to be told you are human. If you run that triggers the idea that they have found food, and they can cover the ground between you at a pace reaching as much as 35 m.p.h., so running is definitely not a good idea. The lecturer reminded us, if we already knew, that female bears have "delayed fertilization". Although they mate in Spring/Summer, they do not become pregnant until the onset of winter, and the young are born in dens during winter hibernation and only weigh a pound at birth, and apparently the mother is not always awake then.

Willow is an important shrub in the tundra and provides food for many, especially for moose. We also learned about permafrost and how it can create the picture of drunken-looking forests that slip slowly down the bank, and also about the taiga, which is south of the tundra and more open with far fewer trees.

We did not see many species of birds, but we did spot golden eagles in the distance and many times what looked like ptarmigan by the road. The Long-tailed Skuas which breed here should have arrived back from their migration, but they were nowhere to be seen.

We did not try white-water rafting, which could be arranged at the hotel; but we did enjoy the salmon bake eatery just across the road from the hotel, which was no more than a primitive wooden hut with a loose glacial pebble floor and a help-yourself salad bar. The salmon was cooked outside on a grill and because the air was cold, we brought the food indoors to eat close to a primitive wood-burning stove.

The next day, before the train south, we had time to try to get closer to the beaver and separately to walk a little way down the main highway, where, on our right, we found a small but definite path up a valley and into the edge of the park where we has been told there was a small lake with a Red-necked Grebe present on it. We were very aware of what we had been told about bears, and about 40 yards up this trail we found bear footmarks and overlying an adult footmark was the footprint of a bear cub –

time for a hasty retreat!

After the return trip by train later that day, we spent another night in the Anchorage B&B before heading to the airport to take off in a 4-prop plane to head west along the Aleutian chain.

The Pribilofs. A crazy wild place. These islands, of which two are inhabited, lie well north of the Aleutian chain; they are about 600 miles from Siberia and 300 from the Alaskan mainland. They were first discovered by Russian fur trappers over 200 years ago. The trapper to land first had a boat named for St. Paul, and he gave this name to the largest island. There are three other islands – but only one is inhabited, and is quite large, and it is called St. George. Note however that these names would have been Russian.

When we visited, St. Paul was said to be inhabited by just over 600 people – sometimes called Aleuts, although many are of true Russian origin. The Russian discoverers knew that the fur seals migrated northwards to rookeries, but they did not know where until the breeding colonies were finally traced to these islands. The ensuing history is not pleasant reading. It starts with the importation of labourers – mainly from the Russian Far East, but perhaps also from the Aleutian chain, and they were enslaved forcing them to "work the fur trade" in this remote and wild island group, where the job to be done was the mass butchery of the seals. Eventually the 'settlers' that remained were apparently abandoned.

Our flight west required us to follow the Aleutian chain to a point midway along the chain and then turn due north for St. Paul. Our pilot explained that we would need a window in the cloud to be able to get down and land, and that our remaining fuel needed for his return direct to Anchorage gave us just 20 minutes to find a gap and land. We were lucky and the first passenger to land kissed the ground! The gap lasted long enough to enable the pilot to climb out and fly directly back to Anchorage.

Since 1982, under Alaskan regulations, the locals are no longer allowed to kill for profit. Only subsistence sealing is allowed, and the animals taken are the 3-to 5 -year-old males. We understood that the skins are burned, which seemed a wicked waste, but presumably there is no market for them.

Apart from a tiny income from tourism the people today have no incentive – or real opportunity – to work, apart from fishing, and many islanders rely on national assistance, much of which reportedly gets spent on drink. It seemed to us that little pride was taken in the island. We saw quite a lot of trash on the beach, but some of this comes in on the tide and is not local. Nylon fishing nets unintentionally ensnare and entangle many seals, such nets are usually then cut loose which leaves the seals, still entangled, to die. The abandoned nets are not biodegradable.

The big male seals are called 'beachmasters': we saw some on shore, but we could only look through windows carefully placed in wooden hides. A beachmaster is a mature male (or bull) seal; these arrive ahead of the females, and each claim a stretch of beach that becomes his territory ready to receive about 12 or more females, which he tries to bully into joining his harem. The females produce their pups within days of arrival, and they are soon receptive to mating again. Like bears they have delayed fertilization.

In some places around the island there are tall cliffs and we saw and photographed many species of cliff-nesting seabirds of which the puffins – especially the tufted variety – were the most amusing to watch. I took photographs leaning over the edge of a tall cliff with Edward holding onto my legs! Near the northernmost point of the island was a tiny lake on which we were fortunate to find the rare Emperor Goose.

Here we were befriended by those who had been

here before. One was an elderly man with a weather-beaten appearance, who has been returning to St. Paul for years. Another was a young lady, who, apparently, had acted as a tour guide in many different locations throughout the States, but who is also drawn back to this wild place.

Later on in the season, the drab volcanic landscape with dry-looking grass is transformed by carpets of wildflowers, which we were shown in slides during an evening lecture. We found and photographed the Woolly Lousewort, but the only other plant we saw in flower was blue and looked like a small gentian.

Among our fellow passengers there were about 6 hard-core birdwatchers, and a few other tourists who didn't quite realize what they had let themselves in for! The one hotel that existed was primitive and the restaurant was a walk away. Until recently the locals were unfamiliar with most vegetables that we take for granted; they did not know what to do with them or how to cook them. Reindeer have been introduced onto the island and the people have learned to eat their flesh. However, attempts to keep cows and pigs on the island have proved to be a disaster.

The Blue, or Arctic, Fox is a resident and one appeared on the skyline and studied us enquiringly.

The foxes raid the birds' nests that they can get to, and they are often found on the beach.

During our three-night stay we did once see some blue sky, but mostly the islands were wreathed in low cloud and drizzle or sea fog. One night the hotel furnace went crazy, and we were nearly roasted alive in our beds, and we were thankful to get out into the morning mist!

We made an interesting visit to a Russian church; Father George told us that the people are very devout – "they haven't much else in their lives". The church is lovingly cared for and maintained. As is customary in a Russian Orthodox church, there are no seats. The services last a minimum of 2 hours, and a wedding can last 8 hours. Father George spoke in favour of bringing back sealing as a livelihood for the people and said that he thought some conservationists distort facts and fail to see other sides of the story.

There is a national weather station on the island, which is linked by satellite to all the other US weather stations, so in 15 seconds one can know the conditions forecast for any given place in the U.S. or its waters. Hydrogen balloons are released several times a day accompanied by a data box which, as it ascends, transmits all the local information. There are about 20 coastguards here and after a posting to the Pribilofs, each can choose any posting in the U.S. they wish as his or her next location. But apparently some people are actually drawn to this place and stay longer than one tour.

We finally flew back to Anchorage where we had another night before departing for Juneau.

Our next stop was centred on Glacier Bay, which is reached from Juneau not far south of which is the border with Canada. We were not going to be staying in Juneau.

On deplaning from Anchorage, we boarded a little Piper "Cherokee" 6-seater plane that I christened Paper Plane. The pilots of these planes all seem to be husky youths, who have had strict training and who now have a good knowledge of these craft. There was room for a third passenger on our 25-minute flight, and with us we had a fisherman enjoying his retirement, who, like us, was on his way to Glacier Bay Inn.

Just after take-off Edward thought he spotted a whale in the bay below, so the pilot tipped the wings and came around so that we would have a better view. But unfortunately we couldn't see it again.

A day or two later the fisherman told us that he had

been concerned for the safety of the boat because whales were leaping about all around it. During his stay he caught a 150-lb halibut, and he had had it frozen; he kindly gave it to us to bring home.

Glacier Bay Inn is in Gustavus, and it is run by a young couple called Al and Annie, who with a true pioneering spirit had moved north from the lower states U.S. They "won" this plot of land in an auction, one of those run to encourage people who wish to settle. They then set about building themselves this home cum hotel. It was built using wood for half of it and is absolutely charming. The final touches were from Annie who had done a splendid job of decorating it beautifully but simply. The hotel can accommodate about 18 people. After the Pribilofs it looked like Paradise.

Just after our arrival we spotted a Bald Eagle perched within 100 yards of us; and while we were admiring him, we realised that we were surrounded by hummingbirds which were coming to a feeder on the terrace. There is just one species of hummingbird that gets this far north, and it is a long-distance west coast migrant. Two visitors, who had just gone upstairs into the turret, spotted a Black Bear strolling across the meadow and we rushed out to get a better look.

Al and Annie's two small children can play to their

hearts content in a cleverly devised playground area in part of the grounds, which include both garden and meadow and in that there is a landing strip for Al's little blue plane, which he uses for his 3-weekly visits to Juneau for supplies.

They have hired a cook, who came on a cruise and fell in love with the place and stayed. He had had experience in France and Germany, and he seemed to specialize in desserts and fish dishes. Salads were served daily, and all the vegetables were from the garden and picked just minutes before the meal. All the bread is home-made.

Gustavus is a small community and locals come to the restaurant if they can establish that seating is available. Annie told us that they had two wedding parties booked for later in the summer and that wedding ceremonies take place under the hummingbird feeder in the meadow. We didn't discuss what happens in winter.

Next day at 7 a.m. our hosts drove us a few miles north along the dirt road to the edge of Glacier Bay where we, like 80 other people (from the main hotel in the area), were to join a ship for a 9-hour cruise up the bay to the foot of the glacier, where smaller glaciers reach the shore on one side of the bay. The ship carried a ranger, who was knowledgeable about the area and gave a talk. He told us that 200 years ago the glacier extended much further down the bay and when the ice retreated it exposed small fjords along the sides of the bay, and the temperate rain forest grew up beginning with small alders followed by spruce and hemlock. The temperate rain forest is a mysterious place with its thick mats of mosses and lichens trailing from the trees.

As the ship progressed further up the bay the vegetation became smaller until it disappeared, and the shore became just rocks and ice.

The climax of the trip was a 45-minute stop about half a mile short of the face of the main glacier, which looked as if it must be 50 foot tall. The ship's engines were turned off so that we could appreciate the cracking and creaking and groaning of the ice and watch the "calving" of huge lumps of ice that bob back up to the surface. Of course, the further up the bay we went the colder it became, and near the ice it was bitterly cold, and we wore everything we had with us! There were mountains further back, but the tops were never visible because of the low cloud.

Soon the boat was bumping into quite big lumps of ice, and we learned that an earthquake had taken place 4 days earlier which had shaken up the glaciers and caused them to calve at a faster rate than usual. Some of the floes had Harbour Seals perched on them and they plunged into the water when our ship came close. Puffins were visible on rocks off to the side.

The boat deliberately kept its distance from the calving cliff face, but the cliff was so tall that it still felt as if we could have reached out and touched it.

We disembarked where we had boarded, and hitched a ride back to the hotel, but next morning we went back there to explore the temperate rain forest. We hunted quite hard to find a Blue Grouse; we could hear booming its mating call, but it was impossible figure out where it was coming from. All around us were Bald Eagles whistling and shrieking. In the forest we did see a Black Bear across a small pond from us and a porcupine that was walking up the trail ahead of us. Next day we travelled back to Juneau and caught our planned connecting flight to Chicago.

Now back in Chicago we are struggling to acclimatize to 95 degrees and bright light, but we shall long remember our holiday in three such different locations in the wilderness of Alaska.

OUR RETURN TO ENGLAND

Early in the Spring of 1988 Edward arrived back from work in the early afternoon and reported that his job at Clintec was at an end. He had been asked to leave the office to go to the Baxter Head Office where he found he was face-to-face with his boss and a senior man from Nestlé. Edward's boss had been unhappy with being reminded that Clintec was a joint venture and that it was being managed as a strictly Baxter entity which Edward saw as inconsistent with the original agreement. That this independent approach was possible was due to the way the deal had been structured.

It was made clear to Edward that Baxter wanted a quiet and non-confrontational settlement, and a satisfactory deal was thrashed out. Edward was to be paid for the third year that he had been contracted for, he was also allowed two trips to England to help sort things out, and Nestlé offered help with finding a job back there.

There was no problem about shipping home all the furniture we wanted: indeed, we could have had our two cars shipped back free as well. As regards the house we had bought at Lake Barrington Shores, Baxter said that they would seek three offers for the property and, without waiting for there to be a sale, they would pay us the middle price, and this turned out to be almost identical with our purchase price. Sometime later we were told by friends that the market turned down quite sharply over the next two years, and that the house sold for some 30,000 dollars less than we had been paid.

On the day of the confrontation Edward heard that his father had died and there was a funeral to go to. Coincidentally, a letter also arrived from Moscow where Philip Warren, one of Edward's friends, was working for Nestlé. He was writing to say that he had noted in the Daily Telegraph that a senior job was on offer at the Wildfowl & Wetlands Trust at Slimbridge in Gloucestershire. He enclosed the advertisement and Edward phoned Slimbridge to enquire if he could still apply! The reply was Yes. If Edward was going to be in England next week, an interview could be arranged.

So, Edward flew to England and hired a car making Slimbridge his first place of call. The interview seemed to go well. It began with Brian Bertram, the Director, a man who has previously worked for London Zoo. Then there was an interview with Sir Peter Scott and the Manager for the Arundel Centre of the Trust.

Next day Edward attended his father's funeral in Ferndown; and had a phone call from Slimbridge to say that he was being offered the job, which was to be titled Head of Operations. Edward called back to say that he was delighted to accept. Now we could both fly home and all our belongings could be shipped directly to Aston Magna, where much would have to be stored in the garage.

In due course our furniture arrived back at Norman Chapel to be stored in the garage and our trusty Opel had to sit outside. Soon we would be catching up with the children.

THE WILDFOWL AND WETLAND TRUST, 1988-1991

Edward's daily drive down to Slimbridge took about 50 minutes if there was no snow. He had to get down into the Severn valley by way of Broadway and work his way across to the A5 motorway, which was usually a fast road.

He found that everything to do with each centre and the captive birds held there was the responsibility of the relevant Centre Manager, who reported to Brian Bertram. They were also responsible for any wintering wildfowl, and at two centres, Welney and Caerlaverock, there were only wild birds. Also reporting directly to Brian were those responsible for the education of visitors, fundraising, finance and accounting, and research. In theory the research scientists were funded by the annual surplus the Trust made. Everything else turned out to be Edward's job.

This included personnel, marketing, journals and the large estate in Devon – an asset that had been gifted to the Trust. The previous owner lived in the big house, and she took an interest in what the Trust did with the estate, including the forestry cycle and the interests of the tenant farmers.

It quickly became clear to Edward that Brian's multiple commitments, which included meeting with the Board of Directors, limited Brian's opportunities to see the Centre Managers and so Edward set himself the task of visiting each of them once a quarter and reporting back to Brian, and both he and the Centre Managers seemed to appreciate this.

Sadly, Peter Scott died in August 1989 and the funeral, held in Slimbridge village church, was well attended, and both of us were there.

It so happened that the Trust was already suffering from reduced visits by school children due to the Education Reform Act and a financial depression. The loss of Peter as the Trust's most effective fund raiser tipped over the balance and in 1988 or 1989 the Trust was losing as much money as it had been used to make as an annual operating surplus.

In early 1990 it was agreed that some redundancies must be made. Both the decision making and the personal handling of the choice of jobs to be made redundant were poor as, predictably, the senior staff asked to identify cuts they could make dug in to protect their staff. Edward offered to leave, but this was rejected, only to be taken up 9 months later when he found that the other senior staff had been told before he was.

During this time, I bought a franchise to run an

after school French club. I started this in three nearby villages having advertised in paper shops and supermarkets. The initial take-up was quite encouraging, and the material provided was excellent. However, I'm afraid to say that some parents obviously found this a convenient way to have an extra hour without a tiresome child!

As anyone who has worked with children will appreciate, it just needs one disruptive little one to ruin it for all the others. It was quite a tiring exercise, not only because it was necessary to go to each venue ahead of time and set up in the previously booked space, but also because some children had no aptitude for the language and were not really interested.

Having said all that, most of the children were lovely and polite, and we had some good times. The parents were also appreciative.

When we eventually left the area I tried, unsuccessfully, to sell the franchise. But all the materials came with me and came in very useful for playing with when our grandchildren came to stay. Sad to say, none of them seem to have an ear for languages.

Norman Chapel

Niagara Falls

The Winnebago

Morning Glory pool at
Yellowstone National Park

Alaska

Thompson's gazelle in Kenya

Philip and Diana's wedding day

Melanie and Steve's wedding
day

Agami heron, Belize

Taj Mahal, India

On the Rio Negro, Brazil

Tony and Christine's Mountain Home
Brazil

PART 3. OUR YEARS IN RETIREMENT
KENYA, 1990

This year we shared another unforgettable holiday with friends who, like us, were celebrating their 25th. wedding anniversary.

We landed in Nairobi and transferred to the Serena Hotel. The gardens immediately provided views of Superb Starlings, of weaver birds nesting in a palm tree and of very vocal sunbirds. One of the waiters amused me by saying that a sunbird usually came to help itself to the assorted cocktails placed on display on a sideboard together with attractive fruits as decoration to entice customers rather than birds.

Just four miles outside the city centre is Nairobi National Park, an area of only forty-four square miles, where they say one may see more species of birds than breed in Britain; but we were to be visiting other larger parks, not this one.

However, we walked into Uhuru Park – not a wildlife park – which is in the city centre and was just yards from our hotel. Edward and I walked over; he was wearing his binoculars on his chest, and I had my camera. There were few people about and we left the valley floor and climbed a slope to get a view and we approached a narrow road. As we did so a car swept up and a man got out and ran towards us. This was clearly an attack; I was thrown to the ground and had my camera and bag snatched, and Edward dropped onto his chest to protect his binoculars and bit the hand of the attacker, who yelped and ran back to the car, which drove off – but not before I had memorised the number plate.

We were shaken but only slightly hurt, and we went straight back to the hotel and reported the attack to the hotel management, who immediately sent us to the Police Station. The police at the desk were not interested; in the station yard however was a parked car with two or three men in it who asked why we had been into the police station. We explained, and when we told them that we had the number of the car to look for, they promptly set off to look for it. A dramatic chase ensued, the chased car crashed into a bus and shots were exchanged and two of the thieves were injured and our 'team', together with a uniformed policeman came to find us at the hotel.

Two of the three men had been arrested, one placed in the cells, and the other who was wounded was sent to the hospital under guard. The third had fled. We were required to go to the cells and to the hospital to identify the men. They had not been masked and we confirmed that these two men had been involved, one – probably the injured one –

had been the driver. The other was only 18 years old. Next, we had to identify the car which was easier.

We were then told that we must go to Court the next day, but we replied that we were due to head out early on safari with our tour group. They agreed we should go, but asked the date of our return and fixed the court hearing for the day after that. Our two friends were thankful to hear all this, having been aghast at the events, and eventually they came to court with us to provide moral support.

Edward had badly bruised and sprained his left hand when he fell on his binoculars during the incident. This resulted in a trip to the private hospital, where, because his hand was so swollen, he had to have his wedding ring cut off!

Next day, as scheduled, we set off on the safari. We left early and drove south to Kilaguni Lodge in Tsavo National Park, from where one has an excellent view of Mt. Kilimanjaro. We arrived for a late lunch and afterwards we visited Mzima springs, where there were hippos bathing.

Next day when we sat down to breakfast, we had to defend ourselves and our breakfast from greedy baboons leaping onto the tables, snatching fruit and

Weetabix. A waiter was called to beat them off with a stick. Red-billed Hornbills came to eat practically out of our hands as did Superb Starlings.

Our next stop was the Serena Park Hotel in Amboseli National Park – a beautiful oasis of verdant vegetation and brilliant plants. Here there were Toyota vans with an elevating roof for safari viewing, and each taking four guests and a driver (our driver was called Peter).

Our 'Leopard Safari' group was made up of five buses. During the afternoon ride, we saw elephant, cheetah, lion, Thompson's Gazelle, impala, Grant's Gazelle, gerenuk, wildebeest or White-bearded Gnu, Coke's Hartebeest and Common Zebra.

Next day's early game drive produced two perched and stately Bateleur Eagles and a Verreaux's Eagle Owl, which is two foot high. By lunchtime Edward had seen 52 species. I think it was here that we had a wild leopard walk through the hotel, which was apparently a regular event.

Our next journey was the longest single drive we made and was northwards, partly over miles of dry lakebed and then onto a road bypassing Nairobi and heading up to Outspan Lodge in Nyeri, where Baden Powell built a bungalow and lived until his death.

On our way further north we stayed at Treetops, the famous lodge where in 1952 Princess Elizabeth became Queen of England overnight, following the death of her father The original lodge was burned down during the Mau Mau uprising in 1953, but the new one can accommodate 100 overnight guests.

The ground level is strictly for the visiting wild animals; above that the lodge has one floor providing small chalet-like bedrooms and above that again is an observation platform on the roof. A warden told us not to make too much noise or we would be asked to return to our room.

Salt is put out daily around the pools and the game troops in as dusk falls, although a few animals are usually comfortable by the pools in daytime.

For me, Treetops will be remembered for the elephants, especially one teenager which wallowed in mud at the edge of the pool for at least half an hour before going into the lake right under water and clearly revelling in it.

Our next stop, which was our northernmost one, was Samburu and on the way there we crossed the Equator at Nanyuki, where a line is marked on the road, and you can place one foot on each side of it and have your photo taken. If you look across the road from the left-hand side, as you go north, you will see the mass of Mt. Kenya with a little snow on it.

Samburu is not far from the Ethiopian border. It is a very dry park, but a shallow river runs through it and our lodge was close to that. This was a brief visit. There were elephants, and we saw a variety of birds including bee-eaters and a Goneaway Bird.

Leaving Samburu, we turned back up the road towards Nanyuki, but soon turned west and drove down into the Rift Valley. Once in the valley we turned north again to reach Lake Baringo where we stayed overnight.

Next day we saw Ground Hornbills and Verreaux's Eagle, and later we drove a few miles south-west to Lake Bogoria. This lake is about five miles long and is said to have the world's largest concentration of flamingos – numbering about 4 million and including two species. It was very, very hot; we stepped out of the van and walked across the dry saline flats towards the vast shimmering pale pink sea of flamingos and watched them parade and took our photographs.

Next day we continued south down the Rift Valley down a bumpy road leading to Lake Naivasha, at 6,200 ft. where there was an up-market hotel in truly superb grounds with ancient and interesting trees, shrubs and flowers, and rolling lawns on which there were Sacred Ibis. These birds are gluttons for afternoon tea cakes!

Down by the lake there was a magical quality to the early morning light on the lily pads and reeds – rather like Kashmir. Years back this hotel was the airport terminal, this was in the days when BOAC used flying boats from Southampton to get here, via Cairo, in a 3-day journey to land on the lake.

From here we had another long drive south towards the Tanzanian border to Keekorok Lodge in the Maasai Mara. Here, having left the Rift Valley, we are in the Western Uplands at 6,000 ft. Our driver told us this was his favourite place, to which I replied, "Yes, because it's the end of the safari and you will soon be able to say goodbye to us"!

By the time we left here Edward's bird count was up to 270 species. We said goodbye to Peter, our amazing driver who had taken us 2755 kms or 1720 miles in 13 days, and we flew back to Nairobi.

Upon arrival at the Nairobi Serena, we were told that the Court hearing was tonight! Paul and Sue were coming for moral support. But the hearing was postponed until the morning as the lawyer for the accused men could not be found. We were fetched by a police convoy of cars, which included that of the three accused men and the wrecked car, and we all drove from the Police Station to the High Court.

We were at the Court from 9.30 a.m. to 1.15 pm. A large crowd turned up, which we thought included the accused men's families and dependents. I had to wait outside while Edward testified in front of the Magistrate. A lady translator was present to repeat in Swahili what was said.

I waited on an open balcony on the top of the building, along with the plain clothes men who had caught the "baddies", as they were also waiting to testify and could not be allowed to hear Edward's evidence. One of these young men was an accountant in his day job. It was he who had had Edward's spectacles fixed for which he refused any payment. These men provide support for the police and apparently do this plain-clothes work for free, presumably because they want to help the government, and perhaps they enjoy the thrill of it.

It all took a long time because they had lost Edward's first statement. Later, while waiting, I was asked to write my own account of what happened – this for the first time. It ran to four pages. When I was called to the witness box, several prayers went up. I was asked if I was a Christian and to swear on a Bible, which then sat there in front of me and just by its presence was very comforting.

While I was in the witness box Edward, Sue, and Paul were sitting off to my right. I did not look at them. I could hardly bring myself to look at the men in handcuffs seated opposite. The room was small and crowded, the wind was blowing the papers about. The Magistrate had to laboriously write his account for Court records.

After I had recounted my version of events, the defence lawyer questioned me slowly – because of the need for interpretation. She turned and gave me a surprised look and did NOT translate when I said I had shouted "God bless you" as God would be their judge, not me! Happily, I was given strength to stand there "in the box" for about an hour and to remain perfectly calm. Later everyone said I had done very well.

None of the exhibits displayed at the trial, including my camera, was ever returned to us despite promises that they would be.

Earlier we had had contact with Jill and Michael Harley. Their home was on what used to be the Karen Blixen estate (Out of Africa) and it was one of the first to be bought after that estate was sold. Jill breeds racehorses. They have a large property and have lived in Kenya for 30 years, employing 44 staff and feeding goodness knows how many dependents. They had given us their phone number in case of problems, and we rang them to tell them that we hoped most of the problems were over, and they kindly invited us to dinner at short notice and then picked us up at the hotel.

We also asked the hotel to move us to another room under a pseudonym, which seemed like a wise precaution.

In the circumstances we were glad to leave Kenya. Our flight to the Seychelles was delayed for about an hour because Marabu storks had to be removed from the runway, but finally, we got away.

THE SEYCHELLES, 1990

Oh! what a breath of fresh air after our recent problems. We had a three-hour flight from Nairobi to the island of Mahe, the main island in the Seychelles, where the runway is built out into the sea. From here there was a transfer to a De Havilland Otter 20-seater for a 15-minute flight across to Praslin Island, where we were to stay for three nights.

These islands are the only mid-ocean granite islands in the world and are said to be 650 million years old. The land is covered with lush vegetation and 40 species of land birds can be found, including the Black Parrot. We were delighted to see graceful Fairy Terns, snow-white against the blue sky.

We hired a mini-MOKE, which is a low-slung buggy without doors, just a windscreen in front and a plastic flap at the back. Paul drove and followed the island road around its north-east corner to the top of the hill, where there was a communications transmitter at about 1500 ft. from which we could enjoy the panorama.

We found the 'perfect' beach, shaded by a Takamaka tree and other palms. The sand was pure white, the sea turquoise and translucent and beautifully warm. We donned masks and snorkels and admired the fish passing quite close to the shore.

Amongst the giant palms here is the 'Coco de Mer', which is a very large and unusually shaped double-sided nut. As we walked through the forest later, fruits were falling around us with a 'plop', but luckily none fell on us.

We were able to take a boat across to visit Cousin Island, where we were told there was a meeting of the International Council for Bird Preservation. There are apparently four permanent members of the I.C.B.P. on the islands, monitoring and protecting the rare Seychelles Brush Warbler. This island also boasts a large population of Fairy Terns and Lesser Noddies.

It was extremely hot and humid. Another transfer from dinghy to boat to dinghy took us to Isle Curieuse, where we joined other groups, and an enormous barbecue had been prepared with delicious char-broiled fish, salads, fruits, bread and iced drinks, without which we might not have survived!

We were shown a Cinnamon tree, and a Vanilla tree – which has to be pollinated artificially as the insect, which pollinates it in its native Latin America, is not present here.

We were rather dismayed to find that there were sewage problems on Isle Curieuse, powerful smells pervaded the pool area of the hotel and the dining room; there was also an open run-off stormwater drain along the sides of the road and this also smelled bad.

Finally, the group embarked again and headed for the very small island of St. Pierre. Lady Scott had advised Edward that this was the best place to see tropical fish. We did indeed see some very lovely fish, although coral is virtually non-existent as, apparently, it does not grow on granite.

After another hot and sweaty night, we went to the dear little airstrip and made the 15-minute flight back to Mahe, the main island. We were then transferred to the Coral Strand Hotel on the other side of the island; this had the benefit of being air-conditioned. Mahe is obviously more touristy than Praslin, and initially we missed the hotel there and its lack of sophistication.

For the final days of our stay, we decided to hire another mini-MOKE to explore the island. There are some attractive beaches here, however the SE winds and strong undercurrents make them poor choices for swimming. We nevertheless enjoyed sporting in large breakers on one beach. Then we ate our tiny bananas for lunch before moving on to stop at a craft center. An excellent, recently tarmacked, road led us up to the cool air of the National Park at about 2,000 ft. Here, at Mission Lodge, we had a magnificent unspoilt view of the sea and the mountains.

After de-sanding and a hot bath back at the Coral Strand Hotel, we drove the mini-MOKE to Le Corsaire, a barn type restaurant said to have excellent service – although we had to wait 25 minutes for our desserts! However, Paul, Sue and Edward all said they had had one of the best chilled soups they had ever tasted.

Next day we took a glass-bottomed boat from which we could see the coral beds and we saw a turtle. The coral was nothing like as good as I had seen when we were in Asia, but it was better than at Isle St. Pierre. Three dolphins appeared and made several leaps around our boat. Most of us swam from the boat, anchored in quite deep water so swimmers did not get into trouble scraping themselves on the coral. There were some nice fish including Parrot Fish, Sergeant Major Fish, Angel Fish, Moorish Idols, Trumpet Fish and Wrasse, and a few crowns of thorns starfish.

On the way out the skipper showed us how many fish behaved like piranhas when bread is thrown into the water, and he even caught one of these fish in his hands and landed it on the boat.

Paul had left the mini-MOKE keys with the hotel reception (along with all his other keys on the keyring) only to find the car had been hired out to someone else, along with Sue's bikini that was still in the back lock-up! We were finally given another car with less petrol than we had had left in 'our' tank. Paul threatened to leave the car "somewhere on the island and not say where" if the car hire firm didn't give us a half-day discount!

Back in the market in Victoria – the capital of the Seychelles – we were amazed at the asking price for the Coco de Mer shells. We had seen them cut in half in the Praslin restaurant where they made lovely serving dishes; amazingly, here looking even more polished they were priced at about £70. Apparently, these rare trees had suffered a set-back on Praslin when a fire burned 100 acres of them.

We met an English lady aged nearly 80 who told us she Scuba-dived regularly and that she wears everybody out with her energetic diving.

Before leaving we made another trip in the glass-bottomed boat, and I enjoyed taking pictures using the underwater camera Philip had lent me.

In the evening, we had a meal at a French

restaurant offering Provençal food, which had attracted Edward's eye in passing; he was paying this time as Paul had paid at the Tamarind in Nairobi – here was just as expensive.

On the last day Paul, Sue and I had one more swim before leaving to catch the plane home, via Dubai, which took 13 hours. "Adieu les vacances", but "toujours du plaisir n'est pas du plaisir".

THE TRUST FOR ORIENTAL ORNITHOLOGY, 1992

Edward suggested to Oxford University Press that there was a gap in the market for a multi-volume handbook on Asian birds in the style of works on the Western Palaearctic, which had been completed – but was not a financial success – and of Australasia, which had recently been launched.

Initially OUP, which did not feel that the Western Palaearctic book was making money, asked Edward to outline how funds might be raised and then to submit two documents, one describing the planned work and the other on financing. The Trust was to be part of the financial planning, and the Press paid good London solicitors to provide the Trust Deed for submission to the Charity Commission for its approval.

Soon I was meeting the recruited trustees and their wives and thus came into contact with James and Sylvia Hancock, thanks to whom we became involved with India, as I will describe later.

Having paid for the Trust Deed, and also for some brochures intended to help raise money for the eventual colour plates, the Press asked for a meeting with the Trustees at which OUP hoped a formal agreement could be signed. However, the Press wanted to an agreement stipulating that if the project failed any funds that had been advanced by OUP would have to be repaid. The Trustees decided that they could not accept that liability.

Along the way the Trust had been promised help from the National Museum of Natural History in the Netherlands (since renamed "Naturalis") and many articles were published in the museum's journals, which were intended to provide a foundation for work on the text for the suggested Handbook. This led to several visits to Leiden by Edward and to our friendship with Rene and Charlotte Dekker with whom we made a special visit to St. Petersburg.

Edward's discussions with OUP also led to the commissioning of a field guide to the birds of the Philippines with Edward as a junior co-author. This, not a Trust project, was a sequel to a 507 page checklist published in 1991, which I helped to type; that was created by Edward, with help from Bob Kennedy, who we had met in the Philippines, and Ken Parkes who Edward had visited in the 1960s at the museum in Pittsburgh where Ken was Curator of Birds, who came to stay with us in Lake Barrington Shores.

A LITTLE INTERLUDE

One which has a rather strange story to tell. It could have been in any one of the places in which we have lived. It was Springtime and I was doing some clearing out of cupboards with the windows open and the sunshine pouring in. A happy day and I was whistling, which is unusual for me. Suddenly amongst the linens I came across a tiny cardboard box that I had never seen before. Curious, I opened it and inside were two small pieces of paper each with a word printed on it. One said "Nous sifflons" (we are whistling) and the other said "siffler" (to whistle). How odd is that?! I still have the box.

PHILIP'S WEDDING, MAY 1993

When at the polytechnic college in Kingston on Thames Philip met Diana Stalker who was managing part of the furnishing section in the large John Lewis store there, which is very close to the bridge over the Thames.

This wing of the large Stalker family – Dick and Elizabeth and their two other daughters, Katherine and Nicola – had moved down from Hertfordshire to Sussex and were living in Haywards Heath, just over 30 miles north-west of us. It was an afternoon wedding at the United Reform church – in the middle of the High Street – and the service was followed by an early evening meal at Borde Hill which was a lovely venue. Edward and I attended, as did my mother, Melanie, Mike Barlow and family, and Ada from Switzerland.

THE DREAM OF AN INDIAN FIELD GUIDE.
JASDAN, 1993

We flew to Mumbai (previously known as Bombay) and joined the long queue of disembarked passengers. The tedium of queuing at the airport was briefly relieved by two devout Muslims (one an airport official and the other a traveler) getting out their prayer mats and dropping to the ground.

Before we left, Carole had phoned to give us the phone number of her sister-in-law who had been given in marriage, by Carole's late husband Tom, to an Indian Anglican Bishop, who is now retired and running a retreat in the foothills of the Himalayas.

Our travel agent was Cox & Kings and an employee met us to say that tomorrow's flight was not confirmed despite what we had been told in London. Apparently, the Royal Yacht Britannia was in port, and a couple from London, for whom Melanie had acted as a nanny, had dined on board. Now, years later, we cannot remember who could have drawn this to our attention. When Melanie was at boarding school one of her school friends was the daughter of the then Captain of H.M.S. Britannia and she and her parents kindly invited Melanie and us to board the yacht when it was berthed in Southampton, and we were shown round it.

It turned out that we could take the planned flight to Jasdan. We were met by Kumar Shri Shivrajkumar Khachar. Jasdan State was founded in 1665 and the Khachar family became its ruler in 1807. His title ranks him as a Maharaja. He brought us to the palace, where eventually we were to be joined by Andrew Robertson; but our visit to Jasdan, and Andrew's, was arranged by Edward's friend James Hancock, who was currently leading one of the tours, that he arranged in conjunction with Cox & Kings, to allow tourists a good chance to see tigers in the wild. He had his wife with him, and this tour was arranged despite him having suffered a heart attack a couple of years ago.

Jasdan Palace is a bit like a fortress within the town, complete with its own huge gates which are closed at night. Satyajit – as we were to call him – spontaneously took us on a tour of the palace showing us several palatial rooms, all with shuttered windows. Some contained family portraits of five generations of the Maharajas, as well as pictures of tigers they had hunted!

Just before dark we enjoyed a magical pink and yellow sunset seen from one of the balconies.

At dinner the food was surprisingly bland – perhaps "Europeanised" for our benefit. Tantalizing dishes of very large and delicious looking custard apples were carried away to another part of the palace whilst our desert was a ginger sponge pudding with a light-coloured ginger sauce that was not very strong.

The mosquito nets did a good job, I had not one bite. However, there seemed to be traffic most of the night, as well as servants flitting about and chatting in low voices, and then the market became alive at dawn.

This trip had been prompted by Oxford University Press, who believed that there was a need for a field guide to the birds of all India and this was either mooted or endorsed by James Hancock.

Edward had first met James at the bird conservation meeting in Thailand back in the 60's. James, who had worked in the oil industry, knew India well and Edward had invited him to be a Trustee of the Trust of Oriental Ornithology established by Edward in 1992. Now we are all visiting Jasdan because James has arranged an invitation for us.

Andrew Robertson is a near neighbour of ours; he lives in Blockley near Aston Magna. He had flown into India some weeks earlier and had been re-visiting Periyar National Park in Kerala, about which he had published a small checklist of birds and animals. It was hoped that Andrew would be able to work with Indian nationals to create the proposed field guide. He arrived today, his flight up from Periyar had been affected by the late monsoon weather. He had been enduring rain almost daily and the birding had been bad.

Edward was there because Oxford University Press had asked him to assess the project.

That morning there were fascinating sights at every turn; for example, I saw a large crow-like bird land on a milk churn that was being carried on the back of a motorized rickshaw in which there were several other churns and the 'lids', which were just bundles of straw that I imagined the birds could easily penetrate. This made me wonder whether it had been wise to drink cold milk at breakfast! Lunch, a vegetarian meal, was at a baronial table and we were waited on by orang-turbaned staff.

After lunch we were shown another part of the building, on one side of the central courtyard, where there was a large room with bookshelves from floor to ceiling containing enough volumes to fill a county library back home.

After the post-prandial siesta, we were driven 20 kilometres with Satyajit and his cousin and Andrew to the fort built by the family hundreds of years ago. It stands on a hill about 1,500 ft. high and commands a view across the plain for miles around. In the hot season in August and September the family moves here to enjoy the cool breezes.

We went for a walk in the nearby Nature Reserve that Satyajit had created, and we saw plenty of birds, two jackals and an antelope. Satyajit also supports the community in various ways and is a Trustee of the local eye-hospital which is said to be the second best in India.

Next morning Edward rose at 6.15 to go back to the Reserve with Satyajit and Andrew where they watched the sunrise and saw many of my favourite birds such as rollers, minivets, bee-eaters and hoopoes.

After my late breakfast with Satyajit's mother and grandmother, three maids glided into the room; one was to sweep, one to clean the bathroom, and the third was bringing me a lime juice. Through the bars on the screen clad windows at the back of the sitting room I had a birds' eye view of the colourful market, where I could see baskets of custard apples drifting by on someone's head and brass water pots and wicker baskets full of gravel.

Edward and the other men are now in the library with lawyers, friends of Satyajit and a senior representative of the World Wildlife Fund, talking about the potential Indian Field Guide.

The sun was high in the sky and as I had left my watch at home, I didn't know the time, but I guessed it to be around 1.30 p.m. The market was over, and the vendors pushed their carts and wares back home. Only the cows are left to forage amongst the remains. The metallic clicking of an angry little squirrel has replaced the merchants' cries.

Later Andrew, Edward and I were given a tour of the bird library and of an exotic locked room in yet another building off a lonely courtyard completely dominated by an ancient tree. This room was like Aladdin's Cave that Satyajit had loved when he was a child.

There were intricately hand-worked coloured cushions trimmed with tiny beads picturing people, birds and animals in colour. There were also larger cushions, dowry chests standing about 5 ft high with vast elaborate brass ornamentations and locks; and a swinging bed anchored to the ceiling by chains, from which hung brass bells and carved elephants etc. Red was the dominant colour everywhere. Running all along the top of the wall, right round the room, was a shelf filled from end to end with brass water pitchers. This is the palace storeroom housing their ancestral heirlooms, handicrafts and so forth.

As we went to bed, we thought that our entire floor space in Norman Chapel would fit into just one of the large rooms we had seen.

Saturday. We were awake for a while that night, but earplugs worked wonders, and we were late for breakfast although an unfortunate servant had knocked on our door four times.

We left about 9 a.m. after farewells and we had a driver who did not speak English to take us on the four-hour journey to Desert Coursers, a resort still in Gujarat near Zainabad and in the Rann of Kutch which had been recommended by Andrew. It was rather like an Indian Camargue and 304 bird species have been recorded over the years. It is also one of the few areas where it's possible to see the endangered Wild Ass.

On arrival we found a collection of rondavel type mud huts with grass roofs. We were greeted by a real Indian meal, our first! What a treat and joy … papaya and lime. There are a couple of Indian parties here too.

The owner, Malik, is due to take us out at 3 p.m., when it is less hot. He is a bird watcher and a keen conservationist who Andrew has met before and whose son Raj helps run the encampment. As I write I am sitting on a swing seat in front of our hut. The mud walls have had different leaves stuck all over them when the mud was still damp, after which they are removed to create an attractive, natural decoration. There is a notice on the door which reads "alcohol prohibited", this being a dry State which will disappoint some visitors. A pair of House Sparrows share our hut; they keep trying to see the mirror, which is in an alcove, and they think they are seeing trespassers. I have turned the mirror round now, but the insistent, restless female has crept into a very small space at the back to continue her watch.

After a delayed start due to a broken fan belt, we set off with Malik and four German wives who were planning a night beside the flooded area. It's very like the Camargue in many ways apart from the flooded flats there are some salt pans and some similar birds. We saw spoonbills, cranes, flamingos, a hoopoe and many waders. The flooded area proved to be a long way away, but it was a pleasant place to see the sunset and we left the Germans to their vigil; they had no tents, just a bedroll and some tinned food. Malik was staying with them but the young man driving us back didn't seem to know the way and after dark it seemed twice the distance away.

Raj's sister and future in-laws were at the camp and were having a party round the campfire. We retired early because we planned an early start in the morning, but before bed we saw a pair of owls which later woke us in the night with their coarse shrieks and cat-like noises.

Sunday. After coffee we left at about 7 a.m. in a jeep. Cotton is the main crop in the Rann of Kutch, its yellow flower reminds me of Lavatera (Mallow). The crop is a slow grower and is harvested in March, so there is only one harvest a year.

In the jeep we fought our way through the omnipresent weedy shrub with spines and acacia-like leaves, and reached dry terrain that was almost desert-like and saw vultures, sandgrouse, various larks and many other species, but not the supposedly common one Edward was hoping to see. There was some good-natured argument between the three men who were with me in the jeep over the identity of a distant duck out on the lake, which proved to be a Tufted Duck. Several distant herds of Wild Ass were visible, but they are very shy.

A fairly strong breeze meant the temperature was comfortable, and we ate breakfast in the middle of the 'desert', returning to camp at 11.30. There is reliable bottled water available all over India nowadays which is a blessing, but the Government has disallowed any invasion by American Fanta and Coke, and indeed it is nice to get away from uniformity!

After lunch we set off in search of the elusive Cream-coloured Courser that Edward had hoped to find, but we saw only the Indian Courser. A storm was threatening so we returned to camp to pack making sure that everything was as waterproof as possible, and we found that the bed rolls had had rice sacks thrown over them because, of course, the thatched rooved huts are not waterproof. In the end no rain fell. Raj was more than relieved and the "no alcohol" sign was removed to make way for a dram of bootleg whisky. The meal with Raj was late but quite jovial; he has planned a six month visit to England which we discussed, and we gathered that his family were putting pressure on him to marry.

Everyone, except me, declined a searchlight trip but during one I was shown two different kinds of nightjar, some Spotted Owls, a Turnstone and a mouse and a wolf!

Monday am. Andrew went walking on his own. Raj took Edward and me to Nava Talava (New Lake) where we had gone last night, and we enjoyed a picnic breakfast whilst watching the birds and we found a Rubythroat.

In mid-morning we departed from the camp and headed for Ahmedabad, but Edward had a bad cold. The journey was a bit fraught! Malik had been supposed to organize a taxi, but none was available. We ended up in the car of a relative, who happened to be returning to Ahmadabad; so, we had four Indians sitting in the front seat and the three of us in the back.

Ahmedabad is located near the banks of the Sabarmati River; it is a vast sprawling town. Little 3-wheelers jostle with cows and camels pulling carts along the roads and across the traffic lights. Anything goes!

Our base for the day was the house of Pria, Raj's sister –a concrete apartment where, that morning there was a servant lying on the floor suffering from malaria. Pria was there and was struggling to teach small children English, and to cope with her own cold, four dogs and a mongoose. The four German women from Desert Courser caught up with us and they had to be put on a train to Bombay.

Edward and Andrew had an appointment with another ornithologist about the proposed Indian field guide. I asked if I could visit a museum, but most were closed, and the driver took me to a causeway over an artificial lake with water snakes and plenty of Pond Herons. When Edward and Andrew returned, we were offered interesting Indian snacks and then driven to the airport for our flight to Delhi.

The plane was delayed until 10.30 p.m.! During the long wait we tried to phone Satya in Delhi to tell her we were supposed to arrive about 1 a.m. She said that when the taxi from the airport got to her house she would come to the door with a strong whisky.

Satya is an Indian pediatrician who Edward had invited to visited Nestlé in Switzerland, where I first met and made friends with her. Her house is in the old part of Delhi across the river Jumna, and our airport taxi needed help from a local taxi to find her house and even he had to ask people. We finally got there at 2 a.m. and were warmly greeted by Satya and her sloppy family dog! We finally got to bed at around 3 a.m. when I persuaded Edward to take a sleeping pill.

Tuesday. This morning, we were warmly welcomed by the family which included Satya's sister, her niece and her brother who lives in New York where he is a High Court Judge but was visiting. Satya told us about her house fire when they might have been roasted alive in the upstairs rooms. She lost some Chinese paintings bought during her trip and was sad about this.

When her young patients began to arrive, Satya offered her "tame" Seik taxi driver to take us to the YMCA building where Oxford University Press has its offices; this being where Edward was to attend a final meeting with Andrew, James Hancock – back from his tour – and six local staff of Oxford University Press about the proposed Field Guide. I think the meeting went well. I had come there with Edward, and, while I waited, I enjoyed looking at some of OUP's publications.

I miss seeing the amusing camels in the traffic jams here. There is no part of the camel which doesn't make me laugh, especially when the poor things are trying to act as transport vans.

After the meeting Andrew, Edward and I were invited to a buffet lunch at the "restaurant in the sky" at the Meridian Hotel. We had super views over the city and an Egyptian Vulture sat just outside the window, but where, oh where, was my camera?

James Hancock invited Edward and I to his hotel for dinner that evening, where I met his wife Sylvia and was introduced to their two other guests, a newly wed young American couple involved with saving a rare species of stork in Assam where they were going to be going with James. The meal was a 5-star Indian meal with an accompanying display of Indian dancing, which I found rather meaningless as I did not understand the movements. James was in fine form telling me all about his friendship with the father of Satyajit, who we had stayed with in Jasdan, his early life in the Army (on the Indian Frontier) and he said that he would be doing less work for Cox & Kings in future and that Edward should take over from him. This would mean that Edward would be leading tours of 16 people to India about three times a year in winter – mainly to see tigers – and that I, like Sylvia, would be able to go along! James told me that he has 3-4 years left out of the 7 since his heart bypass.

Wednesday. A full 14-15 hour round trip to Agra and the Taj Mahal and Satya's Seik driver negotiated a real obstacle course without a bump or scratch, which was a miracle. We saw the Taj in the middle of the day, a time not recommended due to the light, but it was very special anyway. However, we did not enjoy seeing the poor Sloth Bears up on their hind legs tethered to their owners, who hoped we would stop and pay to take a photograph.

On the way we saw the splendid sign "Undertakers

love overtakers" on the back of a lorry! From Agra we headed for Fatehpur Sikri, an abandoned Mughal palace and we picnicked in the car on the way. Fatehpur Sikri was abandoned not long after it was built because the river dried up or perhaps changed course. This is a very impressive building with huge bees' nests high up.

The return journey at about 40-50 m.p.h. seemed interminable, partly because we had a battery problem which added 45 minutes to the trip. But it was extremely kind of Satya to arrange the day.

Thursday. Satya was not feeling well, so Edward and I visited the Red Fort, which Edward had already seen. We hired a guide, who was not very conscientious and was rather difficult to understand. They had a 'Son et Lumière' show in the evening, but Satya told us she did not want us to see it as it did not portray the British in a very good light. There is a lot of restoration work in progress, but the fort is a pretty drab place apart from a small museum. In its heyday it must have been amazing with fountains and a silver ceiling and semi-precious stone inlays everywhere (like those at the Taj Mahal, but without the white walls). Satya insisted on showing us a temple that she enjoys, the Baha'i House of Worship at Bahadur, just outside Delhi. This is a multi-cultural, inter-religious cult established all over the world. It is the latest of seven edifices inspired by the lotus flower and structurally harmoniously balanced based on the nine "cooling" pools surrounding it.

We returned to Satya's home, where her sister, who rises to pray at 3.30 a.m. every day, had prepared a high-quality vegetarian meal of considerable variety. Later some doctor friends arrived unannounced just as Satya was trying to sleep on the sofa, while her brother was already asleep on the floor. Later, a lonely, retired anesthetist came and held us in non-stop philosophical conversation for about 2-3 hours. They all seem to love company and talk.

Friday. Next day Satya was feeling too unwell to attend her clinic. Edward went to a meeting of the Indian chapter of the World Pheasant Association, and I went to the Maurayon Sheraton in the hope of a swim. But the hotel wanted 300 Rupees, which seemed expensive, and the water wasn't that warm; I opted out as it would have been a short swim. At the poolside I became engaged in conversation with another talkative lady, who turned out to be a big noise in the world of journalism and in Delhi politics. Her husband was obviously a senior officer in the Army or the Police. She told me she had been reincarnated five times, and on one occasion that had been in Ireland! She wanted me to visit her tarot card astrologer friend, but I escaped.

Later Satya insisted on taking us to an emporium where she negotiated amazing discounts and we bought 10 small silk scarves, a couple of sandalwood paper knives and a lapis lazuli necklace (£12 reduced from £50!) to replace the one I had lost in the fire in Manila 17 years ago. I also looked at embroidered handicrafts displayed by Franciscan nuns – beautiful work that they have taught the village girls.

Satya's judge brother was scheduled to fly back to the United States tonight leaving after midnight and Edward and I elected to come with him in the same taxi which meant getting up at 2 a.m. Eventually, we spent eight hours first dozing on the concourse floor and later in departure lounge on several comfy seats. Had we known our flight would be delayed an hour we might have tried visiting what we heard was a famous second-hand bookshop not far from the airport.

ISRAEL, 1996

Carole, my oldest and dearest school friend, and I decided to join a tour based on a group from Billericay going to Israel.

The tour was led by a husband-and-wife team; both were vicars who had lived in Israel. We obtained the necessary visas and flew off to Ben Gurion International Airport in Tel Aviv. When we arrived at the airport there were strict controls and everyone's luggage had to be opened and inspected. Our first night was in the King David Hotel in Jerusalem.

It was May and very warm, but we were prepared for that. Joining us locally was an Israeli guide who spoke good English and knew the Bible very well.

We visited all the usual tourist spots and trod in some of the places where Jesus would have walked, and this gave us an incredible feeling and brought to life all the familiar Bible stories. In some of the places, for example, the Garden of Gethsemane, we took Holy Communion in the open air and sang hymns. Of course, we visited the Wailing Wall in central Jerusalem, the hilltop fort of Massada taken by the Romans in 73 AD following a mass suicide, and the river Jordan; and we also floated in the Dead Sea.

We ended the holiday by staying at the edge of the Sea of Galilee in a luxurious hotel looking up towards the Golan Heights. And there, we took a boat to where Jesus had preached to the crowds and fed the five thousand – a church has been erected there with tiles on the floor that depict the miraculous event.

No sooner had we returned home than we received a phone call from Ada in Switzerland to say that we must book tickets to go to Israel because her son Sebastian, Philip's friend, was getting married there before the year end!

We were both invited and we decided to go out early so that Edward could arrange to do some birding beforehand, and after flying in to Tel Aviv, we flew down to Eilat where Edward had made arrangements to meet an Israeli ornithologist who took him around the outskirts of the town and into the desert to see a species of sandgrouse that he had not seen before and some northern migrants that he and Edward expected to find there at this time of the year.

In Eilat we were also able to join a bus tour that took us over the border into Jordan and to a hotel in Petra, where, declining a donkey ride, we walked down into the valley to see the Rose City and the ancient Treasury a 45 m. high temple called Al

Khazneh. On returning to Eilat we flew back to Jerusalem for the wedding.

The bride, Pascale, was then living and working in Israel for the International Red Cross (while Sebastian was working for the same organization in its Swiss HQ). It was a church wedding, after which we all drove down to Tel Aviv for the evening celebrations, and a belly dancer performed.

BOLSOVER COURT, 1998.

Wanting to get away from the winter fog in the Cotswolds in 1997, we began to think about moving to the south of England and visited south Devon to look around. We looked at several properties, and in each case concluded that the opportunities did not appeal.

Back in Norman Chapel we sat down to discuss this and concluded that moving down there would commit us to long trips along the south coast to Eastbourne to see my mother. Edward's mother is also still alive, but she is now in a nursing home and potentially could be moved to one in Eastbourne. We decided to go down to Eastbourne and examine the potential for us to move there.

We stayed with my mother on several occasions while house-hunting and eventually just after a three-hour journey home mother called to tell us about a flat that had just come onto the market. She had been walking home after taking us to the train and passed an estate agent's office where she saw a light was still on and popped in to have a word. A very nice flat had just come on the market; she read through the details and phoned us to say, "you must come back at once; it looks ideal for you". So, we asked her to go and have a look, which she did. Promptly, we travelled down again by train, and we were very impressed. The house is just four down the road from where mother used to go to school with her two cousins. What a coincidence! And one that was not lost on mother when she sat drinking tea, and memories came flooding back to her.

The flat is on the first floor of a Victorian house, which had been divided into seven flats in, we think, the 1930s. It had an excellent sea view looking along the garden from two large front rooms, each of which had double doors opening onto a balcony with cast iron railings and space for a small round table and seats.

It was evident that a lot of work would be needed, but we went straight to the estate agent and offered the full asking price which the seller accepted, and things began to move. We had a satisfactory survey report by early November and a draft contract from the solicitors for the seller just a week or so later.

We put Norman Chapel on the market in the autumn and by October 1997 we had a low offer, but in spring 1998 we sold it for more than our asking price and rewarded our agents with a case of red wine! By this time, we had bought the flat in Bolsover Court. However, the amount of work to be done in the flat dictated that we would not be moving in much before mid-1998.

Melanie, who had done a couple of ski-guiding

winters and become close to an Englishman called Steve Latham who had done the same; and she now suggested that Steve had the skills needed for the work in the flat and that he might be happy to have the work. This proved to be true, and Steve moved into the flat for 5 months while he worked on it – negotiating the budget with Edward.

The drawing room would need to house an upright electric piano and would need an exceptionally large and comfortable sofa. Although the piano had earphones, we needed to minimize noise and we created a gap between the walls and the flooring so that the sound would not travel down the wall. In doing this we discovered that the floor was not just one layer of floorboards but two! The lower layer was shipped down to Salisbury, where Melanie and Steve had bought their first house to be used there.

In our drawing room in the front of Bolsover Court the remaining layer of floorboards was worked over so that each was linked to those on either side with biscuit joints. Lastly the floor was professionally sanded and polished, and it looked splendid.

To obtain a suitable sofa we went to the annual Ideal Home Exhibition in London and haggled on the price for a large 6-seater Italian red leather sofa, which would be shipped to us from Italy.

The bay window in the drawing room held the gate-leg table from Norman Chapel and handsome chairs from Bayhorne, which looked as though they belonged here. We had collected shells when we were in the Philippines; and they had followed us from there to Lake Barrington and on to Norman Chapel and finally to Bolsover Court where we had two glass cabinets for them in the drawing room.

The master bedroom – the second large front room – had been modified to include a bathroom separated by a wall of bricks rising from the floorboards! Steve replaced this with a light-weight paneled wall. The bathroom was accessed from the small dressing room that led from the hall to the bedroom.

The alignment of the replacement wall would determine the width of the bathroom and of our bedroom. We bought two tall clothes cupboards at Ikea in Croydon and assembled them on the left along the wall between the drawing room and the bedroom; the first was positioned just inside the door and the second one just beyond it. Where that ended was the line for the replacement wall.

To achieve accuracy, we erected the cupboards and put them in place; after that everything was easy. The new wall was built, and the bath was equipped with a jacuzzi.

The front hall was quite wide and beside the east wall included a gas fire installed in the chimney in the corner and a comfy area with a sofa and an Oriental carpet.

A narrower passage ran back northwards through the flat, off which on the left there was a WC, a bathroom, a second double bedroom with a window looking southwards alongside the house yielding a view of the front garden and the sea. The room held a double bed, a cupboard and my desk in the window area where the room extended out over a narrow walkway below.

We consolidated the WC and bathroom and made this one room with a door near the hall and another door into the adjoining double-bedroom with a step up.

On the right of the central narrow passage was a space under the staircase that led to the upstairs flats. Here we installed a fridge freezer opening upwards and a vacuum cleaning system with three points in the flat where the active tubular head could be plugged in to make it operational.

Then there was a right turn into another large bedroom and access to the kitchen, both of which looked over the narrow back garden to Bolsover Road and Southcliff Tower, which never seemed to disturb our view.

This big bedroom was converted into a large study for Edward's library and workspace. Edward specified and Steven built some cupboards about 4 ft. tall, designed to hold 4 layers for standard storage boxes where Edward would keep leaflets and photocopies that he needed for the books and articles on birds that he was writing.

Edward's desk allowed him to sit with his back to the window and at the back of the desk was a map chest facing the window. To his right, when he was sitting at the desk, was the wall between the study and the kitchen and it had a gas fire in it. Nearer the window there was room for our two splendid American-bought wooden filing cabinets each having one long tray above the other.

We had enough space on the floor to lay down another of our nice Oriental carpets. When Phil and Diana's all the family came to stay, their two daughters – Jessie and Thea – slept here on a sofa bed; Rufus, their son, slept in a small room originally reserved for the maid which was opposite the utility area in a small room at the back on the east side of the building, close to the installed washing machine and nearby sink.

The kitchen had to be rebuilt; it originally held a

huge 6 ft. long oak table that we bought, which could seat ten, and we could just get 5 chairs round on each side and still have room to move. We eventually sold that and replaced it with something a bit smaller. A new oven and a new fridge were installed, and the work area and sink were new. In time, when we were abroad, Steve – who by this time was employed as a kitchen and bathroom fitter for a firm in Salisbury – refitted the kitchen for us.

To the east of the central passage was perhaps that led directly to iron steps down into the garden; this exit could be reached from a flat above us.

Thanks to Steve's excellent transformative works we spent 18 happy years in this flat and it was perfect for the visiting grandchildren; they had a short walk across the main road to a winding path that led down to the beach. Occasionally, we played shuttlecock or croquet in the garden, but I also remember watching a vixen in the middle of the lawn in broad daylight with six pups suckling!

SABAH, BORNEO, 1999

A NATURETREK TOUR TO BORNEO

Sunday, 3rd. October. Monday. We set off at 6 a.m. from Flat 3 by taxi – an excellent service to Heathrow from Peacehaven charging £30 less than the Eastbourne taxis.

At this stage I hadn't taken on board the fact that we would be making 5.30 a.m. starts throughout this holiday. What is the definition of a holiday? Doing different things. eating different things, seeing different things and meeting different people in different surroundings wearing different clothes and keeping different hours? If this is a definition of a holiday, then we most certainly went on holiday. A trek it certainly was. But a rest it was not.

We took a Malaysian Airways flight headed for Kuala Lumpur (KL), which left about 11 a.m. and took about 12 hours. Allowing for the time zones this got us into KL about 6 in the morning on the 4th.

After a three hour wait at the airport, we boarded a smaller plane to cross from the mainland to Sabah, which is a Malaysian state in north-western Borneo. The plane called at the island of Labuan and then continued to Kota Kinabalu where we landed.

We were a group of 12 plus the English tour leader Nick Dymond, and we were to be joined in Kota Kinabalu by the local guide Osman, a cheery fellow with a good sense of humour, who had worked with Nick on previous Naturetrek tours. We were not the only greyheads.

A keen, fit and sprightly 75-yr. old Yorkshireman kept up with all the excursions and was always Nick's shadow and tried to be first to spot every bird on the trails, but the birds are really worth seeing so it was no hardship, just hard work. This was primarily a bird-watching expedition, but an 80-year old and his wife had joined us at Kuala Lumpur airport and they said that they came primarily to see orchids and other plants.

The plane stopped in Labuan and when we got to Kota Kinabalu, which is on the west coast, a small plane took us over to Sandakan on the east coast where we arrived about 20 minutes later. From the plane we could see the huge palm oil plantations below, the large-scale forest clearance and the milk-chocolate-coloured rivers and their tributaries.

At Sandakan we boarded a minibus for a half-hour ride to the Sepilok Rehabilitation Centre for orang-outangs. The name means "People of the Forest". These apes, like all monkeys, are related to us and are vulnerable to all the same diseases. Here, just a short 10-minute boardwalk into the forest, we were able to see them being fed. This is a protected forest area, which the loggers reputedly left alone to sustain orang-utangs in the wild, so as a refuge for those whose original home forest has been felled.

Although they are free within the enclosure, they are, to begin with, at least, hard put to find food in the forest. Daily returnees are closely monitored by a warden and given medication when necessary. Limited offerings of bananas are made at 3 p.m., a timing designed to reveal to the orang-utangs that there are none left if they do not come back in time. This reduces their enthusiasm to travel back if they are far off and managing well; but the youngest ones are often highly dependent and enough come daily for visitors to see them. We were lucky to see a large male thought to be about five years old.

We left Sepilok at 4 p.m. for a further 2-hour journey to Sukau, through miles of almost nothing but palm oil plantations. The road initially had an asphalt surface, but the final 25 miles were a dirt track. This became muddier as we neared Sukau, which is on the Kinabatangan River, but some way upstream from its mouth. This part of Sabah is not far from the Sulu Islands, a group in the southwest of the Philippines where the people are muslims. These islands have also been a refuge for pirates, and along the Sabah coast talk of raids by Moro pirates is not unusual.

Reaching the river at Sukau, we boarded two small motorboats for the 10-minute trip upriver to the 'Sukau Rainforest Lodge', where we arrived exactly 24 hours after leaving home, having had no more than a couple of hour-long naps along the way.

The area around the lodge is prone to flooding, but in some places the foundations are raised, unlike some other lodges nearby. However, the lodge is rather basic, although the bedrooms have mosquito screens and there is hot and cold water. The dress code for dinner included the option of sarongs and flip flops (courtesy of the lodge). Our initial candlelight supper was in the unscreened main foyer of the lodge, and we were tired and soon headed off to bed.

Edward's eyes were really red and sore looking – mainly due to the air in planes being very dry which is said to cause some loss of body fluids: but eyedrops quickly dispelled any discomfort and he was excited about seeing new Asian birds next morning. The night was disturbed by Bruce who was suffering from a cold with a cough sounding at times like whooping cough. His bed was only a couple of inches away on the other side of the thin wooden panel dividing our room from his, so our sleep was somewhat disturbed.

Tuesday 5th.: began with a 5.30 a.m. wake-up call and the organization of the mosquito sprays, mosquito gels and walking boots required. Life vests too if one was going on a boat. I declined the first boat trip, preferring to sit quietly on a lodge bench until breakfast, taking in all the unfamiliar sights, sounds and smells, and watching tantalizing glimpses of sunbirds and the like.

Identification should not have been a problem with all these experts around! Edward went on this trip and had his first views of the brilliant Blue-eared Kingfishers and of the Proboscis Monkey – since shown to the world in David Attenborough's TV programme on Borneo. The group explored a side passage and found it led to an oxbow lake, beside which there was a nature trail; however, that proved to be very wet, and they began to meet Borneo's leeches. At this point in our holiday, we did not yet have leech socks and some of us suffered the loss of some blood!

After breakfast we both went on a muddy walk in

the forest behind the lodge. This produced one of the most fabulous and lasting images of the whole tour, several fleeting glimpses of a Garnet Pitta, seen both on the forest floor and perched on branches not far above it. Later in this walk Edward saw Black-and-red Broadbill and various other colourful birds.

Early PM was siesta time, when the birds are quiet too; after that I joined the group going up-river, while Edward caught up on sleep. Each boat had a Honda outboard engine and another smaller, battery-operated engine: these batteries get recharged from solar panels, which also provide much of the power needed by the Lodge. The electric engine is very quiet and not very powerful, resulting in slow movement which is perfect for gliding along narrow tributaries and surprising wildlife.

The pilot of my boat espied a large salt-water crocodile on a mud bank, but as we glided towards the creature it raised itself up and slid away into the water. It would not do to take a swim here! Another boat party had seen an elephant, and we made a detour to where they had seen it, but we were not lucky.

We returned to the lodge at 6.30 p.m. in virtual darkness having seen Blyth's Hawk Eagle, many parties of long-tailed macaques and several superb families of the tragicomic Proboscis Monkeys, a species in which the male has a long fat nose, reminding one of General De Gaulle. We were lucky enough to see 2 or 3 Silver Langurs as well.

An evening slide slow provided an overview of lodge history, which only dated from 1996. Every evening the group was to meet to go through the printed bird list provided and to discuss what everyone had seen during the day; not just birds, animals were also listed.

Wednesday 6th·: another 5.30 a.m. alarm, after our first good night's sleep (thankfully next door's cough was somewhat better). After a coffee we donned life vests as usual, along with plenty of mosquito deterrent and set off in two boats heading up a different creek using the quiet motors.

Not much was stirring except a pair of noisy hornbills feeding on a fruit tree. These were a dark-coloured species called Bushy-crested Hornbill: it is one of the smaller species.

Later we splashed our way through the very muddy forest trail behind the lodge again, but we saw very little; I was delighted to find out just how waterproof my French walking boots were.

We had a good sweet-and-sour lunch at the lodge, but then the heavens opened, and a tropical downpour descended. Later we boarded the boats again and crossed back to the landing stage, where we had arrived, and embussed to follow a bumpy road to the large Gomantong caves. These are full of nests of the Edible-nest Swiftlets; commercialized harvesting of the nests began in Borneo as early as the 15th. century, when the Chinese persuaded the Malays to "farm" them.

The most prized white nest is entirely composed of saliva and built by one of the species here, while another species builds a 'black' nest made of a mixture of saliva and feathers. A kilo of this saliva, when not mixed with feathers, which have to be cleaned out later, is worth more than 2,500 US dollars The daring workers learn to climb flimsy bamboo ladders to dizzy heights in semi darkness where they prise the nests off the cavern walls. Not only are they 150-200 ft. off the ground, but the cave is also inhabited by several million bats. The noise is eerie with the squeaks of bats, and the clicking calls of the swiftlets which use these sonar clicks to echolocate as they fly around in the dark. The cave floor is deep in guano and other detritus, which offers a home to other creatures such as cockroaches. The smell of ammonia was very strong.

There are several different varieties of bat, but the most abundant one is larger and is known as the Wrinkled-lip Bat. At dusk every day, wave upon wave of them leave the cave by various chimneys, or roof holes, and this exodus continues for at least half an hour. This is feeding time for the Bat Hawks and Peregrine Falcons which are nearby waiting for this daily feeding event. They circle above the holes where the bats pour out and plunge into the clouds of bats and try to pick out a straggler or weakling.

As the bats leave to feed, the swiftlets begin to enter the caves in numbers to roost for the night.

Black-nest Swifts' nests are also collected, but they are worth less due to the need to clean out the feathers and remaining impurities. The area surrounding these caves is closely guarded for obvious reasons and it lies in the conservation area managed by the Parks Service.

Just outside the entrance to the cave we spotted our first truly free orang-utang, a female on her own, quite high up in trees on the rock face to the left of the large cave entrance. Today was overcast and dark, with rain off and on, and an early sunset, and by then both we and our clothes were dripping. We saw two particularly attractive birds: a Black and yellow Broadbill and an Orange-backed

Woodpecker that I spotted!

Thursday 7th.: Another 5.30 start after only 3 or 4 hours of sleep. No boat trip this morning, but another bird-walk in the grounds around the lodge. The light was very tricky until the mist lifted. Not much was happening except squirrels mating: we watched the female seeking to escape but closely followed by the male, both were jumping very large gaps between the trees.

We crossed by boat to the village where our bus was waiting. Our heavy cases had been sent on ahead of us. I checked out the little riverside store on stilts, so reminiscent of the sari-sari stores in the Philippines. It was very well stocked with Nestlé products, some of them new since our days with Nestlé.

We went back up the dirt road to join the highway, stopping for a treasured view of two very rare Storm's Storks, which we disturbed by stopping the bus, so they flew off; but I was not alert and missed them.

There were plenty of Serpent Eagles about and thanks to Nick's agility with his excellent scope, which he used for spotting and laboriously dragged around for our benefit, we enjoyed superb views of a vicious-looking adult Blyth's Hawk-Eagle with a black and white throat pattern, a prominent crest and orange eyes.

We had an excellent Chinese lunch in an air-conditioned restaurant in Lahad Datu, in Davel Bay on the east coast. This is a bustling little town with an open market, open drains and one very plush hotel. A few of us checked out the cool air-conditioning and marble floors, and four of us sat down to fresh lime juice, a very different drink from Rose's lime juice from a bottle. It was here that we learned from a local paper, that there had been a very nasty train crash in the UK, near Paddington, with about 30 killed and many injured.

After lunch we were taken to the town office of 'Borneo Rainforest Lodge' (BRL), where we were given a short talk by staff before proceeding in two vans, and the truck with our luggage, on the 82 km. drive to the lodge in the rainforest of the Danum Valley.

On these dirt roads and with stops to see birds, this journey took 3 hours. There was no rain this afternoon, but an extremely sticky atmosphere. On the way we had good views of the male Violet Cuckoo with its orange bill and barred underparts, and we also saw the beautiful little Whiskered Tree Swift and some Rhinoceros Hornbills.

Eventually we reached the lodge, where we were to stay for six nights. This belongs to, or is a part of, the Sabah Foundation, a government body that also provides concessions for selective logging in much of the remaining tract of forest assigned to the Foundation.

The lodge took 2-3 years to create and was finished in 1996. The communal area of the lodge is large, well manned and airy, and holds a reception and the main dining room. The meals are buffet style. Tea and coffee are available from urns, as is cold drinking water from containers that can be tapped to fill a water bottle, which is a constant companion for each of us.

Bedroom and bathroom accommodation is in a row of sleeping lodges for individual families. These are spaced out well and they are linked by an elevated boardwalk. Various flowering trees are planted around the lodges, and these proved to be very good for spotting sunbirds and butterflies. The sound of the river, which was visible from our balcony and from the main dining room in the central building, could be heard in the background and on days when it was in spate after heavy rain it sounded much louder.

One of our earliest actions was to go to the gift shop to buy 'leech socks'; these are made of closely woven green cotton and are loose enough to fit anyone; they have drawstrings just below the knee, to be tied outside the trousers. Leeches may still get into the boots, but not through the weave of the socks. We have gladly used them in other jungles since!

The late afternoon walks, along the trail to the nearby suspension bridge, produced good views of a Hawk-Eagle and some of us saw a Helmeted Hornbill which flew over.

Friday 8th.: Osman, or perhaps the security staff, woke us at 5.30 a.m. The bedrooms here are spacious and there are ceiling fans. Each has a balcony with a view of the river and a drying rail for the inevitable wet clothes. Nick had worked out a rota with two groups, one led by him and the other by Osman or Danni, to follow the three main trails.

Our early morning walk with Nick produced Blue-headed Pitta, a brief but reasonably good glimpse of a male on the trail, of Cinnamon-rumped Trogon, and further views of Wallace's Hawk-Eagle. After breakfast, we were assigned to Danni (our local guide), proved brilliant as we saw Scarlet-rumped Trogon, Large-billed Blue Flycatcher, and, as icing on the cake, a male Argus Pheasant measuring some 6 ft. in length –

a very special sight as he pecked his way amongst the leaf litter on the forest floor. We were able to follow him quietly as he worked along the track. and we had several views spread over about 8-10 minutes. Initially, when he was standing still, we seemed to be looking at a log, but, when our eyes became accustomed to the limited light we saw the red legs first, then the shape of the large tail and the dark crest, and finally the small white oscillations. Earlier we had heard him calling loudly.

After lunch, and a rest during the stair-rod like downpour common in the middle of the day in these parts, we set off again; this time with Nick for the canopy walk. This entailed climbing two series of slippery steps up to a platform and then across two suspension bridges linking giant trees. The first bridge was short and not too far above the ground. The second bridge was long and, because the slope falls away below it, the walkway becomes higher above the ground and at a considerable height, surrounded by very tall forest giants. I did not enjoy walking across. However, there were railings on the sides of the bridges, and it is not dangerous, so after a few crossings I got used to it, and the lure of all the birds one might possibly see spurs one on. We heard hornbills, but we did not see them this time. In fact, there was little movement except a trogon that only Edward saw.

After dinner there was a night drive to look for animals and night birds like owls and nightjars. We all stood up in the back of the open truck with Danni, sitting astride the roof above the driver, scanning the bushes and towering forest trees from left to right with a powerful floodlight.

Peter, the 75-yr. old, needed the Rhinoceros Hornbill for his list, having missed it on the way in, and he is getting frustrated. The floodlight produced a pair for him that were roosting on separate branches in a tree not far above the road, and they looked extremely handsome and colourful, a marvelous sight.

We also saw two Greater Mouse Deer, a Sambar and, back at the lodge, a Leopard Cat that had been lured by bait. This small cat is about one and a half times the size of a domestic one and has very beautiful dark markings on a light background.

A 5 ft. whip snake crossed the road in front of the truck. A day or two later we were greeted by a small one in our bedroom. Luckily Edward spotted it as we entered, it was just behind the door beginning to work its way around the back of the beds; we let it go into the bathroom and then asked one of the lodge staff to come and remove it.

Saturday 9th.: 5.30 wake up, and dawn is always about 6 a.m. After tea in the lounge, we donned our anti-leech socks and set off on the boardwalk with Osman and Danni. Because it had rained so much, the tiger leeches were out in legions waving at us from every leaf in anticipation of feeding. Tiger leeches are about one inch in length and, unfed, thinner than a fine shoelace. Once on your leg or arm they make a succession of humped loops to climb upwards until they are satisfied that a suitable stretch of soft flesh has been reached. They can best be flicked off in the act of looping. When undetected they start to suck blood and gradually swell to the size of a fat English slug, eventually just dropping off. This leaves one continuing to bleed for a while because their bite comes with an initial "injection" of an anti-coagulant.

All of us, except Nick, attracted leeches, but we saw most of them soon after they climbed aboard our leech socks that sometimes did prevent them entering our boots. However, a leech sock tied too tight under the knee is not good for blood circulation especially on the long walks, when we might be standing in one spot for up to 20 minutes listening and looking for birds. As far as

I can remember we had no more bites after we began to wear the leech socks.

We saw very little; it was a very dark and humid morning. The birds must have known something because during our post-breakfast walk which was with Nick, and we were only 5 including him, we worked up and down the switchbacks of the poorly maintained East Trail, but produced only one new bird, an Orange-tailed Shama, of which we got a good view.

We tried to be as quiet as possible, in fact creeping along, and talking - even whispering - is discouraged, because, if one wants to see wildlife of any kind one must recognize that it will immediately pick up noise and movement from further away than we can. Bruce (with the cough) and his wife Diana, though keen to see wildlife, are talkative and tend to annoy the others. Today was the "hardest" morning's birding I have ever done, and for virtually no sightings!

The afternoon was disappointing too, with very heavy rain. Edward had set off earlier with Gerry to visit the canopy, but they had got stuck for over half an hour on the road sheltering under umbrellas from the stair-rods of rain. Most of us ventured out after the rain eased off and we went, as a group, along the same road and Danni spotted an orang-utang with a youngster. Soon after that, we met Edward and Gerry returning from the canopy area. We were all under lodge brollies for this walk and had to keep them up till we got home. Our glasses steamed up and the light was very difficult.

Sunday 10th.: A better day with a morning walk with Nick on the 'Coffin Cliff trail' past 'Jacuzzi Pool'. There was dappled sunlight through leaves today and the trails were quite difficult. Another of our groups came part way with us and then took a lower trail, so that they would reach the platform later than us from the opposite direction. So, we were first to climb to the vantage point where we rested overlooking the lodge complex. We were completely soaked through from the exertion of the steep climb (500 ft.).

On the way we passed burial caves in the cliff. Some say these are 'thousands' of years old, but Stephen, the senior naturalist at the lodge and a Kadasan, whose grandfather was buried in these caves, did not make this claim. Some human bones were visible in lower niches, but access to the cave itself was not possible. We only had a partial view from the top of a precarious ladder.

The 'bird of the day' (a "stonker" said Gerry) was the Scaly-breasted Bulbul, spotted by Edward close to the platform (he had seen the species years ago when we lived in Thailand). Two attractive waterfalls were visited on the way down and most of us had views of a Red-capped Forktail. The descent was interrupted by endless waiting around for feeding parties of birds to show themselves and be identified. Most were babblers, which moved through too quickly and unobtrusively to be identified, although Nick tried to lure some with recordings.

The afternoon walks from BRL along the main road and back, was unproductive although we saw movement in the trees, which Danni said was by Red Leaf Monkeys. Later, these were seen several times, but not by me. I saw Pig-tailed Macaques instead.

I quizzed Danni about his family, and he told me he was the eldest of nine and that his great-grandmother was still alive and over a hundred years old. He was to make a pilgrimage to see her soon. He said she could communicate with the spirits, presumably dead ones!

Monday 11th.: After breakfast we were taken by the night-drive truck to the forest edge and we walked back, taking four hours to cover the 2.2 miles. As usual, many tantalizing noises were heard, but not much seen well. I had excellent views of two birds: Rufous-tailed Tailorbird (outside our lodge balcony) and a female Olive-backed Woodpecker (on the walk). Hornbill honkings and maniacal laughs rang out around us, but the callers remained hidden.

After lunch we had torrential rain again, but it was over by midafternoon, when Edward followed Gerry and David in the direction of the canopy walkway. There were birds high up in the epiphytes on the spread limbs of the tallest giant trees; they were small black birds with red heads and proved to be the elusive Bristlebirds, which Osman and Danni had been trying to find for us – and we had found them first.

We opted out of the after-dinner night walk. The intent was partly to find the roost of the Pygmy Kingfisher, and partly for reptiles and other nocturnal mammals.

Tuesday 12th.: 5.30 again. Before breakfast we went up the main road with Nick. A nicer day, but mist and the general greyness hid the colours, although at this time-of-day birds are very difficult to see well. We had sun later and there was generally more movement. After breakfast we did the Hornbill trail. This was not on the map, but it leaves the main road opposite the Babandil trail-mouth, looping back to the Danum [River] Trail.

We met and passed the other group halfway, meeting just where Nick had seen, and was the only one to see, the rare endemic Black-throated Wren-Babbler (which most of us did just hear). Danni, Osman and Peter were in our group, but Paddy and Bunny went elsewhere. My best sighting was a Ruby-cheeked Sunbird.

It was very sticky in the afternoon but there was no rain. We rested and skipped the formal afternoon walk. But a stroll around the huts by ourselves produced our best views yet of the Plaintive Cuckoo.

Later, a young male orang-utang was spotted in the trees next to the restaurant where he was taking his time, slowly plucking leaves and eating them and gazing down at us from about 20 ft. up, and no doubt wondering about us, just as we were about him.

During the afternoon, I was royally entertained by a mother pygmy squirrel and her baby, running along the boardwalk to the huts in and around the posts and along the handrail, chuck-chucking and playing hide-and-seek. These creatures are only about 3 or 4 inches long including the tail, and they look like miniature chipmunks. At the other end of the scale, we caught glimpses of the Giant Squirrel with its chestnut and cream body and very large dark brown tail, warm and musky with spicy smells. We saw Mouse Deer, Sambar Deer and, just outside the official park entrance we caught up with a herd of at least four Asian elephants seen on previous nights on by other groups.

The evening game ride before dinner was very enjoyable this time. It was a lovely starry night and when the truck lights and engine were all turned off, we just waited in the dark, not speaking but listening to elephant grumblings (digestive noises, farts and communication noises). It was very atmospheric and special.

Wednesday 13th.: This was meant to be a day off for me. Edward visited the canopy walkway before breakfast. I visited the canopy with him later and, for a split second, had the most magical view of a gorgeous large green and red bee-eater (the Red-bearded), which perched on the handrail just a foot in front of Edward. Although my camera is permanently hanging from my wrist the souvenir photo of such an encounter is usually only in the mind as one is just not quick enough to take it.

We made a brief boardwalk excursion with Danni and were joined by Nella, a Welsh lady who wanted to search for the elusive and beautiful pittas, which we sometimes heard as they foraged on the forest floor, but we had no luck.

Nella and I later decided to take our swimwear and go across the river to the Jacuzzi Pool for a swim. This was very welcome and refreshing. The pool had a small sandy side to it that was just the right depth, and it had the additional refreshing touch of a good waterfall.

Edward had his last canopy walk and I came within touching distance of a pretty Tree Swift on a wire.

We left Danum valley after a good lamb dinner, coming out of the forest on our final night drive and saw a larger group of elephants, this time on the road. Nick, our leader who had led a group here two years ago, was disappointed not to have seen the Clouded Leopard this time. We drove to Lahad Datu and stayed the night in the new hotel, called the "Executive Hotel" where we stopped for a drink on our drive into Danum Valley. This night's accommodation here was a bonus, apparently not part of the original tour plan.

Thursday 14th.: We had an early morning walk to the edge of Darvel Bay which seemed filthy and dirt strewn. After breakfast we drove to the airport and flew back to Kota Kinabalu on a Fokker propjet. We were back where we arrived in the state. Nick forgot his tripod on the plane, but luckily remembered before we set off in the coach heading up to Mount Kinabalu.

Two hours and 88 kms. later, having passed through paddy-fields and then climbed the long ridge leading up into the Crocker Range, we arrived on the slopes of the hills that surround Mt. Kinabalu. This is the highest mountain in Southeast Asia, reaching just over 4,000 m. (14,000 ft.) and still rising a few millimeters a year.

We stopped en route at an attractive roadside market halfway up to Mount Kinabalu Park, where I bought a small pot of wild honey. Some pots contained many dead bees and plenty of wax. When we ate it later, we realized, because of the strong taste, that the bees had been smoked out of the tree. Here we also replaced Edward's lost green cap with a 'Crocodile Dundee' hat hand-made locally using broad leaves from trees, with the underside of the hat fully lined with material. He still wears this today in England. It rather suits him.

The Park Headquarters and entrance are at Kundasang at 5,000 ft. Here there is an education center and a botanical garden. The area is home to 26 species of flowering rhododendron. 9 species of 'carnivorous' pitcher plant, 1,000 species of orchid, 40 species of oak and over 300 species of birds.

We enjoyed the cooler climate and the vegetation which is so different from down below. One very abundant plant, not seen lower down, closely resembled the Medinilla (which comes from the Philippines) that is for sale in Eastbourne garden centers. The vegetative structure is almost identical, but the berries seem to lack the pink flowers or bracts that come out with the fruits in the Philippine species. Since then, we have been able to confirm that the two plants do belong to the same genus.

In the bowl below the main mass of the mountain there is a little village run by the Park Service and a circular loop road, with one-way traffic, where it is easy to bird-watch. The first afternoon was dry, which we were to find was a rare event, and we had excellent birding that afternoon. The star species were Whitehead's Broadbill, Sunda Cuckoo-shrike, Bornean Treepie, Sunda Laughing Thrush and Temminck's Sunbird.

We were first lodged in Nepenthes Villas (Nepenthes is a generic name for pitcher plants). After two nights Bruce and Diana and the two of us had to move because rain poured in through the roofs and soaked the beds. We had been sharing a bathroom and lodging with David, but after the soaking we were moved to a room in the main building, which meant we had the advantage of getting to meals without going out and getting wet. It was also roomier with loos upstairs and down, and we had it to ourselves.

Friday 15th.: We had good early morning views of the mountain which looks rather formidable. There had been an option when we booked the tour to sign up for the climb to the top of the mountain. Don and Nella had booked a climb on the 17th. but they are the only ones from our tour who are doing so – despite like us being grandparents. This, as they knew, would require them to spend the night in the large 'cabane' which is up in the rocky zone at the top.

Today Edward and I took the Silau Silau trail, which rose upwards along the nearest stream. I briefly glimpsed a shy Sambar, but Edward only saw movement as it crashed away, I also saw a Summit Rat busy in the forest leaf litter. We crossed another path and entered another trail, the Kiao View Trail, which rewarded us with the 'Bird of the Day' another Bornean endemic, called a Stubtail, which is a dear little bird, rather like our wren, but with longer legs, even less of a tail and a reddish cream eyestripe. He was busy plucking moss, perhaps for nest-making. We then followed the ridge trail down and around to the Park H.Q.

That afternoon we had problems over chalet keys and people locking themselves out. There were low clouds and plenty of rain, so we sat on the balcony and listened to the dripping rain, which was not too torrential this time, and saw the occasional white-eye and tailorbird.

Saturday 16th.: Breakfast was 2 eggs in some form or another, a small chicken sausage with 2 slices of cucumber and 1 of tomato. Sabah is officially Muslim and so, for most people, pork is not on the menu. The only pig we saw was a very large wild Bearded Pig, which visited the BRL (Borneo Rainforest Lodge) one evening on a scavenging spree.

This was the day we were rained out; and rained in! Edward's book on the birds of Sumatra, Java and Borneo was on the bedside table and it got soaked, but more of that anon. It was also "Cracking Day" for Nick. His fuse is short, and he can be somewhat volatile: more of this later too.

While I sat on the balcony in the sunshine trying to dry out some clothes, the rest of the party bussed up to the Power Station at the top of the road at 6,200 feet. I saw a Black Eagle soaring above me, but Edward said that it was essential to see the yellow feet to be sure of its identity, and I had not seen them, so it didn't count!

Drying was not easy in the consistent deep humidity in this part of the world, but one becomes increasingly ingenious. I first found the top of the water heater for the shower useful because Edward could reach up to place a plastic bag on top first, allowing me to then spread our damp things on that. Later, after we moved, I found that the large metal kettle could be put to use as a drier.

Later in the morning, I set off on a trail on my own, which I suppose was rather undisciplined, especially as I went without water or maps! But I never intended to go far, and all the trails here are very well signposted. I saw no forest birds, however.

From the Power Station the group split up; Nick leading one party along the Ular Trail, and the rest: Edward, Bruce and Diana, kept to the road. Those taking the road were immediately lucky, seeing a small covey of rare endemic partridges below the road.

When Nick's group got down to the top of the Silau Silau trail and the entrance to the Kiao View Trail Nick tried without success to find the Stubtail for his group. Edward meanwhile dived down the Silau Silau Trail where he was eventually overtaken by Bruce and Diana who, slightly above him on the trail, had just seen the extremely shy Crimson-headed Partridge. Edward, of course, went back upstream to look for it and just glimpsed a single bird in the deep shade of the undergrowth, but he saw no colour on it at all so it couldn't be counted.

He then stayed put to inspect a feeding flock that had suddenly appeared which included treepies, bulbuls and woodpeckers, a pair of very attractive Fruit-Hunters (this being a rare endemic) and the Short-tailed Hunting-Crow (proving that this overlaps in altitudinal range with the Green Hunting-Crow, which we had seen 20 minutes earlier).

Immediately after lunch, as it began to rain, about six of us boarded a minibus with Osman to go far down the mountain, to about 1,000 feet, on the east flank, beyond Ranau, to see a flowering Rafflesia. This is a strange and unusual plant in that it has no roots or leaves. It is a saprophyte not a parasite. It grows on a host-vine, and it flowers only very briefly. The flower lasts for about 5 or 6 days, and then collapses into a heap of compost. The bud, which, over about 9 months, grows to the size of a large round melon, opens to expose the largest flower in the world that sometimes measures a meter across (however, that measurement relates to the largest species of the genus, which is Sumatran), the Bornean species is a bit smaller. The owners of this land guard this rather precious host vine, and, when it blooms, they ask visitors to pay to see it thus providing a source of income, and we were told that some of the visitors' money goes to benefit the entire village. As the flower only appears rarely, and is not common, we were very lucky to see it. The site was rather dark as the vine has been trained beneath towering bamboo stands, and it was protected from the sun and the rain by a corrugated iron roof which helps to prevent it rotting prematurely.

When we got back to the mountain it was to find that there had been a tremendous downpour which had raised the water in the streams by three feet, and it was this rain that had penetrated the roof above our beds. Just as we were moving out, and Edward was falling over in the van and hurting himself, Nick appeared. He had discovered that Paddy and Bunny, the older couple, had been away all day thanks to Osman who had organised a different guided tour for them with a plant specialist. They had gone to Mesilau to see orchids and pitcher plants including the biggest of these: the Rajah Pitcher Plant. It annoyed Nick that this had been done without telling him, as he felt others should have been told that such a trip was available, but it was planned as a birthday surprise for Paddy. Nick's comments upset Paddy, who told us that she and Bunny had visited the Naturetrek offices and been assured that the trip was not solely for birdwatching, and that their interests would be catered for. Apparently, Nik had not been briefed on this and they had travelled independently to Kuala Lumpur to get to Kota Kinabalu. Nick had known it was Paddy's birthday and had suggested

that a cake be organized; but Osman had been
sworn to secrecy about the day trip and had said
that Paddy wanted nothing special.

The problem of food also came to a head today.
Clearly the Borneo Eco-Tour people had awarded a
contract to the catering staff for set menus at a
fixed cost and we were being given bland and
rather boring food every day in insufficient
quantities. So, after some earlier complaints
(including some from Nick, who said that very
good Chinese food had been routine here two years
ago) Osman told us this evening that we could each
chose a la carte up to 15 RM (Malay Ringits). This,
of course, was a recipe for disaster, and caused
further tensions due to the slow pace at which the
food was delivered in the sequence of the orders
placed. Nick, in some dudgeon, actually went off
with my Tom Yum soup, which was the first
ordered, and I had to wait for his, which had been
ordered later! They should send a psychiatrist on
these trips: he would have a field day.

Next day we went back to fixed meals, but slightly
larger and of a better quality. It was possible to
enjoy a large helping of rice with a main dish of
chicken or other meat and a delicious sauce,
accompanied by various green vegetables with
spices and ginger or mushrooms all for a
reasonable price. However, those wanting

European fare had a problem with the prices for that. Our dessert was invariably a dish of pre-cut pieces of watermelon, pineapple or papaya — the red variety and quite delicious. At the market stall on the first day on the mountain I had bought a large papaya for us all to share. However, Edward only ate the pineapple.

Edward saw Red-breasted Partridge, Golden-naped Barbet, Short-tailed Green Magpie and a pair of Black-breasted Fruit-hunters: of which the male seemed longer than depicted in the field guide and the female seemed paler and more orange below), and he glimpsed what he believed was a Sunda Bush Warbler, but he considered that he had not seen it well enough to count it. He did see the Crimson-headed Partridge, almost exactly where Bruce and Diana had seen it earlier in the day.

Sunday 17th.: The day for the climb, and a Larium day again too! This was the anti-malarial pill we were taking. I slept well; having taken a sleeping pill about 11.30 p.m. in the knowledge that we would be awakened at 5.30 again.

We were given picnics and, like the day before, bussed to the Timophon Gate. Don and Nella were to start their climb today and several of us thought we would follow them for a bit. I went as far as the Layang Layang Staff Hut at about 7.800 ft., thinking all the time about the descent in the guaranteed pouring rain. Edward, and two others in the party continued up to Pondok Villosa at 9,652 ft. (a climb of 2,600 ft. for me and 3,400 ft. for Edward.

It soon became clear that a downpour was coming, and we, but not Don and Nella, started down to Timophon Gate as fast as we could, and soon Edward had his leave-based hat flat against both his cheeks! We were all soaked on the descent, which became quite tricky and slippery as some sections of the trail became main drainage channels, and there were some wooden steps which all became more slippery. We were both very wet when we got back to our lodgings. Five times the height of Beachy Head is quite enough for an afternoon stroll.

This is a friendly mountain, and it is constantly being climbed and, on the way, people greet each other in every language. People from all over the world come to train for and race in the annual run up from the Timpohon Gate at 6,200 ft. to Low's Peak at 13.454 feet and down again; a distance which has been done in under 3 hrs. Most people, not running, take time out to look at the rhododendrons, pitcher plants and birds and at the views of course.

On the descent I was accompanied by Osman, and met a talkative Malay, who introduced me to a younger man saying that 2 years ago he was the first Malay to have climbed Mt. Everest. To which I replied that Mt. Kinabalu must be a mere pimple for him.

We learned later that sadly Don and Nella did not quite make it to the top. They reached the hut, but could not get to the top that evening, leaving the remaining hour's climb to the morning. After a night in the hut, a 3 a.m. start is recommended to be at the summit for sunrise if a full descent to the Power.Station is intended. The distance to climb was not great, but it was raining, and Don was feeling the altitude. It sounded quite tricky to climb the steep and slippery shale in the dark even with the benefit of fixed ropes and Nella, who weighed up going for the top with the guide, felt that the push to the top and then the full descent was too much to do in the day.

Bunny and Paddy had been quickly ferried down to see the Rafflesia, and Dave had set out alone down the Liwagu Trail – he saw some good birds, but he reported that the Liwagu Trail was difficult in places.

I spotted the Black Eagle again and this time it was verified by the pros; Edward missed it, but he did see the Mountain Black-eye.

Monday 18th.: The group marked time waiting for the climbers' return. After breakfast Nick took Edward, David and Peter down the Silau Silau trail to the Liwago River, the last stretch of this being precipitous, and came back over Bukit Burung. The main objective was to find the elusive Whitehead's Trogon, which so far had been seen only by Dave on our first afternoon on the mountain. After over an hour's search it was Dave who spotted one sitting quietly above us with its back turned; it would have been so easy to miss.

At this point the group was probably not far from where Dave, yesterday, had found Everett's Thrush (another very rare endemic).

As the group returned for lunch it rained sharply for over half an hour, but the usual prolonged rain after lunch did not fall and we set out to follow a steep new trail along the ridge from the restaurant area to the Kiao View Trail. More climbing for the, by now, complaining legs. It is difficult enough spotting birds in the forest when it is sunny, but sadly the day was grey, and the clouds rolled right over us, and we spent the afternoon in forest thick with clouds and saw little.

The usual gathering in the evening for the bird list

took place. Peter, who has not visited any part of Asia south of central Thailand, has already added about 115 new species to his life list; Gerry perhaps had more; both are indefatigable and constantly at Nick's heels, although Gerry is apt to go off solo. I visited the exhibition over the restaurant, and later so did Edward. There were some stuffed birds, some maps and a few quite nice photos as well as mounted butterflies and insects under glass.

Tuesday 19th.: We all went to Poring Hot Springs, down at about 500 ft., to 'take the waters' and soothe our aching limbs. The main swimming pools were empty of both people and water, which was a disappointment, but a few of us joined the locals in various small tile-lined tubs with individual taps where one can regulate the water temperature because the spring itself is much too hot at source. While there I saw some live stag beetles, but they were under glass, gnawing on some bamboo in the butterfly gardens.

Edward did not 'take the waters' but pushed far up the mountain trail with Nick, Peter and Dave, joined later by Gerry, hoping to see the Blue-banded Pitta. They got into its habitat, at a location where it is known to occur, but the bird was not to be heard or seen. In the early part of the morning, but behind the lead group, I had found half the same climb quite sufficient. And how hot it was in the plains! We replenished our fluid balance with shandy, others chose beer. Today, however, I also drank fresh coconut milk from the nut, but it was not a very young nut and so had no nice tender flesh.

I met a bright green whip snake pretending to be a vine winding itself around the side netting of the suspension bridge and the butterfly garden was clearly in need of some TLC (like many other things we saw on this trip) and we felt sad about it. Talking of butterflies, earlier in the trip, when we were near the Borneo Rainforest Lodge, Edward was very lucky to see a Rajah Brooke's Birdwing in the wild.

Nowhere did we get the sense that there was a general genuine concern for nature, just a desire to harvest the tourist dollars.

Wednesday 20th·: We left the mountain after breakfast descending the ridge road to the lowlands and headed south down the West Coast, going through Kota Kinabalu, where we left our suitcases at the hotel along with our laundry to be done and to await our return next day. Our destination was the island of Pulau Tiga, or "three hump island", which we were told is a National Park.

We stopped for a noodle soup lunch at Kuala

Penyuh where we waited for the boats to be sorted out for the trip across to the island. The soup was good, but we had to watch for splinters of chicken bone as the birds are not jointed in the way we are used to in Europe, they are quite skinny and are simply chopped up with a few deft blows of a machete.

This island is a wild place. It was about 2 miles to Pulau Tiga with the boats, including our limited luggage. We were greeted by an oil slick, actually a diesel spill, which was covering a wide area along the shore. The staff claimed it had been dumped illegally by a 'cruise ship'. Two disgusted Dutch visitors, there for their third trip, and angered by the decline in standards, thought it was caused by the builders of a third-party resort that had been carved out of the forest just along the coast to the south: this seemed likely to be closer to the truth. The development work had interfered with the natural drainage of the swamp near the park HQ, which meant we could not access the main trails because the water was deeper than our walking boots.

Mosquitoes were numerous. There was a dense dark forest on the slopes behind the swamp. Mangroves and similar trees occurred on the muddy swamp edges and there were casuarinas just inland from the sandy beaches. The trails we were able to get to seemed to be unmaintained and the beach was filled with tree trunks and flotsam – the usual plastic bottles and damaged flip-flops. I could have cried for the place.

We slept in dormitory style with bunk beds: two rooms for the boys and one for the girls. Luckily there were 2 fans in my room without which I wouldn't have slept a wink. We had the impression that a marine biology group was attached to this park and had taken over the bungalows originally meant for tourists.

The wildlife, apart from the crabs, consisted of Long-tailed Macaques and a few Hornbills; but Edward managed to see a Tabon Scrubfowl and Nick, Peter and Gerry had good views of a Nicobar Pigeon.

Thursday 21st.: There had been torrential rain in the night, and this continued into the first half of the morning and a brisk sea was running. Perhaps it was this that helped us to discover that down the beach to the north there seemed to be no oil slick, and the sea was clean enough for a swim and even Edward swam! After an excellent early lunch prepared by a friend of Osman's wife – who had come over with the provisions.

There appeared to be a serious rainstorm coming so

Osman persuaded the Park Officer to let us hire the Park's larger twin-engined boat to get us back to the mainland, and even in that the 50-minute crossing was quite scary as the sea had become very choppy.

We got back to Kota Kinabalu, returning by a slightly different route, which yielded a few good birds such as a Malaysian Plover and a Grey-headed Fishing Eagle, a species Edward had missed at Sukau although I saw it there. We checked into the Promenade Hotel and were glad to be reunited with clean laundry.

We had made our own plans for dinner that evening and could not join the group for the evening meal offered by the local tour company. Dr. Angelina Cheong, Ando's Chinese friend from her time in Malaya during the "emergency", flew down from Kudat especially to meet us and she insisted on taking us out to dinner in the Chinese restaurant at the Hyatt Hotel.

Angelina told us how she had met Ando in Kuala Lumpur in about 1952. The Red Cross, for which Ando worked, had identified her father's recent blindness which was due to shrapnel from a communist Chinese bomb in Johore at the time when some Chinese were promoting independence. His wife was in hospital and died of bone cancer at the age of 26 and Ando had helped her by arranging the three young children, one being Angelina, to visit their mother. For four years the children looked after their father and then a woman came along who offered to marry Angelina's father in spite of his blindness. This woman became the proverbial wicked stepmother.

Angelina and her husband, who is of Indian extraction, run separate medical practices – his being in the USA – and they are well off and able to cover the costs of education overseas for their two daughters.

As schools in Malaysia all teach Malay, relegating English to a foreign language, the Chinese and the Indian populations have become unhappy with the effect of this on the opportunities for further education and employment for their children.

Angelina is a Catholic and has financed a junior school and, we have since heard, a senior one as well; she also contributes in other ways to Kudat's prosperity.

After dinner she had a driver take her back home, a 3-hour journey, arriving soon after midnight. In the morning, she sent another driver down with a parcel, which was for her daughter Alina, who was studying for her A level exams in Croydon, along with a handbag for Ando and gifts for us. Typical

Oriental hospitality.

A very nice note to end the tour. Interestingly, Angelina told us there had been a severe drought the previous year. On the plane home Nick told us that he thought that this might account for the lower bird numbers.

Friday 22nd.: Today we flew to Kuala Lumpur and after a few hours we emplaned for Heathrow.

Saturday 23rd: Our flight to London was quite good, the seats were wider to accommodate TV screens but were rather uncomfortable. There was a choice of films to see and good food, and we landed at Heathrow at 6 a.m. where, by arrangement, we were met by the same taxi firm from Peacehaven.

INDIA, 2000

Thanks to our friends Roger and Liz Charlwood in Eastbourne this trip was planned in consultation with General Jimmy Singh (Retired) of Gurungdongma Tours and Treks Kalimpong in Bengal's Darjeeling District. We were to be accompanied, for most of the trip, by our daughter Melanie and her husband Steve – and they joined us in Delhi on February 5th.

January 27th. We flew from London Heathrow to Mumbai on Virgin Atlantic (Premium Economy) which was quite comfortable. Despite a sleeping-pill I only had a short nap. We arrived in Mumbai 4,800 miles away to find a pleasant temperature in the 80s. Many of the locals seemed to be yawning like us. We crossed to the domestic airport and picked up a 1-hour flight on Indian Airways to Hyderabad, where Edward's birding friend Asheesh and his charming wife Smriti met us.

After a hair-raising ride in traffic with constant horn-blowing and near misses resembling a Laurel and Hardy movie, we arrived at our friends' new apartment and met their son Prashast (17) and daughter Prakriti (20) and after a veritable feast of vegetarian dishes we gratefully turned in.

January 28th. Aasheesh took us to visit the Chowmahalla Palace, one of many inhabited by former 16th-17th century Maharajas & Nizams, which is now a museum for the costumes of their wives, their weaponry and furniture etc. We stopped to photograph the Char Minar monument and then visited the old Pittie home now abandoned and due for demolition and to be rebuilt for the two families involved. In the afternoon Asheesh invited three birding friends to discuss a book on south Indian birds, while Smriti and I played Scrabble!

January 30th. Edward and Asheesh went to the big lake in the middle of the city as there was report of a Grey-headed Lapwing (the 1st. record for the city). Other birds seen included Spotted Owlet and Hoopoe.

When the men returned, we all went for a walk in the "National Park". There were interesting educational signs along the path including a quote by Ghandi: "the earth can supply all Man's needs, but not all his greed". Also "God does not throw you into deep water to drown you, but to purify you".

Asheesh's parents came to meet us after another copious breakfast with delicious samosas made by his mother. Later we exchanged warm farewells before boarding a flight to Kochi where we were met by a driver and interpreter.

From Kochi it was a 2-hour drive to a beach resort full of surprises. No hotel here, just two guest houses amongst the coconut palms with hammocks erected outside. It was quite a walk to the beach which was all sand and the water a dreamy temperature, but we did not swim as the waves were too high. There were some rather amusing children living along the beach and they wanted their pictures taken. Our host and his wife Mali and their children were very welcoming. I found it rather reassuring to be in a Christian area here, where the Catholic schools have nicely designed uniforms.

All the rural areas and small towns were very reminiscent of Thailand with small dwellings and sari-sari type stores at the roadside.

We couldn't figure out the remote control for the air conditioner and instead we used the mosquito nets and had the fan on all night.

January 31st. After a wash in the open-air bathroom, Edward and I walked down to the beach where the ocean, here treated in atlases as the Arabian Sea, had calmed down a bit so we had a swim!

Plovers and crabs were scuttling around on the sand. There were several fishing boats around and a stone wall which stretched as far as the eye could see was being constructed all along the beach.

8.30 am. We had rice pancakes, coconut chutney and honey for breakfast. A taxi was called – an old Ambassador – for the drive to Allapula village where one can rent houseboats, and indeed boats of all kinds to ply the numerous waterways leading to Lake Bembenada, which stretches away to the distant horizon. The proliferation of water hyacinths would no doubt completely choke the channels here if it were not for the continuous passage of boats.

Our boat – Yes, we were the only passengers – was a covered one, but after a while we sat on top to get better views of the birds which included Open-billed Storks fishing for snails, Blue-tailed Bee-eater, Purple Gallinule, Bronze-winged Jacana, Anhinga, Indian Shag and White-breasted Kingfisher, and, new for Edward, White-eared Barbet and White-tailed Tree Pie. Later, back at Allapula, we took a taxi, which stopped for me to photograph a Hindu procession that was on its' way to a temple and was accompanied by beating drums and an "anna" (elephant) in a headdress.

I also asked to stop at a dress shop, where models of women were hanging, blowing in the breeze, to display the clothes for sale. I chose a dress which cost Rp. 120 (roughly £1.85), an even better bargain than the Eastbourne charity shop prices.

The local language is Malayalam, and we are the guests of Abi and Mini Arakal in Chetty village. Davis, the young son is such a cheeky little lad, full of fun. Mini gave me a complete facial with an iced vegetable pack that she left on for about 30 minutes, and also gave me a massage. I found this so relaxing – her hands were perfect for the job. She told me she had had to pass an exam in Delhi. It was well worth Rp. 300.

February 2nd. We asked for a 5.45 a.m. call, instead of which Mini knocked on our door at 5 a.m. I had only just begun to fall asleep, having had what the French call a "nuit blanche". We did have the air conditioning on, but an English couple in the adjoining house were very noisy and the man was suffering from "Delhi belly" and the opening and closing of the thick wooden doors of these 300-year-old huts in the night sounded quite like a chain saw.

After an extremely fond farewell of hugs from our hosts we set off in the dark at 6 a.m. We had an Ambassador car with a driver named Ajit, who was excellent, but after 20 minutes on the road Edward, still half asleep, declared he had left his everyday spectacles on the bed! So back we went.

We were heading up to Munnar in the Cardamon Hills, a 130-mile drive which took us about 4 1/2 hours. On the way we saw a Giant Malabar Squirrel, which was dark chocolate brown with cream underparts, and a Dhole (the name for the Indian wild dog).

Once we were in Munnar we contacted a guide called Vinod who we had booked for the next 3 days. He was good at identifying birds and was terribly in awe of Edward when he heard that Edward had published a review of the "Birds of South Asia: The Ripley Guide" by Pamela Rasmussen - which is the book we have with us on our tour.

This area, at about 3,000 ft. above sea level, is famous for tea plantations and the spice cardamon. Although it is the dry season the tea bushes look very green. Cardamon has leaves like a small palm; it doesn't flower or fruit until after the local rainy season in May/June.

Our lodging is called the Olive Brook resort and after a welcome hot shower we ate some toasted sandwiches and set off in the car for a first bird watch, sadly outside the National Park, which has just been closed for a couple of months on account of the breeding season of the Tahr, an endangered species of mountain goat. We managed to get excellent views of the Nilgiri Laughing Thrush and of the dusky blue Nilgiri Flycatcher.

In the evening, we had a cookery lesson in the kitchen that adjoins the dining room of the Resort. Lessons like this each evening are a nightly feature here.

The menu for the evening was fish curry. It was fascinating, but I doubted we would go to all the complex preparation at home! We and the other tourists, which included Spaniards, Swedes, Canadians and Americans, all gathered around as we had the food preparation explained. The result, of course, was quite delicious, aromatic and not too hot, and this was just one of about 4 or 5 dishes served that evening.

When we left the young cook, called Anouk, said he had 200 recipes in his head, gave us his e-mail address and told us that when we were back home, we could seek his advice any time.

February 2nd. Edward was up at 6 a.m. to climb the hill behind the resort with Vinod, who had recruited two locals to help in the hunt. This was not very productive, but we saw Malabar Whistling Thrush, Black Eagle and Barking Deer and heard the rumbling sounds of a nearby group of elephants.

This area also grows tea, and we visited an estate, so we learned a good deal about the harvesting, withering, maceration, fermentation, drying, sorting and grading of tea, which we might remember when we next pour a cuppa!

We read an alarming statistic in The Hindu newspaper which reported that 17,000 farmers had committed suicide in 2006. Apparently, the wives and children of indebted farmers met the Union Agriculture Minister seeking a total loan waiver and guarantees on the procurement of farm commodities at reasonable prices, as well as a ban on the import of wheat and genetically modified seeds and foods.

After Edward's sortie and his late breakfast, Ajit drove us and Vinad down to a waterfall, which was impressive and must be monstrous during the monsoon.

That night we had our second cookery lesson, which was Kerala chicken curry. I counted 21 ingredients. Dinner was laid with the usual array of different dishes all deliciously spiced. The ingredients are always fresh, never kept refrigerated nor made ahead of time. I thought this made us Brits seem very lazy and casual about food. My hand went up mentally "guilty as charged"!

February 3rd. Sunday.   We said goodbye to Munnar at 4.30 a.m. and were given sandwiches, bananas, oranges and water. We were to drive to Thattekad, where Vinod lives on the edge of a Bird Reserve, which is a gated forest area of 25 sq. kilometres. Traffic that early was minimal at that time and we bumped and swayed along for 2 1/2 hours on an endless "snake" of a road.

We stayed at Hornbill Lodge, which is a tented accommodation with a palm leaf roof and a wooden veranda, looking out on the Periyar River where one can canoe or shoot the rapids in an inflatable dingy.

We were offered a variety of curry dishes for lunch, and I much enjoyed the coconut milk drunk straight from the nut. My digestive tract has adapted well to the new diet and quite settled down. As it was very hot, I relaxed in a lounger, whilst Whiskered Terns – which I first saw in Kashmir – circled over the water, but I associate all terns with the sea.

As I was repacking my large case, I found the small New Testament Bible that I thought I had lost. This had been given to Melanie at her French speaking school in Switzerland. I was so happy to have found it; I had been praying to do so and now I gave thanks to the Lord!

Edward returned just after dark having seen the frogmouth which was a major objective here. Hurrah! Vinod had clearly worked hard to please.

February 4th. Another birding day in the dry deciduous forest at the end of which we said farewell to Vinod and settled up, and he saluted "Edward the Guru" with a "namaste" touching our feet in reverential style!

February 5th. Another early start. I am not too sad to be leaving the hard beds and the endless zipping and unzipping of the tent. By 7 a.m. we were on the road with Ajit heading for Cochin airport.

We were due to board a Jetlite plane for a 40-minute flight south to Trivandrum to pick up a flight back up to Delhi. When the plane came in and we had boarded we were kept waiting for a while. But eventually we started to roar down the runway, only for the brakes to be slammed on and return to our start point. Another wait followed with no announcement from the captain. Meanwhile the cabin temperature began to rise alarmingly. Everybody started asking the stewardess for information, but all we got was just "a problem". Finally, the doors were opened, and I went back to one of them trying to find some breeze. The outside temperature was 90 C. and a 10-month-old baby in the seat behind us had a bottle of water poured over it. Finally, we took off and reached Trivandrum for a flight to Delhi, which was there to board – it may have been one later than planned; but we arrived safely in Delhi, dropping through a pall of pollution, 2 1/2 hours late.

Melanie and Steve were out when we arrived at the hotel that had been booked for us, but we had a happy reunion when they got back. They looked fit and well after 2 weeks in Barbados followed by 2 weeks on the ski slopes in France!

As planned, they had arrived yesterday and had already visited Dr. Satya Gupta's home and been given dinner by her niece. Melanie said the place was filthy and mice were running around the kitchen! It seems that since Satya's sister died the housekeeping standards at the house of this lovely, vibrant lady had slipped. I have mentioned her before when reporting on our visit to India in 1993.

Meanwhile, Edward had been in contact with an American diplomat called Peter Kaerstner, based at the U.S. Embassy, this had been mainly to thank him for his very favourable review of the 3rd. edition of the *Howard & Moore Complete Checklist of Birds of the World*, published in 2003. Peter is one of the few ornithologists who, in his travels, has seen and identified over 7,000 bird species. He now collected the four of us from the Amanotel, and we set out to find somewhere to eat, and Edward and I had had hardly anything all day. We found a restaurant and enjoyed a good meal and Steve was in his element with Indian food.

The people in Delhi were going about in woolly hats, anoraks and gloves because the city had recently experienced temperatures below zero for the first time ever and it was still cold.

February 6th. Ash Wednesday. Yesterday seems to have taken its toll, what with extreme temperatures, emotion and irregular mealtimes. I felt rather shaky. Edward disappeared at 6.30 a.m. to meet an Indian bird watcher who he had previously corresponded with by letter and e-mail, and he had promised to take Edward to Sultanpur Jheel, or pond, which is about 25-30 kilometers away. Edward came back later, happy to have seen Indian Spotted Eagle, Yellow-eyed Babbler and Painted Storks.

Soon after lunch the four of us entrained in a 1st class air-conditioned train for Jaipur (City of Victory), which is SW of Delhi and in Rajasthan state, a trip of about 3 hours.

Jaipur is on the eastern edge of the Thar desert and is the capital of the state of Rajasthan, the largest state in India. It is a city of palaces, with architecture that was of special interest to Melanie. We were again met by a driver and guide with a notice "Welcome to the Dickinsons and Lathams".

Here we were to enjoy a "home stay" in the home of a retired Rear Admiral; he and his wife had a lovely garden and a labrador called Sheru.

The air, thank God, is clean and fresh, and we could actually enjoy some sunshine. Our first visit was to a War Memorial; later we were taken to the famous Rambargh Place Hotel, which is very definitely 5*, with marble halls, sweet smells of spice and impeccable staff in turbans. The cheapest single room is £400 per night.

One of the staff came over and spoke to us while we were taking tea in the gardens. He spoke impeccable English and had been with the hotel for 27 years. He had spoken with Prince Charles and Princess Diana, on their visit, when they came here due to a polo tournament and apparently Charles has since visited with Camilla. He also told us about the English cricket teams that have stayed here.

That evening we ate dinner in an Italian restaurant just across the road from our host's house.

February 7th. Thursday. Oh dear! First casualty; poor Melanie was up all night, vomiting and on into the morning. We suspected the mushrooms in the risotto at the Italian restaurant. The Admiral asked if we wished to call a doctor, but Melanie declined and stayed in bed whilst we and Steve went out with a driver. The Admiral assured us that Melanie could call him at any time during our absence. Over breakfast he told us about his role in the India/Pakistan war in 1971, where he had to put in place a blockade off Karachi which was very successful and shortened the war.

The buildings in Jaipur are all a "Pompei pink" and the streets are wide and laid out with square-angled crossroads in a N-S and E-W configuration, thanks to Sawai Jai Singh II, a keen scholar, statesman and patron of the Arts. Work on the walled city began in 1727 and the walls took 6 years to complete. An impressive dam was also built which created the Man Sagar Lake, where succeeding rulers built and maintained a summer palace on an islet.

We visited an open-air observatory called Janatar Mantar (1728-34) which displays 16 instruments which look like giant sculptural compositions some of these can still tell the local time down to the last second. We also visited a fabric emporium where cloth is patterned by hand using colour blocks. Every piece here is handmade, not machine-made.

In another shop we saw carpets being made and looked at a huge collection; some from yak wool, some from camel wool and some from silk. Downstairs we watched them being scorched by a blow lamp which removes excess hair and firms up the knots; after that they are washed liberally with water and hair shampoo and finally brushed repeatedly with an enormous brush.

Edward fell for a carpet and bought it and they will ship it to England. Wow! The vendor claimed he had always liked the British and respected them for all the things they had taught the Indian people.

Back at the Admiral's house, we checked on Melanie, who although still vomiting declared it was on the wane, but we still felt anxious. Then the three of us found a local shop for a delicious vegetarian lunch and we paid for the guide and drivers' lunches; a total cost equivalent to £8 for the five of us.

Later Edward felt unwell, so Steve, Melanie and I went downstairs to dine with our host and his utterly charming wife. It's not every day that one dines with an Admiral! He showed us the large bronze model of the Bombay Fort, which he had helped restore to its former glory partly by removing many surrounding buildings.

Melanie bore up bravely and managed a mouthful of a special bland restorative dish specially prepared for those recovering from illness. We enjoyed a true sailors' drink of rum and hot water. Steve thoroughly enjoyed the meal and made up for all our lesser appetites. We discussed many things: the Anglo/Indian relationship, their daughter's wedding last week and so on. A fascinating evening.

February 8th. Friday. Began very sunny with clear, crisp, cold air. Melanie is much better. Edward marginally so and happy to visit the Amber Fort, a 16th. century blend of Hindu and Muslim architecture, considered amongst the best hilltop forts. There were two ways to enter; we drove up to the back of it while most visitors choose to mount on elephants and join the file of elephants toiling up the path in single file, with the tourists in the howdahs and colourfully turbaned mahouts perching on the back of the elephants' necks. We could see this looking down from the fort, what a sight!

We decided to pass on lunch, and after very cordial farewells to the Admiral and his wife, we set off for Agra in two cars by way of the Bharatpur Bird Sanctuary, which we will visit tomorrow. There was an increasing number of camels on the road pulling loaded carts and jostling with the traffic.

Our driver wasn't going to stop on this 3-hour journey, but I insisted on a comfort stop.

Our lodge was just on the outskirts of the Sanctuary. It was not bad, and I had a bath, but there was barely any water.

February 9th. Saturday. One needs many layers of warm clothing here to venture out at 7.30 a.m. at this time of the year and I wished I'd brought my ski pants.

After breakfast a Sikh rickshaw driver took Edward and me to the sanctuary gate and we started walking along the dry and dusty paths. A Maharaja of Baroda wanted to shoot wildfowl, and originally tigers, and he built the grounds in the 1920s, when he was able to welcome Lord Curzon and his generation for shooting on the many lakes. In winter it now accommodates thousands of migrating birds. We found the lake level very low and displaying a lot of red algae. Nevertheless, we saw spoonbill, ibis, kingfisher, Spot-billed Duck and Comb Duck. We also saw some mammals: Sambhar, Spotted Deer, monkeys, Nilghai (a large dark-gray antelope) and jackals, whose shrieking had awoken us this morning.

There is a small area of dry forest at the far end of the grounds and a walk there produced a Dusky

Eagle Owl sitting on a nest high up with just the large erect "ear" tufts visible.

We were caught up by Melanie and Steve who had taken rickshaw rides from the gate, and they seemed delighted with the morning. On the way back Melanie persuaded her driver to sit in the back and let her do the last bit of pedaling back to the gate while he rode in the seat!

In the afternoon we looked inside the crumbling shooting lodge, now overgrown with tree roots. There is a stone monument in the park listing when, and what they shot when they came here from the 1920s until 1965.

Here are two strangely worded quotes from a book by Hindi gurus, placed in our bedroom: one reads: "Worship of other gods: driven by the properties of their nature, they who fall from knowledge desire worldly pleasures in imitation of the prevailing customs, worship other gods instead of the one single God" and the other "Those whose intellect has been robbed through enjoyment of worldly comforts, such foolish persons tend to worship other gods than the Supreme Being".

February 10th. I'm suffering from loose bowels thanks to so many lentils. We are all heading for Agra, and this leg of our journey completes what is known as the Golden Triangle.

We, in our car, met Melanie and Steve in theirs at the Mughal Hotel in Agra. They were delighted with their young lady guide who took them to the other side of the Yamuna River to see the Taj at sunset, which allowed them to take some stunning photographs.

Edward and I, having been to the Taj Mahal on our previous visits, went to it with Melanie and Steve when it opened in the morning.

Then we all visited Fatehpur Sikri, where a fort cum palace had been built, but due to the loss of its water supply the intended town was never completed. Edward and I had been before as I have reported, but now our guide was able to add quite a lot that I had missed. The ruling monarch, Akbar, came here in 1570 to see the Sufi to pray for a son. He had three wives, one Christian, one Muslim and one Hindu, and 14 children and the Hindu wife was the only one to give him a son.

This was not as interesting to Melanie as the Jaipur palaces, but she found a central fluted pillar in red sandstone, intricately carved which was quite remarkable. Back in Agra we left Melanie and Steve to tour the Red Fort.

We left Agra that evening and caught the 8.30 p.m. 1st class sleeper train headed to Jabalpur, on the way I was up five times on an otherwise comfortable night.

February 11th. The huge railway station at Jabalpur was extremely crowded. Outside the station was an overpowering stench of urine. Two vehicles were there to meet us and take us to Bandhavgarh White Tiger Lodge to arrive by about 4 p.m. Edward had been here before twice when he was leading the tours that James Hancock had set up with Cox & Kings.

However, our start was not auspicious; first we had one puncture and then a second – with the spare tyre, which was clearly substandard. We were stuck in the middle of nowhere whilst Hari hitched a ride to the nearest village. Poor Hari, the driver was very dismayed at our luck.

A large herd of Indian cattle passed peaceably by with their little hooves clicking softly on the road. No farmer was in sight. Hari told us later that he had asked several people coming our way to pass on news of what was happening, but nobody did.

Finally, another tourist office vehicle turned up and we set off again and arrived at the lodge run by the State Government. It was rather run down with tiles falling off the roof, and the rooms were not too clean – despite the manager shouting at staff and throwing his weight around. I managed to sleep for 7 or 8 hours, which is something I haven't done for years.

Melanie and Steve are great companions, full of jokes, taking everything in their stride; Melanie chatting up the locals and enjoying the enormous contrasts everywhere.

February 12th. Tuesday. After early morning tea was sent to the room, we left at 6.30 in an open Jeep with Hari and a local guide picked up at the gate. We were extremely cold.

Guess what? After about 45 minutes the Jeep started to cough and splutter, and then gave up completely. The driver peered into the engine and declared it "kaprather ut". Not again! Hari, our guide was devastated and here we were sitting in a stalled jeep in the middle of tiger country! Mobile phone signals lack a network here, and the staff don't use walkie talkies, which is a good thing as the chatter would disturb the animals. After a discussion between Hari and the driver, the driver disappeared on foot heading back to the gate, leaving Hari with the jeep and the local guide to walk alone with us. Happily, these guides carry rifles.

We didn't walk far; we hitched a ride with a couple of Swedes and their guide and returned to our boxed breakfast and were then able to catch up with about 25 other Jeeps often noisy parties of passengers who had heard that a tiger was moving around on foot. We tried to find it, but while Steve and I caught a fleeting glimpse of startling bright orange in the dense bamboo, neither Melanie nor Edward did.

In the afternoon we visited one of the elephant camps, which are set at the edge of the camp just inside the loose stone boundary wall, where the mothers stay with their young. There was a two-year-old sleeping in the mother's shadow and, the mahout called him, he got up and came to see what was happening. He was quite feisty and even a youngster like that could very easily bowl you over if he chose. Lovely though they are near to I find them quite scary.

We were shown the elephant "cakes" of special heavy wheat chupattis that provide extra nourishment for the working elephants! Because Hari was quite well known here, we were allowed to feed the mother and baby. As we left in the Jeep the little one started running after us making an endearing trumpeting sound and his mother immediately trumpeted to order him back to her.

Later Edward was very pleased to catch sight of an elusive Malabar Pied Hornbill, which promptly flew towards the mountain and perched about ½ mile away.

That evening there was a power failure and so no room heaters, and it took ages to warm up in bed in spite of our thermal wear. Sleep was not assisted by a large party of Indian LPG (gas) salesmen and their extremely loud music, thumping and singing far into the night, right outside the window.

February 13th. Wednesday.   A 6 a.m. start with warm blankets in the Jeep and a new driver and guide, but Hari, faithful chap, was still with us.

We saw a wild boar quite early on, which is supposed to be a good omen for sighting tiger. We were told Hari did not want to be involved in another "shouting circus" so we went our own way.

We saw a leafbird, sambar (deer); jackal and Spotted Deer (Chital). Then suddenly Hari got news and took us to a place where a tiger had been resting and which others had already been seeing. Between the road and the depression in which the tiger lay was an elephant, and when a group got off its howdah it was our turn to climb on.

We were helped to climb on to the howdah from

the jeep. Melanie pulled me up and Hari pushed from behind! And then, settled in the howdah, we were looking down on a tiger resting in the little clearing. WOW! My position on the howdah was not ideal; I tried to take a picture by twisting round only to find that my view was gone. Not to worry, Melanie had taken several so everyone was satisfied. Later, the elephants were taken down to the river for bathing and we heard them trumpeting.

Edward seems to be surviving on thin air and his trousers are falling down! His diet seems to be an occasional banana, an egg and some cashew nuts.

In the afternoon we visited a shrine to Shiva, the god of plenty. Hari talked at length about all the legends and fairy tales behind the Hindu religion.

We saw good views of wild boar chomping on greenery at a small pool, and excellent views of Spotted Deer and Muntjac or Barking Deer. At dusk Edward saw a Painted Spurfowl, another new species for him.

February 14th. Thursday. We said goodbye to Bandhavgarh Tiger Lodge at 8 a.m. and set off east in the direction of Varanasi (or Benares as the British used to call it).

Hari was his usual cheerful self, and the driver

assured us that he had two new tyres on the vehicle! The distance to cover was about 400 kms. at a speed of about 40-50 m.p.h. But it was sometimes less, as the route varied from a tarmac surface to dusty tracks and rocks helped us to ford a river.

We crossed at least three mountain ranges and passed through endless dusty villages where shopkeepers were peddling their wares at the edge of the road: we saw an outdoor barber, aluminium water pots, saris and sweetmeats on sale, and a lady cobbler crouched over her lathe in the dust; as well as women working on the roads. Hari admitted the village men are lazy or drunk most of the time.

We visited a crumbling Maharajah's one-time lakeside palace called Govind, which was now being restored. Our lunch break was at an "oasis" restaurant; the food was a long time coming and they quite forgot my order for spaghetti, so I had a slice of Edward's pizza. Bananas and cashew nuts were always available.

In the afternoon the drive became tedious, our bodies had had quite enough of being thrown around all day. Tempers became strained and when we finally arrived in Varanasi we struggled to find the Ganges View Hotel, which nobody seemed to have heard of. But we made our way through an impossible maze of side streets and hovels at the edge of the river and came to it and found it to be a real oasis. It had been a private villa at one time. Edward and I had our first really pleasant meal for some time and then turned in. Melanie and Steve went to bed without eating.

Boys here start chewing betel nut leaves by the age of 10 and a couple of years later they will be addicted. Their teeth gradually rot and the gums are coloured scarlet. By the age of 40 they will have lost all their teeth. Everyone spits!

February 15th. Melanie and Steve set off early for a sunrise boat trip on the Ganges. Edward and I enjoyed a lie in until they returned, when we all had an excellent breakfast on the sunny terrace. Melanie and Steve then set off once again to explore the town, whilst Edward and I strolled down to look at the extraordinary sights everywhere. There are foreigners (Westerners) who have "gone native" and who look even weirder: hippies, druggies and dropouts with matted hair and unwashed clothes.

Our guide returned and offered to take us on the river in a hired rowboat to witness a daily ritual taking place at one of the ghats, areas of endless wide steps leading to the river. Ghats are where the dead are prepared for cremation. The whole air is thick with the smoke from the ghats, and there are 28 ghats at Varanasi!

There is an extremely noisy, yet orderly waving of enormous bowls of smoking frankincense to North, South, East and West, to the sound of drums and sitar; all watched by hundreds sitting on the steps or in boats on the river.

Two of the ghats are where the dead are cremated on wood piles at the rate of 200 a day. This goes on all night at the edge of the water. A specific caste takes care of keeping an "eternal fire" burning as it has for the past 200 years. People pay them for using some of this fire to light the pyres for their relatives. One is not allowed to photograph the burning ghats themselves.

There is now a government-run electric crematorium on the spot, but this is used only by people who can't afford the wood fire.

People not allowed to be cremated are young children under the age of five, pregnant women, holy men, snake bite victims and lepers. Such people are all considered innocent of sin. They have a stone tied around them and they are tossed into the middle of the river.

This is also where people come to bathe, immerse

themselves, wash clothes and purify themselves spiritually.

Near dusk we took a boat onto the river opposite the main ceremony and watched the whole ornate evening ceremony, which had a backdrop of pulsating neon-lit parasols and other coloured lights, and the sky was full of tiny paper kites flown high by small boys.

After watching this extraordinary scene, we followed Vimal into town through life-threatening traffic and streets of bazaars like Chinatown. I photographed a bull lying very peacefully on the floor against a counter at the far end of a shop selling clothing materials – this was apparently his usual place in daytime.

At 11.30 p.m. we took another overnight train from the station and were given spotless starched bottom sheets, a pillow and a blanket. The coaches were airconditioned and we slept for five hours. Early morning tea was followed by breakfast with tea, coffee and hot milk (no cold milk for Steve's cornflakes), a vegetarian cutlet and boiled vegetables and finally bread, butter and jam. No complaints!

February 16th. We arrived at a huge rail station in New Jalpaiguri in mid-afternoon. The platforms look as if they are about ½ mile long and apparently the diesel engines usually pull 18 to 20 carriages.

We expected to be met, but no one appeared! We seemed to be surrounded by beggars of all ages, which Melanie and I found very hard to cope with.

Edward made a couple of phone calls, and an hour later a driver arrived with a large vehicle. In this we climbed up to Kurseong at nearly 5,000 ft., and the temperature was pleasant, as there was plenty of cloud cover. This hotel, Cochrane Place, was our first stop on the way to Darjeeling, It had once been the residence of an Hon. Magistrate. It was a quaint old-fashioned little hotel with lots of antique furniture, but it was clean and had modern plumbing. A small pot-bellied stove, smoking mightily, provided heat for which we were grateful. There was confusion as to whether we were on full board or not.

February 17th. Sunday. We had breakfast out on a terrace in weak sunshine and misty conditions created by high cloud cover.

We learnt from the guide that, due to "political reasons" the "toy train" from New Jalpaiguri to Darjeeling, which we had expected to take, was not running and hadn't been for some time. So, after a

334

breakfast of juice, porridge, baked beans on toast, honey and pancakes, a new driver turned up. He brought a guide with him, and we said goodbye to Kurseong and left, heading uphill on a winding narrow road, with continually honking vehicles, passing through tea plantations on the mountain slopes and above then an increasing variety of pines, deodars etc.

At one point a large crowd had gathered at the edge of the road and we learnt that yesterday a packed taxi had gone over into the ravine resulting in two killed and many injured.

The physiognomy of the people around us has changed completely and we now see some ruddy cheeks and more Mongolian features.

After about 50 minutes climb, we stopped at a R.C. Franciscan Mission, where we were shown how 40-50 underprivileged young people are educated, especially being taught how to grow their own vegetables in plots like miniature allotments measuring 1 meter square. Everything is completely organic. The very large, run down building revealed utterly basic dormitories.

There were "solar panels" for water heating constructed on a metal disc with simple coils of metal piping the water. Many on the roof were leaking.

We were also shown how more elderly or physically or mentally handicapped people are taught to make clay bricks. Next was a room containing curious round plastic bags stuffed with hay which had been boiled and seeded with mushroom spores, some of which were already sprouting mushrooms.

The Irish/Canadian Jesuit who started this Foundation is old and not so well now, and the government has withheld funds prior to bureaucratic checks. We were offered coffee by the one-time priest, now Director Fr. Tommy Sasac and saw from the visitors' book that plenty of Brits and other foreigners have visited and some have stayed with their families. It was all too basic for me I'm afraid!

Back in the car we continued to follow the railway tracks in the road all the way up to what used to be the highest railway station in the world at 7,000 ft., called Ghoom; but we heard that the Chinese have recently built one, that is nearly twice as high. We then dropped a few hundred meters and came into Darjeeling, and all the way have been in the state of Bengal.

I had imagined that Darjeeling would be more

sophisticated, clean and orderly because it had been a hill station used by the Brits for decades. I was wrong. Filth and deprivation were everywhere, rubbish is often just tipped over the slopes, but there are piles more left in the streets.

We were booked at The Mayfair Hill Resort, once privately owned, but bought two years ago and expanded into a hotel. It was as far removed from the outside world as you could imagine. We were upgraded and had the Lotus suite with a balcony, and Melanie and Steve had the suite opposite without a balcony. There is no central heating, but the bedrooms all have electric heating of some kind. There was a marvelous bathroom and bath with piping hot water, but the tiled floor was freezing.

A few stores were open, and Melanie found a woolly hat for about £1 planning for their upcoming trek in the Himalayas. The buffet style breakfast opened at 7.30 a.m. and the guests included several Chinese tourists. After dinner we discovered the library, which had two fires and it was possible to get really warm for the first time since Kurseong. Many beautiful coffee table books and encyclopaedias were available as were many hundreds of rentable films. Each room has a TV, but we were warned that there are often several short power cuts.

The political gripe is that the Gurkhas and Nepalese population living here do not wish to be part of lowland governed Bengal (governed from Calcutta by Bengalese). Here we are in a tiny "bubble" of India squashed between Himalayan Nepal, Sikkim and Bhutan and Bengal in the plains.

One lasting image of my day was that of a man lying under a blanket in the filth of the road shivering uncontrollably (perhaps due to malaria) and moaning piteously, possibly near death. I prayed the Lord to take him quickly and found that I could not look the wounded Christ in the face.

February 18th. Edward seems to be starting another cold. After a hearty breakfast Melanie, Steve and I left him and set off to be shown a 150+ year old monastery in Ghum by our guide. The walls were crammed with frescos of all kinds of mythical and frightening looking lions etc. Prayer wheels turned around in the draft of candles and the atmosphere was thick with incense. A huge benign-looking Buddha faced the entrance, swathed in scarves and flags and surrounded by offerings of food. Many other incarnations of Buddha stared out of glass cabinets and two of the walls were packed with "holy" scriptures all wrapped in cloth. Bowls of rice, sweetmeats and breads of all kinds including pitta bread lay about. There was also a large photo of the Dalai Lama, who visited here two years ago. There are five colours that are meaningful for Buddhists. Yellow for sun, green for earth, blue for water, white for air (or spirit) and red for fire.

Melanie and Steve went their own way while I rejoined Edward, and we found a good little eatery and sat down to soup and chow mein, then we bought two sweaters for Edward for the equivalent of about £8 each.

February 19th. Tuesday. I had breakfast with Melanie and Steve prior to their departure on the 4-day trek with an excellent guide and a porter. They declared themselves totally unfit after all this sitting around in Jeeps for two weeks.

Edward, in spite of his cold, had the driver take him out to Tiger Hill at 6 a.m. This is well known for montane birds. After about 3 hours the driver came back to pick me up and Edward and I went for quite a long walk through the bamboo forest.

In the afternoon there were claps of thunder and hailstones, so the place was living up to its name; but it didn't compare favourably with a past visit we had made to Fraser's Hill in Malaysia. Back in town Edward kindly bought me two lovely pashmina shawls that had been made in Kashmir.

We soon learned from the guide that a general strike is planned for several days starting at 6 a.m. tomorrow after which no vehicles will be allowed on the road down to the plains! So, our tour operators through the guide told us that we would have to leave at 4 a.m. or we would be stuck here.

We were then supposed to visit the Botanic Gardens and "old" Darjeeling, where all the locals buy their food and after a tortuous drive with several tight turns amongst people carrying long bamboo poles, old women wrapped in shawls, school children looking reasonably clean in uniform. When we reached the Botanic Gardens, we found the gates firmly locked because of the strike, so we rode back to the hotel, ate a simple evening meal and headed for bed.

February 20th. Wednesday. We were woken at about 2 a.m. and told to be ready to leave in half an hour – which we were. We set off in our car and got back up to Ghum, where we found that there were people already forming a roadblock. However, the road leading down into the deep valley to the east of us was accessible, and from the valley we would be able to climb up the hills and get up to Kalimpong.

First, we had to descend from 7,000 ft. in Ghum to 5,000 ft. in the valley, keeping to first gear practically all the way, in a series of endless bends taking over half an hour to get down as there was quite a bit of snow on shady descent.

Just before we reached the main road in the valley two or three young men saw that we were foreigners and tried to make us stop; they started banging on the car whereupon the driver accelerated rapidly out of their range.

In the valley the main road leads north to Sikkim, the border of which is only about 5 kms. north of where we reached the valley. Crossing this we soon began to climb again and eventually reached Gen. Singh's guest house called Gurungdongma at Kalimpong at 10.45 a.m. We were made very welcome and there were hot water bottles in the beds. Bliss!

Catherine, the tour operator with whom we have been in touch throughout, appeared at breakfast and she is fairly confident that we should all be able to proceed to Lava as scheduled in spite of the strikes. However, she spent part of the day getting permission from the strikers for us to leave tomorrow.

After lunch we had a gentle four-hour bird walk with a guide. This is an army base, and it includes a lot of land, and at one point we were told not to use our binoculars.

Later, there was further discussion about the way through picket lines of the strike. How early would we be allowed to leave in the morning, and would I feel well enough to go?

I had an uncertain digestive system and a headache, so I went to bed – the only place to get warm.

February 21st. Thursday. I felt a bit better as I slept well. Indeed, I felt well enough to agree to go to Lava with Edward; the idea of staying in Kalimpong by myself did not appeal We were driven to Lava (7,000 ft.) without hindrance thanks to an official letter that Catherine had obtained from the regional strike committee, but it required the driver to take us there and to come back without us the same day.

Lava offers lush forests of pines and bamboos, but birds seem to be few and far between, probably due to the cold. We said goodbye to the driver, who had been absolutely excellent and gave him a good tip, and then we had to walk the last 4 kms. into the village, where we were to stay in a lodge called Yankee Retreat (the honeymoon suite, which was very basic). Edward joined a party of seven birders from Canada but didn't claim to have seen any surprises.

I stayed wrapped up in all the layers possible, plus a blanket from the bed and I sat on the balcony overlooking the mountains which were lit by weak sunshine, and I watched the antics of the families in shacks below. The children played for hours with a wooden paddle and empty plastic mug, which got me thinking of all the elaborate toys western children have at their disposal.

Oh! the squalor, the grinding poverty, the filth. Clothes that have never seen hot water. How do mothers cope with cleaning their babies when they are cocooned to keep them warm?

I wondered how Melanie and Steve were getting on; it is now day three of their trek. They should have been able to see the tops of the Everest range today. This morning, we caught another glimpse of the famous Mount Kanchenjunga (also known as K2); it was a bit less clear than when we saw it from Darjeeling.

Supper was soup and other dishes, which seemed to have more black pepper than anything else. My stomach was churning, but at least there was hot water in the tap, so I sat with my feet immersed in a bucket of it. Edward never even undressed that night.

February 22nd. Friday. At last. Sunshine and clear

blue skies. I actually managed a walk along a winding path through varied forest. We had good views of distant peaks, but the birds were again difficult to see. Poor Edward!

At lunchtime we heard of more disturbances due to the political tensions, this time including violence and even some killings it seems. Now there are more roadblocks. The Canadians, who were to have gone back to Kalimpong cannot get there and they have been told they must depart at 3 a.m. and go by another back way, for which they have been given permission.

The latest disturbing news is that internal airlines may be striking on the 26th, the very day we are supposed to be flying back to Delhi. And what about Melanie and Steve? How are they going to meet us? Edward will have to get on the phone to Catherine again.

I had another bad stomach this evening; I can't face the dismal dining room or the awful food. I ordered a boiled egg and milk and honey. I couldn't get the poor girl to understand the word honey, so I had to go and look for it myself. I was up seven times in the night, putting heavy boots on every time to go to the bathroom.

Meanwhile Edward has told Suresh (Catherine's

brother) that he must feel embarrassed to have been double booked to look after us as well as the Canadian birding group. But we also thought that they could have invited Edward to join them. They made many outings (and Suresh knows his birds) and saw some good ones that Edward would have liked to see.

Later we also learned that the tour company has three pairs of binoculars, but Suresh had not lent a pair to our patient young guide. But the next day when we were on our way back to Siliguri, Edward, who had previously lent his spare pair to the guide, open his packed case, took them out again and made him a present of them.

February 23rd. Saturday. Breakfast for me consisted of a rehydration sachet! We finally left Lava with no regrets and set off, part walking, part driving down, so that we could birdwatch on the way. The rising sun made the jungle and thickly forested slopes look very attractive. Birds were more active than yesterday.

We heard that the strike committee had granted us a four-hour window from 10 a.m. to 2 p.m. to get down to Siliguri, which, down in the plains, is outside the troubled zone.

We made a tortuous detour around Kalimpong as

we were told it was "heaving" with people who had not been allowed out for some days. The descent to the plain was only about 50 miles, but it took several hours due to the state of the road and the frequent S-bends. Roadworks were extensive with women pounding rocks and carrying them in wicker baskets, and there were dizzying drops with no barrier at the edge of the road.

Just as we thought we were coming down to river level we found we were climbing up yet another valley. Thanks to medication and starvation my inside has quietened down, so we did not need to make any pit stops on the way down, thank God. I felt sorry for the poor driver having to make the journey back to Kalimpong.

We were booked into Hotel Cinderella in Siliguri where we were reunited with Melanie and Steve who were looking well. They had much enjoyed their trek up to the Nepalese border and had had two days of clear weather and fine views of the Kanchenchunga Range with Mount Everest visible in the distance.

They too had had problems with the effect of the strikes but had been rescued safely by another driver.

February 24th. Sunday. Edward went out at 6.30

a.m. with Suresh. I joined them after breakfast to visit the nearby forested area, supposedly sheltering 200 elephants, but with much of the area off limits. There was a viewpoint looking over the enormous floodplain with the river Teesta looking mighty turgid in some places although this is the dry season.

Another more open area near a village produced a new bird for Suresh (Tawny Pipit) and we saw a Chestnut-headed Bee-eater, and an Ibisbill (a species which Edward had first seen in China).

Suresh had to go to the airport to meet incoming tourists and to confess to them that they would not be able to go to Sikkim due to the roadblocks and the current political problems. After a delicious lunch with Melanie and Steve, Edward and I sat round the almost empty pool in the pleasant garden surrounded by a variety of trees. I was trying to see what I saw yesterday, my second Rubythroat, not seen by Edward on this trip. It is certainly nice to feel warm again.

February 25th. Monday. After our buffet breakfast Sudesh appeared to take us to the airport where we arrived without incident and sat about waiting for our Jet Airline flight back to Delhi. The journey was only supposed to take 2 hours, but we were stacked up over Delhi and circled for a good half hour before landing.

We were met by a driver who fended off and shouted menacingly at illegal luggage touts outside in the parking area, which, as usual, stank of urine. It was during the rush hour traffic that we headed to the U.S. guest house of Peter Kaestner, who we had and had a meal with soon after our arrival in Delhi, and whose guests we were going to be for the night.

Peter, a career diplomat, told us he has visited 115 countries and has now seen more than 7,400 bird species and only two other people have seen more! Peter arrived later and regaled us with tales of his recent visit to Bandavghar for birds, but also to show his daughters a tiger. Like us, he hated the circus of endless Jeeps and elephants all jostling for prime views and chasing each other through the dust. One of his daughters joined us for a welcome salad and spaghetti Bolognese supper, and a hot bath was extremely welcome.

February 26th. Tuesday. Our final day in India was beautifully fresh, with blue sky, a comfortable temperature and a breeze. What a difference from our previous visit. We counted at least fifty kites soaring in the thermals. Melanie suggested a way of usefully spending part of the day as Edward, through the tour company, had organized a van and driver to go somewhere.

Unfortunately, the vehicle Melanie and Steve had had before was not available. The new driver's English was limited and so was his knowledge of Delhi, but we managed to make a few visits.

First, the magnificent Sir Edwin Lutyens buildings commissioned in 1911 and finished 20 years later, now housing the President of India, the Government and the Defence Department etc. Beautiful symmetry, wide avenues, fountains and distant views of the India Gate.

Second, Purana Qila. The old fort with its crumbling surrounding wall. This old site has been inhabited since 1000 B.C. It comes with a pleasant grassy area with plenty of trees, and a lot of friendly schoolgirls who wanted their photo taken. We also saw a couple of Hoopoes, which have been in short supply while we were in the hills.

Third, an area with several good restaurants where Melanie had been before. I enjoyed a raita (yoghurt mixed with onion and cucumber) and some of Edward's fried rice with chicken. Upon leaving we saw our first snake. It was a cobra in a basket and belonged to one of the "pipers" and would raise its head when the lid was lifted.

Finally, Melanie had been really impressed by Humayun's tomb and felt we should see that before leaving. It is a mausoleum to the 2nd Mughal emperor and is set in 40 acres of gardens along with final resting places for other family members and nobles. A series of water channels cross the grounds. This is a place where schoolchildren are brought for one of their main history lessons. It is also one of Unesco's 22 World Heritage Sites as is the later and more famous Taj Mahal built in 1592 by order of Shah Jahan to commemorate his wife Mumtaz Mahal, who died giving birth to their 14th. child.

When Peter returned from work, the restaurants he preferred to take guests to were closed, so I asked if we might eat in the U.S. embassy restaurant. We had to show our passports and walk through metal detectors, but it was very worthwhile as we enjoyed one of the best meals we had eaten in this country.

We wanted to pay for Peter and everyone, but credit cards were not accepted! Peter kindly charged it to his account and Edward gave him the equivalent in rupees, about £50, which more than covered everything for the seven of us!

After packing, Steve, Edward and I set off down the road taking Rocky, the Kerstner's lovely labrador with us for a walk in the nearby Lodi gardens, leaving Melanie to finish her packing. The gardens were created in 1936 by the removal of a village and they are now considered the best urban gardens in Asia – a kind of local Kensington gardens.

Eventually it was time to head for the new international airport, currently under expansion and chaotic. Edward reminded me that the last time we were here we had to leave Satya's house travelling with her brother at 4 a.m. and that I then slept on the dirty floor. That terminal is now the domestic airport.

Virgin Atlantic flew us to Heathrow in eight hours, where we said farewell to Melanie and Steve, and caught the train to Eastbourne arriving at Bolsover Court at about 10 p.m. Rob and Dawn, who live below us, heard us and Rob came up to welcome us back.

Thank God we are back home!

Macaws, Pantanal, Brazil

Turtle, Barbados

Squeezing sugar cane, Barbados

Cave, Barbados

Island Sky

Cape Horn

Torres del Paine, Chile

A ride in a Zodiac

Fox in Chile

Chef's artistry onboard Island Sky

Alhambra: cathedral within a mosque

Shepherd in Lesvos

RUSSIA, 2000

For some reason I took no notes of our brief trip to Russia; so, about 23 years later I can only offer a compilation of notes from memory and some contributions from Edward, but neither of our memories may be very reliable.

We had to obtain visas through the Russian Embassy in London; that required a letter of invitation which Edward obtained from Vladimir Loskot, who we were going to visit in the natural history museum in St. Petersburg. I believe we had to go up to London to get our visas stamped. We flew to St. Petersburg with British Airways.

We had booked a hotel through our travel agent and took a taxi from the airport. The hotel was spartan in character suggesting a continuing communistic situation; indeed, we suspected that the hotel was partly staffed by the KGB. After being shown our room, we were concerned about the risk of fire and I enquired about a fire escape, but when we were shown it, we found it was locked, and we were assured that if need be someone would be there immediately with a key!

It turned out that we were too late for supper in the hotel, but we found a little café over the road with a dining room down a few steps from the road and after a snack we went straight to bed.

Our friends Rene and Charlotte had managed to book into a real tourist hotel and the next day we set out on a tram to find their hotel and then we all came back into the centre of town, where Edward, Rene and I sought out the Natural History Museum. Just inside its door was a stooped lady (a 'babushka') to whom we explained that we were invited by Vladimir (the Curator of Birds) who she rang, and he came down to meet us.

Upstairs in his office and the adjoining rooms he showed us some of the large, well-curated collection of bird skins. Each skin was carefully wrapped in cotton wool and placed in one of the wooden cupboards. Rene and Edward were invited to come again over the following days when they would be able to examine some rarer species.

At this time Edward was puzzling over the composition of an important illustrated work on birds in French that had been published by Coenraad Temminck in over 100 parts, each containing six colour plates. The puzzle required examining as many copies as possible and Edward eventually wrote several scientific articles about his findings. Vladimir was able to show him the St. Petersburg holding.

I rejoined Charlotte and we went to the famous Hermitage Museum. Here we had to join groups to be shown round the important collection of paintings, which were nice to see but they told us little or nothing about Russia. However, a day or two later Edward and I discovered the Russian Art Museum, which proved to be an absolute delight, it was uncrowded and very unlike many museums in London, where one always must peer over several peoples' heads to see anything.

On leaving we came across a local watercolour artist displaying his pictures by the footpath, and we were delighted to be able to buy two framed paintings of St. Petersburg. These, despite "downsizing" from Bolsover Road to where we now live, these pictures are still in our hands.

I have a clear memory of visiting the church in the Moscow's center, where a lady dressed entirely in black indicated that I must buy a candle, which of course I did, but I did not stay for the service. On another day we visited the impressive French style Summer Palace of Peter the Great. This has large gardens in which one can walk down to the edge of the sea. One certainly feels dwarfed by the scale of everything.

One evening Edward and I passed the Marinsky Ballet School Centre and walked on to arrive at a very pricey-looking restaurant. We thought we weren't dressed smartly enough, but we enquired, and they said we could dine there if we went upstairs. We discovered a very small upstairs space where two musicians, a cellist and violinist, were playing. Their delightful music was a splendid accompaniment to our meal. In fact, everywhere we went there was music to be heard and once we found a lady pianist who was willing to play whatever one wanted.

In restaurants we saw no menus in English, but we did not eat in a tourist hotel. In one shop I ordered what I hoped was a borscht soup. Having made borscht many times myself I expected a beautiful, thick, creamy, attractively pink soup that would probably be cold; when it came, I was dismayed to see a bowl of hot, watery soup with floating pieces of beef and a slice of beetroot!

Our next trip was an overnight train to Moscow; but our Dutch friends were flying home. We had a sleeping cabin with two bunkbeds, and we placed our suitcases in the overhead racks and locked the door. However, just as we were about to go to sleep the door was forcibly opened by the conductor who wanted to see our tickets - which we had had to show. In the morning, we were offered hot, black tea.

Our friends Philip and Judy Warren, who we had known in Switzerland had offered us a room in their large Moscow flat. We had first met the Warrens in Aberdeenshire, but they moved to Lausanne and Edward helped Philip to join Nestlé. He had written to Edward about the Wildfowl Trust, as I mentioned earlier, but here he now was in Moscow overseeing the Nestlé factories across Russia. They had been in Russia for a few years and had a country dacha or weekend escape. His wife Judy was taking classes in icon painting, or iconography.

We were impressed by the Moscow underground railway which we found we could use to get about without much difficulty. Judy took me to various tourist spots such as Red Square.

Edward was visiting Pavel Tomkovich the Curator of Birds at the Zoological Museum of Moscow University, and Pavel provided him with an introduction to a very senior and more or less retired ornithologist called Leo Stepanyan. During Edward's visit to the museum one of Pavel's staff took Edward to meet Stepanyan. Leo gave Edward a copy of the new second edition of his book on Russian birds. After he returned to the museum the book was accidentally left at the museum, but one of Pavel's staff rang to say that he'd found it and would deliver it personally and he asked for the room number – not for a flat number – which revealed that Moscovites often live in just part of a flat.

Piers Cumberledge, son of Peter and Shirleyanne, was also living in Moscow and one evening he and his wife invited us to a Moscow restaurant for dinner. Edward had first met Piers as a boy about 3 years old in 1962 soon after he went to Thailand and his family had become great friends, and at times Piers, as a small boy in the Thai jungle, had been happy to be piggybacked on jungle walks.

We had last seen Piers when he and a couple of his fellow university students visited Peter and Shirleyanne at their home outside Draguignon in the south of France. There Peter and Shirleyanne had retired, and they had found 'buried' olive trees, and after clearing the scrub around the trees so he could collect olive oil for refining locally, Peter was delighted to find wild orchids. Before moving to the Var on the Cote d'Azure, Peter, after Thailand, had been posted to Greece, Belgium and finally to Shell's Head Office in Holland.

Piers and his French wife had two young daughters, who were growing up speaking Russian with their nanny. It was an excellent dinner with very pleasant music. By the time we visited Moscow, we had become regular visitors to Peter and Shirleyanne in

Evanton, where Peter was invited to shoot and could fish whenever there was a suitable opportunity.

MELANIE'S WEDDING, 13 DECEMBER 2003

Melanie and Steve researched wedding venues and decided to get married in the church next to Lulworth Castle – which had only recently been converted to serve as a luxury wedding venue. To be married here required Steve to live nearby and he was able to stay for the requisite time with the vicar of the church.

Melanie wanted to plan the entire event and invited over a hundred guests. Our great friend Margaret Houston, who came with Heath, her husband, had kindly offered to see to the flowers, including the table arrangements. Ivy was flowering at the time, and we were able to apply gold paint to some of the berries. I offered to make gingerbread biscuits in the shape of a castle with peoples' names as place settings. Several other couples from our circle of friends were able to attend too.

The service itself took place in the nearby church, just yards away from the reception venue. Fortunately, the weather was mild for December, wind and rain free. Melanie's dress had a 'bolero' and she wore the long veil with an acorn motif that I had worn at Edward's and my wedding. Steve's mother and father, Pat and Gordon, were there along with some of Steve's siblings and their children.

Melanie had ordered fireworks which were set off after the meal when it was dark. There was dancing to a live band and Steve's two nieces from Australia were hot on the dance floor; but many of the guests danced before heading off to spend the night wherever they had booked their stay.

BRAZIL, 2005

Edward and I arrived in Rio de Janeiro after a crowded and delayed 11-hour flight from Paris, and we were met by Tony and Christine. A piggy-in-the-middle seat on the plane and the delay left me feeling very delicate indeed.

Tony's Toyota Overlander was already packed with gear for their mountain home Cantagalo in the Vale di Cuiaba, north of Rio. A small poodle called "Mocca" also accompanied us, they had inherited her from their son Andrew, who had recently found a job in England.

We stopped en route to buy provisions for our stay and climbed to 1300 m. with a ridge above and behind the house at 1800 m., and, ahead of us were vistas of the distant mountains.

Just 24 hours after we left our Eastbourne home, we are in a most beautiful mountain home, designed and built, with some help, by Tony.

Friday 28th October. After breakfast Edward and I had a gentle walk and sat on a stone in a riverbed, where the water was running low. A hummingbird hovered right in front of us which was magical!

The house has a large balcony on the valley side of the building. Behind the building and on either side is forest, and we enjoyed a lazy afternoon watching bees coming and going in under the roof.

It became progressively darker, and a storm followed bringing plenty of lightning and fresher air. After we had eaten, Tony, who had been down to the office, arrived back after a difficult drive in the rain. He lent me a book to read called "Man's Eternal Quest", about the Father of Yoga in the West called Paramahansa Yogananda (1893-1952), an Indian whose beliefs seem to have been very much Bible-based and Christ-oriented, but although in general he makes very good sense, I personally, found his views on re-incarnation a stumbling block. Tony, however, is a follower of Paramahansa.

Tony has a Grotian Steinweg grand piano in the living room and he plays very nicely, though infrequently. Christine served us some excellent "home grown" vegetable stew, wild rice, gravalax and fruits of all kinds. Her homemade marmalades are excellent. Christine's "family" comprises two guineafowls, a cockerel and various hens. Thanks to the hens there are fresh eggs for breakfast, which is wonderful. However, occasionally, snakes – including the very poisonous fer de lance – come to steal them. Mercifully, we did not see any snakes during our stay.

Saturday 29th. The storms are over, and everything is looking a bit fresher. Of course, all the birds are new and puzzling. Tony, Edward and I walked down to a small lake with a nearby ancient generator, which hums away year in, year out, to supply four homes up here in this privately protected bit of forest.

In the afternoon we went to collect another hen to be company for Emily who, as a recent newcomer, is being ostracized. However, Emily turned on the newcomer, who is called Dorothy!

In the evening, we took the Toyota down to Itaipavo for a lovely meal at an "inn" full of artefacts including some ancient pottery pieces. Later, in the headlights, we saw an armadillo on the road. Christine says one keeps digging up her vegetable garden at night looking for worms. We also saw a small porcupine. When we left the restaurant after 11 p.m. people were just arriving for dinner! As in Spain dinner is eaten late.

Sunday 30th. We awoke to a really cool damp day with low clouds, but the birds have enjoyed the rain and it's the start of the breeding season. Edward, Tony and I set off down the hill with Mocca and within a short distance saw a party of Tufted-eared Marmosets chasing each other around. They have dear little faces like Halloween masks. There were good views of a large woodpecker with an outrageous red hairdo, but Mocca couldn't make out why we kept stopping.

Christine cooked a great Sunday lunch of salted cod, which had been steeped in cold water for two days and then baked; it was served with potatoes, onions, tomatoes, herbs and olive oil.

Afterwards we packed and set off down to Rio where they have a new and charming smaller flat with a balcony looking out on a nearby cliff with trees full of birds, and fruit-bats which visit the bird table for bananas. Their maid laid the table, and we ate sushi which was brought in. Edward and I slept on a sofa bed in Christine's study.

October 31st. We were up early after a breakfast of fruit and eggs (laid by Christine's birds), said goodbye to Mocca and took a taxi to the airport, for a one and a half-hour flight to Sao Paulo, where we disembarked and changed to a smaller plane heading to Campo Grande in Matto Grosso del Sul. There we were met and driven several miles to a tiny rural airport where we boarded two small single propeller planes. Each could take 3 passengers as well as the pilot; we were taking a one-hour flight deep into the Pantanal. Edward flew with Christine, and I flew with Tony.

There were huge temperature changes; cool in Rio but sunny and hot as we flew west at about 30,000 ft. over curious luxuriously wooded flat-topped mountains.

The Brazilian Pantanal covers 1.8 % of the entire country of Brazil and is recognized as a World Ecological Sanctuary - one of the largest fauna and flora reserves on the planet.

It is home to the largest variety of flora and fauna in the Americas, 1,650 species of plants, trees and shrubs, 1,500 catalogued animal species of which 650 are birds, 80 mammals, 50 reptiles and 260+ fish. It is in a plain which floods every year; the Pantanal also extends across the Paraguay River into that country, where it is much more limited in size. We arrived at a cattle farm-cum-guest house run by a Swiss named Lucas Leutzinger, who is married to a local lady and has two small children. He has a website where he displays his photographs of Pantanal wildlife and advertises his property.

Adding to these notes 19 years later we are happy to know that jaguars, which were usually hunted in 2005, mainly because they occasionally killed cattle, have become recognized as a major tourist attraction. The tourists come especially to see them, so they are rarely hunted and are now much more frequently seem out in the open; and, of course, tourists bring spending money.

Between the four of us we have half of Lucas's guest bungalow. A couple from Zurich are in the other half of the lodge. There is a very large mango tree just in front which is dripping with green fruit, which we hoped would ripen. In the bathroom there were cute little frogs with sucker feet.

After a 3 o'clock lunch we set off with Lucas, and his driver Fernando, to visit two local lakes, now, at the end of the dry season, they are shallow and smaller.

There was quite an astonishing amount of wildlife to see: Capybara (the largest mammal) and Caymans in the river, rheas, vultures, hawks, Hyacinth Macaws, kingfishers galore, and a huge and colourful Burrowing Owl, as well as waterfowl including Tree Ducks, Coscoroba Swans, Roseate Spoonbills and Whistling Duck. There were two young Jabiru storks sitting on a nest and we also saw Red and Yellow Macaw, and a Bat Falcon catching dragonflies.

November 1st. Just after dawn we walked to the river and saw Chachalaca and little Red-headed Cardinals. After a splendid breakfast we took a boat along the river. The engine was very quiet, but in due course we switched to an electric engine which made no sound at all, perfect for birdwatching and to surprise wildlife.

We saw some neotropical otters quite close to us devouring fish, a superb Orange and black Troupial and a Tiger Heron. The river is called the Rio Negro and during a high spate it has been known to rise about 20 ft. and to flood much of the field between the river and our lodge.

We were invited to lunch at the farmstead of another family and Lucas's wife drove and the children came along; the baby had a seat on Mum's lap as she drove for about 40 minutes along a track which was sometimes overhung with palms. There were deer on the path.

There were quite a few overseas visitors arriving for a training course at the nearby International Conservation Station. I was fascinated to see an ancient cashew nut tree with pinkish, lantern-like fruit from which a fruit juice is produced daily. The fruit is at the end of the nut; it has a delicate smell.

The nights were sufficiently cool for a sheet. The daytime temperature is hotting up; last night it was 35 C under the mango tree.

November 2nd. We were provided with an

abundant breakfast including coconut bread. We would have taken off on our explorations sooner had it not been for a political discussion with our Swiss hosts, who were expecting an inward flight of six people (Swiss German, Portuguese and English).

We saw a flock of brilliant Red and Green Macaws looking marvelous in the early morning sun and then set off in the van towards new territory across the savannah, past several lakes shrinking by the day but full with many bird species the larger ones including Jacana, Yellowlegs, Stilts, large Yellow-billed Terns and egrets. We were treated to a momentary glimpse of Howler Monkeys. By 10 a.m. it was too hot, and I left the others and returned to the van for a much-needed drink of iced water, after which I promptly fell asleep flat on the back seat.

After an excellent fish lunch, the Zurichois left by plane. Tony and Christine went fishing in the canoe after Christine had been horse riding. Edward set off on his own and I lay in the hammock under the mango tree. Sadly, we are about two weeks too early for the fruit.

Our hosts and their extended family own thousands of hectares of farmland here, so one sees lots imported Indian cattle and a few sheep. The family is committed to conservation long term.

At 4.30 p.m. we set off with Lucas and a young local, again driving along tracks across scrubby vegetation, through boundary gates and wooded areas, where the van with its bull-bars took everything in its stride. There was a brief glimpse of a Giant Anteater, and a well camouflaged cute little owl sitting at his "front door" hole in a tree. Wild pigs dashed through clearings and across our path, as did a little buff and grey fox.

We eventually reached a special lake, unlike the others because there were no reeds, no fish and algae of a greenish colour. The water was extremely soft and no doubt good for our skin, it was also slightly salty and very warm (perhaps 25 C.). Edward and I just paddled in it, but Tony decided to strip and wade in for some rejuvenation! We all sat on the wide sandy beach and admired a magnificent sunset, sipping drinks until it was virtually dark.

We could just see our way back through the forest. We discovered a Potoo sitting motionless on a fence, thanks to our spotlight; this is a very weird looking bird! There were also plenty of nightjars. A marvelous night sky and the trees were alight with fireflies flashing and looking even more beautiful than Christmas trees.

November 3rd. The day began with a boat trip and a gem of a bird: a Blue-crowned Motmot. Fabulous, what fun the Lord has had with His paint pot! Another Potoo looked exactly like a branch of the tree where he was perched and where he remained completely motionless. We saw kingfishers of varying sizes, and our first Jacamar which, although it looks very like a kingfisher, is insectivorous.

We got off the boat a bit further upriver and had a very hot walk home; we had hoped to see Giant Otters and possibly a jaguar; we saw no otters and could only claim recent paw marks made by a jaguar.

In the afternoon we all crashed out in 35 C and stayed indoors to avoid the many biting insects. In the early evening, we set off again in the van and returned after sundown having seen peccaries and wild boar, and plenty of Cayman.

November 4th. We left our base at 5.30 a.m. after a night with air-conditioning. There is now a cool southerly wind. We were lucky to see an ocelot dash across in front of van; this small cat has beautiful markings. We missed the tapir, which was seen by our driver, Fernando.

We breakfasted on sandwiches we had brought

with us, watching kingfishers between bites and then we set off in three canoes: Lucas in his own, Tony and Christine in a second one and Edward and I in a third. Edward was naughty and, sitting behind me, left me to do most of the paddling!

This was a first for us! We had only 10 kms to paddle and the current was with us. Sometimes we stopped paddling and just drifted, whilst watching nature go by: we saw Jabiru (Brazil's national bird), Pigmy Kingfisher, Sun Grebe and Osprey to name just a very few; we also saw the nest hole of a jacamar in the bank. Once a Cayman gave a loud roar just behind us. I thought it was a jaguar rushing out of the forest! We saw a very large grandfather Cayman on the bank with very many teeth exposed.

The weather was perfect because it was cloudy and not too hot. This trip would have been impossible yesterday. However, after five hours in the canoe my neck, back and bum were aching – at least we didn't capsize!

Brought back home by road while someone must have loaded the canoes to bring them back, we settled in for a restful afternoon nap: sometimes awake and reading under the mango tree. A handsome woodpecker (a species of flicker) came to the post supporting the hammock in which

Edward was dozing and stared at him for at least a minute.

A later drive took us along new tracks to more lakes, all different having their own atmospheres. On the way home Fernando caught an armadillo to show us; a female which was puffing and panting, and clearly distressed. A small snake was revealed to us in the spotlight by a fox which was dancing around it. The sunset was very lovely and very luminous with bands of orange radiating across a pale blue sky with a wispy moon and the evening star.

Not a very good night's sleep, I must have overdone it yesterday. Poor old grandma!

November 5th. I let the others go off on the morning drive and just did my own birdwatching, mainly from the hammock. A lovely pair of curassows came right by, they were very different and handsome in their way. Later I walked down to the river, sat in the boat and watched the macaws and a vulture very delicately picking a piece of prey to bits on top of a post; as well as the brilliant Red-headed and Black & White Cardinals. which came virtually within touching distance.

After a cloudy morning at 29 C, with distant thunder and a gusty wind, the weather cleared in the afternoon. Edward and I donned hats, sunscreen and insect repellent and took a walk to try and identify some parakeets making nests in nearby palm trees. There is a tick problem here so every time one walks through long grass, especially where there are horses all around, it is necessary to check our legs for burrowing ticks and pick off any that one can find before they bite.

The afternoon/evening drive was quite productive. Troupes of coatis were seen on two separate occasions. A Rosy-billed Duck, which may have been new to the area, was seen on a lake along with at least 18 or 19 other species of birds – a beautiful spectacle, especially with the evening light on the Roseate Spoonbills.

Edward then spotted a Tapir, so we all got quietly out of the van and had splendid views of the large young male, which watched us for a long while before thumping off into the forest.

We ended the day as usual enjoying a cool drink with Lucas and Fernando while watching the sunset over a lake as the moon and Venus appeared. The air here is lovely and pollution free, and when the van's wheels crush the grasses there is sometimes a smell of camphor.

November 6th. Sunday. We were up at 5.30 and

away in the canoes before breakfast with a lovely sunrise.

This time Edward sat in front in our canoe, and we found it a bit cramped. However, we cruised down the river and saw about 12 to 15 beautiful motmots beside the river grouped together in the treetops. Lucas had thought that this species was rare and was surprised by this sighting.

After an hour and a half, we disembarked at a pre-arranged spot where Fernando met us, and we returned to the lodge in the van. We had an early, light lunch and packed our bags as the Piper planes were coming back to pick us up. The Piper that Edward and Christine climbed into wouldn't start, due apparently to a flat battery! Initially the pilot for Tony and I did some low circuits over the bungalows, while the pilot was trying to hand start the prop! Eventually after at least half an hour we could all fly on to Campo Grande and from there to Sao Paulo, and a change of plane to get back to Rio. We arrived back at the flat quite tired, but Mocca was absolutely delighted to see Tony and Christine, who ordered another sushi meal.

November 7th. Next morning Tony took his 3-4 km. walk along Ipanema beach. Edward, Christine and I followed later with Mocca, and the beach offers interesting sights of all kinds, dressed and undressed. A very clever person had made a unique sandcastle village, complete with doors half open, but sadly my camera was not with me.

We offered Christine lunch at a pay-by-weight restaurant where the menu included all the delicious fruits and juices, especially papaya.

In the afternoon Christine suggested we make the most of a break in the clouds and take a taxi up the mountain high above Rio to the famous statue of Christ the Redeemer designed by two sculptors – Paul Landowski and Heitor da Silva Costa. Up here you have 360-degree views.

There were many steps to climb from where the taxi dropped us, but the climb was well worth the effort, and we got back to the flat just in time before the clouds descended. There were numerous coatis at the top, but it was the views that had our attention.

November 8th. Next morning we set off in Tony's van heading north out of Rio, past the docks and the polluted and stinking bay, where it was said that there would be Olympic rowing races in 2016, and then along the road northwards to arrive in pouring rain, after lunch, by way of a branching dirt road, at Guapi Assu Bird Lodge, a conservation area established by another Englishman, called

Nicholas, who is resident in Brazil with his wife Rachel who is from Argentina.

There is a swimming pool and some quite luxurious guest rooms and the evening meal with Nicholas was very tasty. This is a serious nature reserve in the making – at this point awaiting gazetting – which will adjoin and complement the Tres Picos National Park.

Nicholas told us that he was hoping to be able to buy more land along the slope where his property adjoins the park. Volunteer English conservationists have begun coming out to help.

Tony, Edward and Nicholas and one of his field staff set off to climb some way up the slope taking a picnic lunch with them. They claimed they were too late to run across any hunting parties of birds and were probably too noisy as well because we saw very little.

An English couple of honeymooners just arrived and we learned that the bride's parents came from Eastbourne, which was a coincidence, but the coincidence was much greater as the couple had just been married in Lulworth Castle and had a party lasting over three days. This was the venue where our daughter Melanie married Steve.

Nicholas (guardian of the conservation area) and his wife Rachel (pronounced Raquel) who is Argentinan took Christine and me on a walk around the flooded lake with Mocca. She showed us some fascinating trees, including one that flowers only on the trunk, followed by enormous fruits like a smooth, i.e. non hairy, hard coconut-like shell which, when ripe, is filled with pulp like passion fruit. This tree is commonly called the Cannonball Tree (*Carapita guianensis*) which describes the fruits perfectly.

The men didn't return until 5 p.m. by which time I had had my swim. After supper there was a slide show.

During my night visit to the loo a small frog grinned at me from the lavatory pan. When I whisked my towel around, he promptly disappeared into the water with a plop.

November 10th. To-day it is grey and raining, which is a pity especially for the honeymooners.

We departed after a good lunch, but yams are definitely not my favourite vegetable, even when mashed with cheese. They take 9 months to mature, and their green leaves can't be used.

We headed east NE to Macae de Cima (in the state

of Rio), to the municipality of Nuevo Friburgo, which was colonized in the 1800s by the Swiss, who built the dirt road up the mountain. From there it took us an hour to cover the 23 kms to reach Tony's "other place", such is the state of the dirt road. Here, at the road's end, in the wet Atlantic Forest, there is a cute little chalet at 1,000 m. which Tony owns. It is a simple hut converted into 3 cozy rooms with bunk beds and wood burning stove in a small living room.

There were plenty of river views and the noise of burbling river, and an invisible Bellbird calling "pong" repeatedly, sounding like a metal worker. Mocca was dressed in her knitted coat, and we were glad of the fire. It now seems incredible that we were baking in the Pantanal only a few days ago.

November 11th. It's raining again. Nevertheless, we managed to get had good long-distance views of the Bellbird with his resounding ponging calls; we also saw 2 or 3 hummingbirds and a woodpecker feeding young.

After a welcome coffee Tony and I set off for a swim in the tumbling river water which was rather fresh (14 C) and so clear that we could safely drink it. Tony was going to chicken out, but I shamed him into taking the plunge, after which I set off back to the cozy cabana for a piping hot shower in the excellent bathroom.

Nicholas and Raquel and some guests of theirs, turned up after our spaghetti lunch and we took more walks with them and Tony – who later went down the road a bit to the trout farm to buy some fish for our candlelight supper.

Next morning the two of us set off on another trail which was the best yet. Edward spotted and then showed us an enchanting display of Swallow Manakins, 3 of them dancing around as all manakin species do. This is a blue-black bird with a bright red crown. Then we saw a Trogon which was bright blue on the head, green on the back and white on part of its tail. To be looked up!

In mid-morning we packed and left the cabana and headed downhill bumping and lurching on the unmade track. Lunch was at a hotel near Novo Friburgo inside because outside it was raining again; here the garden held many sugar feeders which, after the rain eased attracted dozens of hummingbirds of several species, they dashed around us, inches away, incredible speed, flaunting their iridescent colours.

From here it was not far to Tony's large mountain home above Itaipavo by way of Novo Friburgo and

Teresopolis. We all wanted hot baths, but the recent local weather had been so unusual that the solar panels had not been heating the water. There was a back-up system for the boiler, but as it had not been used for years Tony had to get help from his caretaker, who came up on his motorbike.

Meanwhile, there is discord in Christine's Hen Palace! The cockerel was being persecuted by the Guinea Fowl, who were pulling out his fine tail feathers.

November 14th. A clear day. We repacked and set off north for Minas Gerais state, and an old colonial style town called Tiradentes (meaning 'puller of teeth') which Tony wanted us to see. This was a four-hour drive, winding our way northward around the (rounded) mountains, following the river, and swaying from left to right in the Toyota.

The following day was to be a public holiday and the hotel Tony had wanted to go to was fully booked. I sent up a prayer and we found a place which agreed to take us, but no dogs! However, after seeing Mocca and hearing Tony tell them that he had brought us all the way from the UK the objection was waived.

Huge electric gates opened into manicured grounds with a 250-year-old house and buildings, a swimming pool, a lake, ducks, shady trees and porticoes and columns around a stage, where outdoor concerts are held.

The Toyota was parked in a garage with curtains that could be drawn to hide it.

We were the only guests there and I thanked the Lord for answering my prayer. Away from the noise and bustle, it was a haven of tranquility. We were asked to look at the rooms and choose, and I found one with two beds, a small balcony and canopies. There was even a stove we could have asked someone to light.

Tony and Christine went looking for a restaurant while we looked after Mocca. I swam and Edward birdwatched. Then at 8.30 p.m. we bumped back out over the cobbled road and entered an eatery which was full of artefacts dug up when the building was renovated: old medicine bottles, silver photo frames, coins, pottery etc. all on display. It was very atmospheric. The male staff were dressed in black; the food was excellent, and Edward had a steak, Christine and I shared a paté. I then ordered a cream of leek soup, followed by mango flambé. To finish I enjoyed an unusual liqueur sorbet.

November 15th. We did a little early birdwatching in the garden in glorious sunshine with mountains as a backdrop.

An enormous breakfast buffet was laid for us in another ancient, spacious wooden building. Tony, as usual, was doing a good job with his digital camera. It's nice that he's become enthusiastic about birds. We walked into town and visited the tourist shops looking for Christmas presents for the family. Small ponies pulled canopied "taxis" through the streets some of which were quite steep, one led up to the Catholic church.

Tiradentes was originally founded by the Portuguese over 300 years ago and the area was enriched by gold mining.

After shopping we had a drink in the square and decided not to eat lunch after such an extravagant breakfast, so we fetched the van, said goodbye to the hotel and started to wend our way back south towards Rio.

It was about 5.30 p.m. when we got to Itaipavo and we learned that tourists were put off during this public holiday by the earlier bad weather and by the scare of a tick fever outbreak, from which someone reportedly had died. So, we headed back to Rio to Apt. 52, 38 rua Perana, Leblon for a brief final stay, and time for Edward to do some accounting with Tony.

November 16th. On our last day in Rio Christine kindly took me, and a reluctant Mocca, to photograph the sandcastle maker at work. We stopped for a lovely cool coconut drink straight from the nut.

Edward sat on the balcony at the flat compiling a Brazilian bird list which totalled 234 identified species and perhaps a few more to add when Tony forwards the photos by e-mail.

After a last lunch, Tony came from the office at 4 p.m. to take us to the airport, whcre we were delighted to be upgraded to seats upstairs with more leg room in the 747. Hurrah!

Absolutamente fantastico! Bless you, dear Tony and Christine, for the most marvellous holiday.

NAPLES AND CAPRI, 2006

In April 2006 we flew to Naples intending to explore the region, but in particular to explore the evidence of the eruption of the stratovolcano Vesuvius in 79 AD. The highest point in the city is the Camaldoli hill, which reaches about 450 meters above sea level. We had booked a small hotel in the south of the city away from the center of the town. At the airport we took a taxi to the hotel; a drive that was memorable for the rubbish everywhere – because the rubbish collectors were weeks into a serious strike.

On day one we were able to use the local train to reach Herculaneum which was only partly accessible for tourists. The 79 AD eruption deposited masses of ash but the damage to Herculaneum was due to a river of mud. A few houses had been excavated and some important wall paintings were visible. The occupants would have been asphyxiated. Some of the wall paintings were still vibrant and some of the mosaics of peacocks and deer had been carefully preserved. Intact amphora for wine or oil were on display.

Next day we took the train to the station near to the ruins of Pompei where the population had been smothered by the very heavy ash fall, presumably associated with unbreathable air. We hired a guide which was sensible. One fascinating object was an enormous marble plate with inscription all around the edge. It was interesting to see the streets with cobbled roadways – built to allow chariots to use the specially constructed deep ruts on the sides of the streets to move along the streets. Some buildings were obviously shops. The artefacts salvaged from the ashes and displayed were numerous and some skeletal remains were quite distressing. The volcanic blast was so sudden and violent that it is thought that most people were "frozen" in whatever position they happened to be in at the time. In fact, the eruption may have occurred when many were abed. With the help of our guide, we took a lot of photographs.

Next day we visited the volcano itself; a bus took us quite far up the volcano, but we had to walk up the last 300 feet to the rim. From here we had a clear view of Naples laid out below and to the north.

Later, we visited a museum in town to see some very important relics from Pompei and Herculaneum as well as attractive ceramic and silver objects.

We took a boat over to Capri where close to the landing beach there were a number of expensive shops. We walked up the hill on the road that runs along the spine of the island. We also paid for a motorboat to take us into the famed Blue Grotto which lived up to its name and we enjoyed the beautiful coastline with sparkling blue sea and sky.

Finally, we took a bus tour south to Sorrento and the Amalfi coast.

BARBADOS, 2009

Melanie and Steve asked if I'd like to come to Barbados and whether Jane would come too. We both agreed and Jane flew over from Switzerland and stayed a night or two before we all left together on a flight from Gatwick.

Melanie and Steve were to stay with her Bajan friend Fran, who had been a fellow architectural student with Melanie at Oxford Brooks University. Jane and I were booked into a place near the sea. Oh! With the clear, warm water and sandy beaches, this was going to be a marvelous holiday.

In fact, our lodging was to give us so many laughs that we became almost speechless, with tears rolling down our cheeks. Why was this? I went into my bedroom to find a basin with taps, but no water. We went into the bathroom to be greeted by an enormous planter with a large thoroughly dead plant. I opened the cupboard over the basin and the whole panel came away in my hand. We looked in vain for egg cups in which to place the boiled eggs we had made, but as there were none so we each ended up using a loo roll instead. As we ate breakfast, the overhead fan, hanging at an ominous angle, turned slowly and made us wonder if it would crash down on us.

After consultation with Melanie and Fran, we

moved to much nicer accommodation overlooking the sea called Southern Surf Holiday Apartments which had its own swimming pool. Fran hired a catamaran, and we all enjoyed a trip further up the west coast from Bridgetown where we all plunged into the clear waters, sometimes spotting a turtle if we were lucky.

Melanie hired a car, and we visited the Eco-Adventure Park at Harrison's Cave, where one is driven around in special cars to see the stalactites. We enjoyed meeting Fran's parents and had lunch together and were delighted to watch them dance to the steel band.

When we weren't swimming, we were lounging on the beach, thinking how fortunate we were to be there, or sipping coconut milk direct from the shell.

We found the locals very welcoming and were not plagued by vendors. All in all, a delightful holiday.

LESVOS, 2010

Thursday April 22nd. After a week of indecision on account of an active volcano in Iceland, when skies over Britain and parts of Europe were "no fly" zones, on Wednesday evening the experts decided it was safe to fly again.

We wondered if they were bullied into it by the airline industry losing millions every day. Hundreds of thousands of people were stranded all over the world, some people taking five days to return overland to the UK. Just as we thought our holiday wouldn't happen, lo and behold a miracle took place and we were the first Thompson flight direct to Lesvos.

Saturday. April 24th. We flew in from Gatwick and rented a car to drive to Skala Kaloni Village apartments where we unpacked. This resort was only completed at the end of last season and in fact isn't quite finished. We think the owner is the manager of the nearby cement factory,

The first morning we awoke to the song of nightingales. There is a small river nearby which suits the house martins which are busy building nests under the eaves of most of the bungalows, but not ours. The island at this time of migration is host to hundreds of English and Dutch birdwatchers, mostly retired folk. There are guided tours of people carriers which congregate at stops known for certain species. Out come the long lenses, tripods, telescopes. In fact, one lady remarked that it is like the paparazzi after a starlet.

We are surrounded by small, gently rolling mountains. Ascending any slope on our first day proved to be a problem as the gear box on the little Hyundi was clearly "shot".

We had been over to the east to meet our good Dutch friends René and Charlotte Dekker with whom we have stayed on several occasions, either in their Castricum seaside home or in a flat in Amsterdam that belongs to the family. Just ten years ago we had a memorable trip with them to St. Petersburg. Now however, it was quite by chance that we learned that we would be visiting Lesvos at the same time.

We set out to meet them at their hotel which was virtually on the coast, and we agreed to head off on foot to look for birds and to find the taverna that they had had recommended to them. Finding one we first investigated the kitchen, as is the Greek custom, and decided on 6 little fish each, and these were to be grilled, accompanied by various Greek salads and a squid for René.

The best birds for me today were the Glossy Ibis,

which came quite conveniently close to the hide looking resplendent with their green and mauve sheen. There were plenty of flamingos in the salt pans, but they were mostly juveniles and rather dull in colour.

After we parted from René and Charlotte, we set off home, with me driving, until the engine virtually expired on the hills and an unpleasant smell of burning pervaded the car. Edward took over the wheel and, praise God, coaxed the car home just before dark.

Sunday. April 25th. The day began by getting the agents to bring over a replacement car! I'm really struggling with the Greek language despite my time in Athens. It reminds me of my first months at Mittie's in Switzerland, when I was full of French grammar and quite unable to string sentences together or to answer questions quickly. Very frustrating. I would like to spend a year here and have the full immersion language course. But one can get by with English here, although that is also irritating when communication is limited.

We met Andy and Jill Swash at a hotel in Skala Kaloni as planned and agreed to meet for dinner. They are good friends of our friends Roger and Liz Charlwood in Eastbourne. They have been here before and they proved happy to offer us advice on where to go.

Later, we set off heading for Mt. Olympus and drove up until we were within 300-400 ft. of the summit. On the way saw Kruper's Nuthatch at its nest site in a rotting pine stump in the forest. Care was needed on the dirt roads with crushed boulders that had us worrying about losing the suspension. We climbed the last 400 ft. on foot and enjoyed splendid views. There were some run-down buildings and military radar installations at 967 m., or about 3,000 ft., and here we saw lizards a foot-long with colourful markings in green, yellow and blue.

One town we passed through, Agiassos, had tiny-cobbled streets and people sitting at tavernas on little wooden chairs which we "brushed" with the car as we drove uphill in first gear at an alarming angle. Occasionally another vehicle would be heading downhill towards us! That was fun, especially when we had to make an immediate decision about whether to turn right or not!

On the way back, at the Lisvori spa, one of the dozen volcanic springs on the island, I had to laugh – for 3 euros one could take the waters and, of course, I had to try them. There were 2 small concrete buildings, each with a sunken concrete tank about 15 x 12 ft. The water was dark and extremely hot. There were no showers and the whole place was distinctly dank and unhygienic. A lady, completely nude, was on a towel laid out on the side which was dirty concrete. I gingerly sank into the water without putting my costume on. Health and Safety in the UK or Switzerland would have fined me on the spot. A film of what was probably sunscreen floated on the top of the water, which overflowed through a hole in the concrete into a very sulphurous and almost stagnant creek. There must surely be better spa outlets on the island.

Getting back to Skala Kaloni we enjoyed a meal with Andy and Jill in a more cosmopolitan restaurant overlooking the sea.

Monday. April 26th. René and Charlotte have moved to stay on the Kaloni Gulf coast in the north of the island and we drove over to Petra to meet them. The large rock (petra) with a church on top that rises over the town gives its name to the town.

There are said to be about 11 million olive trees on the island. Other common trees were chestnut and pine, some really ancient and dignified. Statuesque fennel plants about 6 ft. tall adorn the hills, they are in flower with lighter green tops.

Later, it rained, and a cold wind blew. But it cleared

up sufficiently for us to have an evening meal on a sunny terrace with octopus arms hanging on a line to dry! We drank a pleasant local white wine called Limnos.

Tuesday. April 27th. Our neighbours, not birders, showed us an incredible nesting site of the Rock Nuthatch which was only about 4 ft. above ground. The pair had crafted an 'entrance' tube protruding from what must have been a fissure in the rock which leads to an inner chamber,

Later we set off southwest from Skala Kaloni and picnicked in the shade of trees just west of Parakila from where we had a view down to the bay. Afterwards we continued further west past Agra, climbing and turning endlessly to reach the area around Mt. Ordimnos.

In doing so we came to what can be described as the gateway to the very different volcanic area that makes up most of the west of the island. The landscape loses its trees and becomes barren and reddish. We headed down to the coast, and turned down to Skala Erresou searching for a Penduline Tit where we walked up and down several hundred yards on each side of the river until we eventually saw what we were looking for. The nest was carefully grafted onto a willow branch and was swaying madly in the wind. We waited, arms aching, with binoculars at the ready until finally the duller coloured female arrived and disappeared through the nest hole.

We then made the long drive back to our base near Skala Kaloni.

Wednesday. April 28th. We were up at 6 a.m. and away at 7 after a good breakfast, heading west again on the northerly road around Mt. Ordimnos with René and Charlotte. It was really chilly, and I was glad of my cardigan and anorak. There are no barriers at the sides of the road so driving round the hairpin bends can be hair-raising.

On Mount Ipsilou there is an abandoned monastery perched atop a rocky outcrop and our visit there produced a Little Owl and a Golden Oriole for Edward. We also met our first crop of wind turbines on the way down to Sigri, which is the most westerly town on the island.

Before going on down to Sigri, we met up again with the Dekkers and detoured southwards to see the petrified forest caused by the historic volcanic activity – this is renowned as a World Geopark and protected area, what we saw being just one of 17 similar spots in this half of the island. It is a wild and desolate place. One must imagine a forest of giant redwoods ten million years ago, while actually looking at a vast expanse of bare rock.

Charlotte and I visited the museum and saw the fossilized remains of an impressively large tree and the skull and teeth of an ancestor of the elephant which had backward-facing tusks also petrified from that time.

After an expensive fish lunch in Sigri with René and Charlotte we set off, after a coffee, along the coast and eventually did some birdwatching in a sheltered valley. We bade our friends farewell as they will be leaving the island tomorrow.

Thursday. April 29th. A 'cultural day'. The Moni Limonas monastery is the largest one on Lesbos. In 1523 the Sultan of Turkey, who then ruled the island, requested the services of St. Ignatius of Kaloni. The Sultan's son had a deformed hand and Ignatius was asked to heal the boy. Upon the miraculous recovery from the deformation, the Saint asked permission to build the monastery and was given land for the sanctuary and it has been a sanctuary ever since. Today it houses a superb library and museum of religious artefacts. There are over 40 individual churches of worship here and beautiful courtyard gardens with peacocks, and trees laden with oranges and a very laid-back atmosphere.

We had lunch at the "2 Euro" café, where we shared a plate with 2 kebabs (chicken today) and some tomato and cucumber salad, with yoghurt and a few French fries - all for 4 Euros.

Edward took the car and went off, while I ventured into the sea for a swim. The water temperature was about 19 C. Afterwards I swam a few lengths of the pool, again with no one around, but with swirling House Martins overhead.

Friday. April 30th. Early morning light on some of the birds at the salt pans was a joy to see.

After breakfast we set off to try one of the recommended walks in the splendid little book by Brian and Eileen Anderson, which our daughter-in-law Diana had found for us. Walk No. 7 starts from Agiassos and led us through woodlands of pine and sweet chestnut, and fruit and olive orchards. Saw several species or orchid, including *Ophrys umbilicata* (looking like a Bee Orchid); *LImodorum abortivum* (Violet limadoire); a white specimen of *Orchis tridentata* (Toothed Orchid), and *Serapius vomeracea* (Tongue Orchid). We picnicked in a little orchard surrounded by nightingales in full song, and we met no-one.

Then we drove to Pesos Waterfalls and began another walk, initially down a stepped way into the hillside as far as a viewing platform from where there were views across to the bay and a small waterfall. Then the path wound down into the valley through pine woods.

Back at the car we both felt quite weary and headed for Skala Kaloni to enjoy a fish soup at a table out in the open, while we watched the local fishing boats sailing out to bring in the night's catch. I tried ouzo for the first time since living in Athens in 1962.

Saturday. May 1st. Kalo Mina! Or happy first of the month as they say. I had a dip in the sea. It was still rather chilly and I'm missing my plastic shoes because it's not all soft white sand here.

Today is a public holiday and all of the people at Skala Kaloni Village Apartments are invited to lunch by the owner so there was much activity at the bungalows. Awnings and tables started to be arranged as early as about 8 a.m. and an entire lamb started turning on a spit.

Dozens of locals turned up for the barbecue who, we learned, were relatives spanning 3 or 4 generations of the family of the cement factory and resort owner. The lamb on the spit turned out to be a pig, not a lamb! Plate after plate of salads and other Greek dishes arrived, including an excellent local sausage.

Dorothy, the local Thompson agent, never appeared, which we thought was rather a poor show. An old boy struck up on an accordion. Edward drank the red Krassi wine on offer – which knocked him out for 3 hours afterwards.

At sundown we walked along the beach with neighbours and sat chatting with them on an observation platform.

Sunday. May 2nd. We headed towards Petra and a wildflower field Edward was keen to revisit. It was ablaze with camomile, other yellow flowers, poppies and Lavatera. Being such a warm day it was also perfect for butterflies and – horrors – snakes! We encountered three, one which was about 6 ft. long, had perhaps been sunbathing on a rock and shot past Edward at neck level as he was opening the gate into the next field. Luckily these were not the vipers which inhabit the island.

We found a picnic spot on a stone under a tree looking down onto Molyvos on the north coast. Then we drove down a little used track, or rather we lurched and bumped over stones and plants until we came to Eftalou on the coast, where we enjoyed the second half of our picnic. The oranges here are really good – succulent and not pithy.

Monday. May 3rd. Out early again, we drove west towards Sigri, but we took the southern dirt road, where we met the Swashes along the way. We lunched at a totally laid back taverna where we were told by the owner that her son had gone to Anessa for supplies, and we would have to wait for his return! Eventually, the usual tomato salad appeared followed by good tuna steaks.

We returned via Moni Ipsilon monastery which is perched high up on the Mt. Ordimnos range with 360-degree views said to be right across to the Greek mainland, which seemed unlikely given how far east we are.

Two abandoned puppies had been picked up and taken to the vet by a German lady staying at Kaloni. She brought them to the bungalows, which was a bit cheeky as the staff already have dogs and quite enough to do. However, the puppies are very cute.

Tuesday. May 4th. The two pups were going around, seeking attention, playing, and eventually falling asleep in the shade. We discovered that all the electricity was off and learned that there is a general strike. Greece is struggling financially, and the EU wants bigger taxes to help them out of the slough, so the unions are protesting. Because of the activities of the strikers, we stayed in our resort all day.

We ate a late supper over at the center and met Steve and Sue. Sue is a committed Christian and told me how Steve had not been one when they married. The local Welsh community were very critical of this. For 8 years Sue tried to bring Steve round and then gave up, but the Lord came to Steve, and they now worship together.

Wednesday. May 5th. Edward went out early, but later we took a picnic and attempted to walk to the Roman Aqueduct, a new area. It was a really hot day and we walked down into the airless valley through deserted-looking olive groves and past farms where all was quiet except for dogs barking to announce our passing. We didn't complete the circuit, but after stopping to eat our picnic at a second river, which was quite fast flowing and pleasantly shaded, we returned the way we had come. We were glad to get back to the bungalow for a shandy and a swim. Then it was time to begin the packing.

We spent the evening with 4 other couples at the Ambrosia restaurant in Kalonis, where a jazz band was playing on a raised platform in the square.

On TV we saw scenes of serious rioting in Athens with 3 killed and a bank fire-bombed. The whole of the EU is in financial turmoil and in Britain we go to the polls tomorrow. Also, activity has increased at that Iceland volcano and parts of Scotland are already no-fly zones. Will we get away?

Thursday. May 6th. We settled up at the bar for our various ices, drinks and occasional meals, and learned that the abandoned puppies are going to fly to Holland to a family with 2 boys, all paid for by the German lady who was concerned and "rescued" them.

We left for the airport at about 9.30 a.m. and soon discovered that there was a diversion due to a political protest on the main road and this forced us to take a dusty, unmarked track, that we hoped was leading in the right direction. How is it that we seem to attract these situations wherever we go. Remember Darjeeling? Everyone in their individual cars managed to find the way, and we all met up at the seaside airport in Mytilene where Edward I enjoyed a sweet Greek coffee.

Mercifully, the flight home on April 6th. was trouble-free, and we were in time to vote at the village hall in Meads. I was miserably cold for 24 hours, but it was good to be back safely.

THREE GENERATIONS VISIT SWITZERLAND, 2011

I wanted to show this beautiful country to my granddaughter Jessie (13) and hoped that she would come to love it as I do.

Melanie came with us, and we hired a car at Geneva airport. We drove to Jane's amazing cliff-hanging apartment above Montreux where Jessie and Melanie would share Jane's spare room, which had two beds, while I would go upstairs to a spare room where the landlord had kindly offered me a bed.

One of the first visits we made was to one of the nearest tourist spots, the Chateau de Chillon, a castle on the lakeside.

We headed down the valley crossing into the Canton du Valais with the objective of finding the famous St. Bernard dogs to show to Jessie. We did not need to go up into the mountains for this because here in the Valais they are bred and reared. I hoped that Jessie and the puppies enjoyed the cuddles.

Next, back near Montreux we met up with my friend Margaret for a walk on Mt. Pelerin and admired the beautiful spring flowers. Jane's nephew, wife and two children were on holiday here at the time, so we joined them and with Ada along as well we walked to the Glacier du Trient along the easy, flat, path following a 'bis' (a narrow water channel) through the valley; this is one of my favourite walks. The glacier has retreated massively since I first came here; now one needs to climb up the valley from the level water channel and to pick one's way over the boulder-strewn valley to reach the foot of the glacier; and Jessie and the youngsters reached it and soothed their aching feet in the icy water.

The next excitement was the Chocolate Train leaving from Montreux on the MOB, the Montreux Oberland Bernois railway leading to Interlaken. We were only going to Gruyere to see where that world-famous cheese is produced, and to Broc for a tour of the Nestlé chocolate factory, where we sampled far too much!

Melanie and I also introduced Jessie to a real Swiss fondue and took her to visit the hot spring at the spa at Lavey-les-Bains. Jessie's father was a playmate of Sebastien, Ada's son and so we visited the little French village just over the border near Geneva where Sebastian lived with his wife and two sons, Robin and Pascal.

Given all the family linkages I'm sure Jessie will remember this holiday with affection.

PISA AND FLORENCE, 2011

We flew to Pisa and had our obligatory photo taken beside the leaning tower. We also marveled at the Baptistry of San Giovanni – everything was looking resplendent in the sunshine.

From there we took a coach to Florence, through which runs the Arno River. We arrived at a large coach station and from there took a taxi to our hotel.

Our friends Barry and Jane were with us, and we stayed in a delightful hotel with a huge, high ceilinged dining room where we breakfasted in a room that was almost empty. The best way to see the city is on foot, and we soon found the Uffizi Art Gallery and paid the fee to visit it and to go in we passed through the Ghiberti doors, also known as the Gates of Paradise; the two doors contain the twenty-eight gilded panels depicting the life of Christ and give the door its name.

The old two-storey bridge across the river was quite close to our hotel. The upper level leads across from a palace on one side of the river to another palace on the opposite side so that the Medici family could cross without being seen to do so; there are no shops at this level. By contrast, on the lower level there are shops on each side. One was a super ice cream parlour, others sold garments or jewelry and in one of the latter I showed a ring I had brought with me which was Mittie's engagement ring and which I understood had been crafted by a jeweller on this bridge. On the far side of the river was the small natural history museum where Edward was due to attend a conference. Further still and up on a hilltop was a large garden which Barry, Jane and I explored.

As it was November and not too hot, we all had the energy to climb Giotto's Gothic bell tower next to the cathedral. I don't remember how many steps there were, but the view from the top was well worth the effort of the climb.

Two sculptures remain in my memory: first, what is known as the Pieta by Michelangelo, carved between 1547 and 1555, and second, David, also by Michelangelo, this original is, I think, in the Accademia Gallery, but there is a second copy of this in the Piazza della Signoria (Duomo Square) and that was the one we saw.

Jane and I climbed to the church of San Miniato. This church has been described as one of the finest Romanesque structures in Tuscany. It is at the highest point in Florence from where one has a panoramic view of the city, the road being punctuated with the beautiful pines familiar to this region.

We returned to Pisa airport by bus for the flight home.

WALES, 2013

Philip and Diana kindly invited us, together with Melanie, to join them on a holiday to Wales. We were to spend a week in a hire cottage, a comfy long barn style, just outside Caernarvon, and Melanie drove us there in her car. This gave us a good base from which to explore.

Our first visit – apart from a visit to the local supermarket – was to Caernarvon Castle, one of King Edward I's ring of strongholds placed around the coast of Gwynedd, north Wales. This is a World Heritage Site, and it replaced a previous Norman castle and, prior to that, a Roman fortress. Building the castle was finished in 1330 and it was besieged several times, including one battle or uprising when the castle was held by few men against the English army. It is where the investiture of 20-year-old Charles, son of Queen Elizabeth II, as Prince of Wales took place on 1 July 1969.

The beach on the Irish Sea was only a short drive from the cottage, and, although it was the end of July, and not very warm, Rufus and Thea were the only two brave enough to take a dip, and it had to be a short one. The rest of us on the beach amused ourselves by creating 'art' with stones of different colours and sizes. Diana was particularly good at this. Several of us were lured by the ice cream van.

When it rained and we were at the cottage, we amused ourselves with the owners' films, puzzles and games. Thea, I remember, was convinced her calling was to be a singer, and she was warned that singers have to practice a lot!

When the rain cleared, Philip and family headed off to the copper mine for a tour, whilst Edward, Melanie and I went for a walk in the hills further east from Caernarvon; we climbed up one valley turned east and came down the next valley, from where we could get back to the parked car.

Snowdon beckoned, and Philip and Diana, plus Jessie and Melanie, were to climb its western side from the south. Edward and I, together with Rufus and Thea, opted to take the train to the top, and we were to meet the others when they got there. We had timed our train up with some idea of when they thought they would get there. On the valley floor, there was a small lake at Llanberis close the base station for the Mountain Railway which has been running since 1896, and Edward and Rufus enjoyed a row in a small boat on the lake near the base station and Thea and I looked in the nearby shops.

At the summit, clouds and cold winds prevailed, but when the clouds lifted, the view was spectacular.

The Visitors' Centre, Hafod Eryri, at the top of the mountain was designed by Ray Hole Architects and the building won an R.I.B.A. award, partly due to the use of the space inside and the way it sits and gives dramatic views of the valleys below. It was opened in June 2009.

We picnicked against the upper wall of the building in the cold clouds. Melanie had brought a thermos of hot water which took off the chill in the air, but we didn't stay long. We thought the crowds were surprisingly large.

On another, more clement day, we visited 80-acre Bodnant Gardens in the Conway Valley. This is hailed as one of the most beautiful gardens in the world. A big claim, but well deserved. I guess the house is about 40 or 50 feet above the stream in the dell at the bottom of the garden where there are several tall redwoods and rhododendrons of various colours. It seemed from what we heard that a few trout breed in a small lake. When we arrived at the estate we were met by a very impressive laburnum entry tunnel about 15 yards long.

Conwy (or Conway) town: here we explored the castle and then Plas Mawr, which is one of the most complete Elizabethan town houses in the country; it was built by Robert Wynn, in three phases in the late 16th Century and had recently been entirely refurbished. We found this very interesting, and we were amused by the various carcasses of game hanging in the kitchen!

One of our final ports of call was Portmerion, the Italianate village creation by Clough Williams-Ellis the arts and crafts architect who bought the private peninsula in the late 1920's and dedicated the rest of his life to 'improving' the naturally beautiful site. It is, of course, also known for its pottery.

Melanie decided she had wanted an old-fashioned train ride, and she took the Caernarvon to Porthmadog steam train, travelling in style.

All in all, a most enjoyable and varied holiday.

PRAGUE, 2013

Edward had signed up to attend a conference of European ornithologists with museum connections in Prague and I invited our friends Barry and Jane Mansergh, from Eastbourne, to join us, but for tourism and not the meeting. We flew over together and took a taxi to our hotel, which was just a short walk from the Natural History Museum where the meeting would take place.

Jane, having lived on the Continent for part of her music studies, was already familiar with the city. Edward spent the next day at the museum and Barry, Jane and I worked our way down the hill to the Charles Bridge where several musicians were busking; but we did take a look in the museum first. Much of the way down the hill the road was wide with interesting shops on both sides. It leads on down to the main square, but on this bit the road is much narrower.

In the main square near the river the three of us found a large café with a grand hall and high ceiling and we ordered lunch. Jane was horrified to see the grand piano sitting there laden with trays of ketchup and dirty dishes and felt obliged to have words with the waiter!

Edward's Russian friend Vladimir Loskot, who we had last seen in St. Petersburg, was attending the

European Ornithological Conference and we were able to take him out to dinner; he had very kindly brought us a bottle of Russia's best brandy.

We found that there was a concert in a nearby concert hall and we were able to get tickets to attend it.

There was a high-rated up-market restaurant not far from the hotel which was at the top of an ancient belltower, and I believe there was a lift to get up to the restaurant and we went up to examine the menu, and we booked dinner for four the following evening. The meal was excellent and well worth the effort.

BELIZE, 2015

February 3rd. Tuesday. Slight snow flurries were seen from the train on the way to Gatwick. There was no need to wait in line to have our luggage taken away. Curiously, for the first time, my metal hip did not set off an alarm. We had access to the Angel lounge and spent a very calm hour in there which made for a good start. This is not a direct flight to Belize; we must spend a night in Mexico.

We boarded as the wings were sprayed with anti-freeze. During the flight I watched a memorable movie about a 109-year old Holocaust survivor called Alice Hertz-Somner, who lives in London and plays the piano all day long. She had been a concert pianist, and her son is a famous cellist from Prague. She still entertains, laughs a lot and has a wonderfully positive attitude to life. What an example!

We landed in Mexico at Cancun airport where our cases were examined, but the transfer to our hotel, despite a clement temperature, was not a smooth one due to much waiting around. For some reason we had to pick up another couple at another terminal and then travel some 20 miles into Cancun and the Oasis Palm Hotel, by which time it was 1.15 a.m. UK time, and we were exhausted. We mislaid Edward's anorak en route.

The hotel was alive with a mass of tourists. It was a huge, cavernous place of extreme noise and seemed to have dozens of restaurants around a vast swimming pool. Each one had queues, so what a mercy not to be staying here. We ignored the food and chose bed!

February 4th. We watched the sun rise over the sea, grabbed a buffet breakfast and found some swimming trunks for Edward in the hotel shop with sea life swarming all over. "I'll only be wearing them 2 or 3 times" he complained.

We waited and waited for the ordered transfer to the airport and eventually took a taxi. Then, once the driver had found the new terminal, we discovered, after asking, that this region of Mexico had decided to align its time with New York, making only 5 hours difference with Europe. So, our watches were wrong, and the driver had come and waited 15 minutes and gone again; but we were not late for our flight although we did have to go without lunch.

After a torrential downpour a Tropic Air twin prop 14-seater plane eventually took off and we had a bumpy first 30 minutes getting above the weather system. 1 1/2 hours later we arrived in Belize City and were welcomed right away by a driver. It was nice to feel the "English" atmosphere and to know we were being understood.

Sadly though, our driver mistook the place we were going to which was well across towards the Guatemalan border and he turned off left on a bone-shaking ride only to realize he had gone wrong and that he had to get back to the main road – having wasted about 50 minutes. Eventually, at about 30 minutes before midnight UK time, we crawled into Black Rock Lodge. It had taken us 40 hours from home, and we made it!

We had a great welcome from Petra, a South African lady, and it was time for dinner at a table of friendly Brits and Americans. Everything here is eco-friendly; the water for drinking and cooking is spring water and all the vegetables are grown on the spot. Bedtime found us unprepared for a real nighttime dip in temperature. Blankets were available and we dug out a vest to add to the pyjamas.

February 5th. A good breakfast, but too much really. Edward made the acquaintance of Alan Poole from Cornell University, a well-known ornithologist who comes here on a regular basis to help with local research. His retirement is not far away and Alan plans to spend 3 months a year here. Cameron, the American owner of Black Rock Lodge, who flies down from the USA quite often, is going to build Alan a special cabin.

We sorted out our schedule for the week with Petra, the Manageress, and decided we would climb Summit 1 today, this being the mountain directly behind the resort. A big mistake! It was a difficult, steep rocky climb and not really advisable for people our age. But we made it somehow and arrived back drenched with sweat and totally spent.

Later Edward spent some time with Jorge, a Mayan guide who had long pigtails and one pierced ear holding a large wooden ring. He showed us some of his excellent photographs on a laptop. Jorge told us about the Ceiban tree, the trunk of which is covered in stubby spines. The Mayan people are supposed to have believed the roots are the stalactites in caves and the tree holds up the heavens. The spines are to prevent men from climbing to heaven, the domain of the gods, so these trees have spiritual meaning and will never be touched or felled.

I went for a dip in the mineral water pool which refreshed me. A sudden rush of strong wind announced the arrival of rain.

Cameron showed us a stunning Keel-billed Toucan through his scope, I saw a Black and White Warbler and have renamed it "the Mint Humbug bird" because that's what its stripes reminded me of.

February 6ᵗʰ. Our planned early bird walk was cancelled because of heavy rain, and we had a Continental breakfast with excellent honey. As the weather cleared, we were able to do some birding from the balcony.

In mid-morning three small canoes entered the river. Carlos was our guide and paddler. We waited until the dam water had been released; this is done every few days because if the flow of water is too low the canoes cannot pass the various rapids on account of rocks. It was very peaceful on the river; we saw kingfishers every few minutes, but they were difficult to photograph. Iguanas were seen resting on rocks; they are very shy and disappear rapidly – with good reason, as apparently, they taste like chicken and the hunting season for them only finished at the beginning of this month. My best photographic scoop was of the rare Agami Heron under shade on the river edge moving slowly along the bank, and Carlos was able to bring us within a few feet.

We stopped for some lunch at a café with an elevated board walk in the trees, after which Carlos took us for a further 15 minutes down river at which point we each had a go at paddling and then we disembarked at the Botanical Gardens for a tour. We had travelled 6 miles on the water and were pretty stiff. In the garden we saw the National orchid which is black, and we also stepped carefully over a big tarantula about 4 inches long which was in a rain channel down the middle of the path. I took a good photo of this. A car came to fetch us and take us back to the lodge.

In the evening, after a dinner of lamb, we had a night drive. Cameron stood in the back of the vehicle with the spotlight while Alan, Edward and I were inside. We saw a wide-eyed Potoo sitting on a fence post and as a group we quietly walked right up to it as it sat there. Later, we saw another one catching moths and other insects and its eyes shone like red lamps in the torch beam.

February 7th. Edward made an early start. I was supposed to be ready for an 8 a.m. departure to the San Ignacio Market, an important local event. However, my breakfast took some time coming and the long walk back to our cabin meant that I kept a minibus-load of Americans waiting nearly 15 minutes. I apologized and then discovered that the two ladies next to me came from Chicago.

At the market I walked for an hour or more round huge sprawling displays of brightly coloured spices, clothes, vegetables, fruit and souvenirs etc.

There was certainly a rich mix of ethnicity too: elegantly attired Mayan women, local Belizians and there were Menonite men in matching black trousers and blue shirts who were selling their cheeses. The Menonites were not communicative, which was a pity as I would have liked to learn more about their lives and what the children think about continuing to live in isolation without modernization. I tried to take representative pictures of people without being too intrusive, which was not always easy.

I waited in hot sunshine for a return ride with Alan Poole and an American girl from Chicago. It later transpired that I had been supposed to wait another hour and go with the Americans to a chocolate farm to see chocolate being made and to try to make some myself, but I have seen enough chocolate making in Switzerland.

Anyway, I was glad to be back for lunch with Edward and before that a refreshing swim in the pool, which is a spring running continuously and using no chemicals.

At lunch the custard apple I bought at the market was cut open and brought to me at table; it looks dark and has a hard exterior – completely different from the Asian ones. Observers said it looked like "roadkill"! It was certainly not as nice as Thai custard apples.

We have now been moved to a de-luxe cabin, nearer the restaurant, with the sound of rushing white water just below.

February 9th. Just the two of us with Carlos again. Carlos loves birds and is very knowledgeable, which makes him a super guide.

What was good about this drive was the fact that fence posts and telephone wires provided wonderful perching places for birds, and we saw some beauties. The aim was to visit as many different habitats as possible.

The first was El Pilar, a Mayan temple that has been purposely left un-excavated to avoid disturbing the wildlife, so the entire place is a series of huge mounds surmounted by trees, a sort of Angkor Wat disappearing into jungle. Next, we reached a place called Spanish Lookout. From here one sees the Maya mountains stretching away into the distance.

We had a close view of Howler Monkeys – a large male eating leaves and a resting female – but my camera needed charging and I was unable to take a picture.

Apart from the wilderness most of this area is farmed by Menonites – said to belong to quite a modern sect.

We picnicked halfway through the day and ended up visiting yet another habitat which is normally marshland, but a lot had dried out or been drained ready for planting rice. However, this area was different enough to produce different birds.

When we returned to Black Rock Lodge, we had been birding for eleven and a half hours, and Petra said she was just starting to get anxious for us.

February 10th. Today we leave Black Rock Lodge and ride to a tiny local airport for a flight with Tropic Air for just 4 passengers to Ambergris Cay. After 40 minutes we stopped at a small cay to disembark a young couple going diving and then turned north for a final 5 minutes to land at San Pedro on Ambergris Cay. Thank goodness, today the tachycardia rhythm of my heart has calmed down.

A taxi took us through San Pedro to a jetty where we had a 45-minute wait to be collected by a Sapphire Beach boat with very powerful Yamaha outboard in which we rode north along the coast for 45 minutes reaching Sapphire Beach resort just before nightfall. There is much construction work being undertaken at this resort, with a dozen new bungalows half finished. Our chalet was fully airconditioned and had comfy beds.

February 11th. We were given masks and snorkels to wear, but soon discovered that this beach is not the place to try them out. The sea is shallow, full of sea grass and sand mounds and the water is murky.

To see the fish, one really needs to get beyond the reef; here that would have meant taking a kayak out several hundred yards to the reef and then finding a way across. We did not feel confident about that, even less so after a young American staying here with his wife and a baby told us that one year two of his friends did just that and the kayak overturned in choppy water, and they both died!

We took several walks around the property and saw ospreys claiming ownership of a pylon where they intended to nest. In the evening, we had a good view of the Great Horned Owl which had been hooting earlier.

We walked north along the beach and found that as soon as we went beyond the property the shoreline was heaped with rubbish of every kind of plastic, including a loo seat! We were told that cruise ships were part of the problem. Does no-one care about this disaster? Who is going to clear it up?

February 12ᵗʰ. At 1.45 p.m. we were picked up by a boat from "No Worries" Resort just south of here and after a short ride with others from there we were dropped at "Mexican Reef" where we were fitted up with flippers and snorkels. We found the coral a little disappointing and rather colourless apart from some fan coral. But we did not cross the reef to the deep water beyond which there would have been much more coral and many more fish.

We saw plenty of small sting rays and Sergeant Major fish. I can't help thinking how much more there was in Thailand, but it's no good comparing!

Back at the bungalow we saw what we thought was a peccary scuttling round. Sarkey, the manager at Sapphire Beach resort later told us there are racoons in the forest, both north and south of us and that we should be wary of them. Even though we are not on the mainland the swamp here has resident jaguar, ocelot, peccary and crocodiles, all within less than a mile of the resort.

February 13ᵗʰ. Another trip to the reef. When we reached Hol Tan, we stripped to swimming costumes and T-shirts again, and we were told that at this new site there were bigger fish and there was more to see.

When we jumped into the sea, we found it was

fairly choppy with quite a tide race (especially where the reef had gaps), a strong lady was appointed to look after our group, and she recommended that we clutch onto buoy ropes that she could use to pull us over the area – still inside the reef – where we would see more. We did that and were very impressed by her strength and we saw plenty of fish, a turtle and a Moray eel, which was winkled out of its hiding. There were quite a few small Nursing Sharks, which moved around just above the sand. They took no notice of us above them. Edward, who is not a strong swimmer, did really very well!

Lunch was provided on board, and we were glad to change and put on dry clothes.

Back at the bungalow we discovered an American couple had line caught a huge barracuda, which was being attacked by the cook with a machete and was subsequently barbecued and everyone was invited to join the feast, which was very kind. It was caught by one of the ladies, who arrived today, on her 60th birthday, so I got Sarkey to bring in a dessert with a candle for her.

We learned from one of the guests that we could have taken a 10-minute boat ride further north to a really pleasant swimming beach with an accessible reef just a few yards offshore! But we did not have our own fins and snorkels.

February 14th. St. Valentine's Day.

We began our trip home today with a boat ride into San Pedro over a calmer sea. This dropped us and our luggage fairly close to the airport, to which we could walk.

At the airport we expected that we had tickets for the transfer to Belize where we would pick up the flight up to Cancun. The airport staff however, had had us booked on yesterday's Tropic Air flight – this turned out to be a mistake made by the Guatemalan travel agency used by Dial-a-Flight. The situation required a phone call to Dial-a-Flight's emergency number, so Edward went into the High Street and found a friendly American guy working in a real estate agency, who very kindly allowed Edward to ring Dial-a-Flight in the UK.

Eventually the flight connections needed were fixed and we made the transfers. Edward had to get out his credit card and pay all over again, which we knew Charlie at Dial-a-Flight would refund for us.

Had we not resolved the flight issue we would have missed the Cancun flight home across the Atlantic. But in Cancun we finally transferred aboard the Virgin Airlines 747 to Gatwick at about 8 p.m., thankfully, this time it was expected to be only an 8 & 1/2 hour flight, as we would be blown along by the jet stream.

Much to our delight Philip and Diana were at Gatwick to greet us and drive us home. Diana's idea, bless her. A real lifesaver as there would have been bus transfers as it was Sunday with engineering work on the railway.

Two days of green apple quickstep ensued for me, which the doctor said could be due to nasty bacteria in the warm sea water and that they are sometimes resistant to antibiotics.

Edward had developed a sore on his ankle and a swollen foot and was put on antibiotics anyway. It took us a few days to readjust, and I think it took more out of us than we would care to admit. The forest part of the trip was the best, we could have passed on all the rest.

THE ISLES OF SCILLY WITH MOTHER, 2015

On the spur of the moment, I decided to treat Mother to a holiday in the Isles of Scilly.

It always seems as though one is stepping back in time there, because although it is only a journey of just under 3 hours by boat to the main island of St. Mary, it seems almost like a foreign land. There are also small planes that go back and forth from Penzance to St. Mary's. Life there is at a slower pace and there are no cars on the smaller islands. An old-fashioned bus is available.

We stayed in a small guest house and did quite a bit of walking. What thrilled Mother was the fact that birds seemed so tame and came to share food if one ate out of doors. A boat took us to Tresco to the famous gardens which benefit from the climate tempered by the Gulf Stream.

It was a successful visit and I felt happy to have given Mother some pleasure.

PARIS, 2015

My dear school friend Carole and I decided to make a quick trip to Monet's Garden, which meant going to Paris first. We were accompanied by Edward, who was going to the Natural History Museum to examine specimens there. We all stayed for three nights in a rather strange hotel.

Carole and I took a boat trip along the Seine, which is a nice leisurely way of sightseeing. We visited the famous Gallerie Lafayette and here we became rather childish. We decided to try on some of the fabulous wedding hats, and we had already taken several photos of each other doing this before a sales lady came over and ticked us off!

One memorable visit was to the Sainte-Chapelle, built in the mid-13th. century by Louis IX at the heart of the royal residence, the Palais de la Cite, to house the relics of the Passion of Christ. The access is up steep and winding steps and is quite challenging. Once one is in the church one is immediately overwhelmed by the extraordinary number of stained-glass windows, each depicting a bible story, and on a sunny day the light pours through.

We boarded a train for the short journey to Monet's Garden. The collection of roses was especially wonderful; this was a delight and at this time of year looking at its best. The house itself is immaculately kept and it too was fascinating and well worth the visit.

In the evening for dinner, we met up with Edward and his Dutch friend René, as well as my friend Maria and her husband Henri.

It was the weekend of the U.E.F.A. League Championship finals, which meant Paris was hosting more visitors than usual and there was a lot of flag waving.

FUN WITH PUBLISHING, 2013-2015

When our daughter Melanie visited us in Eastbourne, she would often remark, drawing on her architect's training, on the number of high-quality buildings, and she persuaded us that there was enough material to create a book similar to the one she had helped to create for the Salisbury Civic Society. Their book was called "Salisbury in Detail", which had a proportion of picture pages to text pages of about 5 to 1, and the pictures were excellent photographs of architectural features such as doorways, chimneys, ironwork, gables and eaves, old signs and suchlike.

The Society deliberately excluded everything to do with the cathedral, because there were already several books on that. The organizer and designer of the book was Richard Deane. Melanie was a member of the Salisbury Civic Society and had been involved in discussing the project, and, when the pictures and text had been arranged, she was able to use a computer programme called In Design to set up the work for printing.

We thought that a book called Eastbourne in Detail might be successful and discussed the idea with a small group of potential helpers, including a local architect and a print designer, and we asked the Eastbourne Society whether it would welcome a visit by Richard Deane to tell them about the

Salisbury book and how it might be a suitable example for a work about Eastbourne. We explained to the Society's Chairman that we would invite Richard to come and discuss the idea and his visit was arranged and he duly came and made the case, but when we told the Chairman that a selling price below £40 would not be profitable because of the many colour pages, he said that a book selling for over £30 would not find a sufficient market. However, our little group decided that we would take the project forward without the Eastbourne Society.

Edward, who had set up a publishing company for some bird books, took the chair at a series of Committee Meetings held in our spacious flat in Bolsover Road and made himself responsible for keeping the project within budget and meeting the eventual deadline when we set one. The committee comprised Richard Crook, the local conservation architect, Nicholas Howell the professional graphic designer, as well as Edward and me. We soon co-opted Susan Body who manages the local interests of the Duke of Devonshire, whose family had been one of the two major landowners here and the promoters and developers of the town. Indeed, they had established the local by-laws, one of which ruled that there should be no shops along the length of the sea front, much of which was to be occupied by hotels. Not only could Susan talk to the duke's family, she was also well known to many local businessmen who pay ground rent to him, and some might agree to become sponsors.

Between us we secured six major sponsors and another 28 minor ones and thanks to their generosity we were able to maintain the planned sales price and thanks to the modest second impression we made a profit, partly thanks to many sales subsequently made by the Eastbourne Society.

We were all quite excited to explore the town on foot to identify buildings and other suitable subjects for the photographs; this was definitely a job to do this way. Richard proposed a list of chapters with their subject names so that each chapter subject came with suitable colour photographs. Richard, Nicholas and I all took many photographs and ten others also contributed so we often had choices to make. I built up a collection of photos arranged by subject, and I was thrilled when forty-two of mine appeared in the printed work.

In total several hundred were submitted and a small subcommittee arranged groups laid out by subject, and Richard and Nicholas scrutinized and compared pictures and eventually made the final choices.

Edward had had his two-volume Checklist of Birds

of the World printed by Imago, where his contact was Michele Draycott, and she was kind enough to provide advice on the printing. The quality of the colour printing was vital, and Michele arranged for a proof to be printed in London which the reasonably priced Croatian printers were required to match. It was a hardback book with an initial print run of 1,000 copies, and the format matched that of the Salisbury book. The six copies required by law to comply with Legal Deposit rules were duly dispatched to Edinburgh. A small second impression followed which, for no explained reason, was packed 13 to a box instead of 12!

We planned an evening launch event which took place in the Grand Hotel with the Rt. Hon. the Earl of Burlington – who is now the Duke of Devonshire – as guest of honour, and the lady Mayor, the local MP, some celebrities and all our helpful sponsors were invited as well as about 30 other guests.

Earlier, in the afternoon, our local MP, Caroline Ansell, rode in a goat chaise on the western lawns which made headlines in the *Herald*. This was one of the modes of transport on offer here to Victorian and Edwardian tourists. Each mode had marked stations showing where they parked and took on passengers and these sites were signaled by tiny place markers that can still be found close to ground level on the seaward side of King Edward's Parade, opposite Wilmington Square. No goat chaise could be traced locally, but Edward cleverly discovered a breeder of goats in Dorset who could provide one and she came to make the event possible.

I really enjoyed this satisfying project.

CLASSICAL SPAIN, 2016

Edward and I joined a Riviera Travel trip to "Classical Spain" which entailed flying to Malaga where we arrived quite late and boarded a coach to take us to a hotel, a 40-minute drive away, where we stayed one night.

On day 2 the coach took us to Ronda which is built on a high ridge and a very impressive gorge divides the town in two. The two halves are linked by a massive 18th. century stone bridge. The coach parked in the center near the bullring, and we set out on foot to explore. The first few strides took us to the edge of the huge cliff that runs behind the bullring, which has a huge bronze statue of a bull outside the bullring – where fights do still take place. The arena here is said to be the largest in Spain. From the edge, a drop of perhaps 150 feet, there is a splendid view down into the valley.

Ronda is a location where terrible acts of brutality occurred during the Spanish Civil War (1936-1939) when Nationalists were tossed over a cliff into the gorge below.

We noticed a sign saying Paseo de Hemingway which reflects the interest of Ernest Hemingway the novelist in Spain and indeed in Ronda where he lived for some time, studying and writing about bullfighting. After lunch our bus took us on to Seville.

Day 3. We had a tour of the city of Seville and closest to our hotel was the Plaza de Espana, the most famous square here, created for the Ibero-American exhibition in 1929 to symbolize peace with Spain's former colonies. There are 52 benches with Andalusian tiles that represent all the Spanish provinces, and all this with rain coming down on us like stair-rods. Next we were taken to the fortified Tower of Gold, so named because it was used to store the plunder from the Americas brought across the Atlantic, from La Guiara near Caracas in what is now Venezuela, by the famous treasure galleons, then we also saw the bullring and the cathedral, where there is a backdrop of gold to the altar, which is a series of 'windows' into the life of Christ. To us it all seemed rather 'over the top'.

Day 4. We were given free time today to explore the city as we wished. We explored the town center looking particularly in a shop selling fans in and another selling mouth-watering pastries. The 'Mushrooms of Seville' is a strange, enormous wooden construction dating from 2011 complete with a pantomime ceramic terrace, a walking path and an archaeological museum. Nearby there was a good place for a drink.

Our hotel was in the district of Triana and quite close to it was a theatre where, in the evening, we enjoyed a show mainly of flamenco dancing and heard music typical of the region of Andalusia.

Day 5. The bus drove us east to Cordoba, another of Andalusia's classic cities. We had a special guide to take us on a tour of the Mezquita (Moorish Mosque), which is quite extraordinary in that after the defeat of the Moors the mosque was not damaged, but had a catholic cathedral built inside it.

Leaving Cordoba, the main road passed through large estates of olive groves, and we began to see spectacular views of the Sierra Nevada mountains beyond Grenada where we arrived at the Alixares Hotel which is high up within walking distance of the Alhambra Palace and with steep roads or steps leading down into the town.

Day 6. We awoke to see the distant mountains soaring up to 11,000 ft.; here we are closer to them, and they form a perfect backdrop for the Alhambra Palace which is extraordinary. The guided tour of it lasted 3 hours. There are other tours ahead of us and behind, and each is required to keep to a timetable and there are staff to monitor the crowds and chivey us along. One needs to be fighting fit.

Day 7. Back to Malaga and our return flight to the UK.

CENTRAL ITALY, AUGUST 2016

This was a family holiday which included Philip and Diana and their children and separately Steve and Melanie travelling with us. Everything went remarkably well. We flew to Pisa and hired a car, which involved quite a long wait while they processed the requests of those who got off the plane before us.

Once on the road we drove south down the west coast to pick up a ferry to the island of Elba where we landed at Portoferraio. We had booked a hotel for a night on the edge of the bay. We had fine weather and drove over the hills to Porto Azzurro for a ferry back to the mainland. We then worked our way east to the walled town of Lucca where we parked and found a restaurant for lunch and then explored the views from the walls, but we did not look at the Roman amphitheater. After lunch we drove further west to meet the main highway towards Perugia.

Our destination where we would be for about a week was a small town called Resina, where we did our food shopping.

The house that Philip had rented was well outside town in rolling country; it had an excellent swimming pool which was a great success with us all. A flock of bee-eaters must have nested locally for we saw many of them in the immediate area. By this point in August the young birds had presumably fledged.

On our last evening the owner came and demonstrated how to make spaghetti, which we all ate with him.

One day we drove up to Sienna to see the racetrack for horses in the Piazza del Campo and a tall 14th century tower. We entered the city through a gate at the foot of the hill and walked up to the Piazza, where we lunched.

The city comprises 17 'contrade' who on special occasions, and the day of our visit was one such, the male members of the 'contrade' parade separately in the town, nowadays in a routine and peaceful and relatively quiet way. We did follow one such group for a while.

On another memorable day we drove north to Assissi, which is the home of the Basilica of St. Francis, a massive, two-level church, consecrated in 1253. Inside there are 13th. century frescoes portraying the life of St. Francis, which we were able to see in the lower church. Seen from the main road as we drove up, the whole town seemed to be a pristine white and very striking. We split up to explore, and Edward and I had a super lunch at a table in the open in the middle of the main street.

Our return journey involved a drive straight through to Pisa to hand in the car and fly home. I think Philip and family, including Jessie's partner, drove down from England and back up again.

BARBADOS, 2017

27th March. I looked forward to another trip to this wonderful island. This time is different because Edward is with me, as well as Jane and Ada from Switzerland. We are staying at Southern Surf holiday apartments, on the eastern side of the island; it has a pool and looks out on the beach and the sea beyond with only a road, admittedly a busy one, to cross to get to the beach.

Melanie has had to drop out because Steve is unwell. We are hoping to see Fran Cadogan who studied architecture with Melanie at Oxford Brookes University and has become a close friend of hers.

On arrival at the airport Jane, who could not use the portable steps rolled up to the exit door, had to be lowered to the ground from the galley door.

It wasn't very long before I became unwell too, because of my heart arrhythmia.

For a year or two I had been suffering from tachycardia and was hospitalized on several occasions to try and regulate my heartbeat. Once with cardioversion, which basically means stopping the heart and restarting it.

The problem occurs when the electrics are

malfunctioning. I have twice been on the operating table to try and rectify this problem, but without success. Eventually I was fitted with a pacemaker. After that was installed, I was dismayed, and presumably my surgeon was too, to see that I was, once again, experiencing tachycardia. Finally, the surgeon decided to approach the problem by entering the artery through my groin directly into the heart and "disconnecting" the rebel electrics. Hurrah! That worked and I have had a steady heartbeat ever since, thank God. But that was after this visit to Barbados!

I think a second glass of white wine set off the problem this time! It is an unpleasant sensation and although I try to stay calm, my heart rate sometimes soars to inappropriate levels. Luckily, Fran's mother gave us the particulars of a doctor experienced in heart problems, and we were able to organize an urgent appointment.

I was given some intravenous medication, which sorted things out temporarily. I then had to go back twice for further help, always driven by Edward who became rather familiar with the route past the island's principal cricket ground on the way into and out of Bridgetown.

In between times, it is great to be warm and to enjoy some sea swims. The fact that turtles are sharing the water is a bonus. Indeed, even Edward swam with us, however, he forgot that he had put the key to our rental car in his swimming trunks which gave it a thorough soaking, so that the car refused to start. The garage has been quick to provide a replacement vehicle, but the key is beyond repair, and we will have to pay for a new one. The car is important because we want to be free to explore the whole island.

On my previous visit Jane and I sailed in a catamaran with Fran for a short trip to another beach further up the coast. This time Jane, Ada and I have rented another catamaran, which is a bit less roomy. Sadly, Ada felt a bit queasy and did not enjoy the voyage along the coast, and the beach we visited was not inviting for swimming, so nobody ventured in this time.

One of our early car trips was to a restaurant called Atlantis about halfway up the east coast of the island; this shore faces the wide open Atlantic and can have huge waves rolling in. We are hosting Fran and her mother, and we have all had an excellent meal and enjoyed ourselves. We came across a rural cricket ground and found a team of English schoolboys is playing a local school and we watched them for a while.

At the northernmost point of the island, where a

rocky terrain replaces sandy beaches, is a cave that one can visit by steps down into it. It is called the "animal flower" cave and there are sea anemones in the internal rock pools and the tide floods the cave twice a day. We ate lunch at a nearby café.

A third trip took us to Hunte's garden where one parks in the road and walks in almost directly into the owner's house. We were made welcome and discovered that he had a loud-speaker down in the garden broadcasting classical music from the house. Here one is well below road level and in an expanse of flat garden with many attractive flowering plants – including orchids – and a few birds coming to feeders. We came back down the east coast, which is built up almost all the way back.

We did not always eat out but took turns to shop and cook in the apartment kitchen, making sure there was always a plentiful supply of ice cream. When we did eat out in the evening, we went to Champers just 50 yards along the road which was very popular and smart with a good menu.

We flew back to England on April 2nd.

CANTABRIA, 2017

It's October. We are setting off on this adventure with our friends Barry and Jane. The travel company was Woods Travel, but the coach and driver from a firm called Galloways came from Norfolk with half their coach filled.

Day 1. We were collected by taxi from Eastbourne very early in the morning and taken to the roundabout near Lewes where the Woods Travel coach was waiting; it picked us up and took us to a meeting point somewhere along the A3, where we transferred to the Galloway coach en route for Plymouth to catch the afternoon sailing of Brittany Ferries to northern Spain.

We found everything about the ferry was excellent: meals, accommodation and on-board facilities, and we had good weather for the crossing.

Day 2. We arrived in Santander, cleared customs and rejoined our coach for the journey to the Hotel Juan de la Cosa near Santona, where we are to stay for seven nights with dinner, bed and breakfast included in the cost of the tour.

The long beach here is patronized by windsurfers riding the giant waves. We explored the full length of the beach and at the western end we climbed up the hilly headland. There was another coach party at the hotel, and they ate in one dining room while we ate dinner in another. The bar had a Happy Hour when drinks were free. Our room looked out east along the beach.

Day 3. A full day excursion by coach to the mountain range called Picos de Europa. It became apparent that the coach driver had been here before as he was entirely comfortable with that the twisting roads which took us through several valleys to the market town of Potes, which has a river down the middle of it with parts of the town on either side. Here there were shops full of stuff for tourists, but we were able to find coffee and look at the river before continuing to Fuente De, where we took a spectacular cable car ride angling up from valley to quite high in the mountains.

At the top Edward managed to trip on his bootlaces and fell over, a temporary wound dressing was handled by the cable car people, but we had to leave our hotel in Santona and go into town next morning to get the wound dressed by a doctor.

Edward had hoped to see a Wallcreeper in the Picos, but none was seen.

Day 4. Apart from going to the doctor in Santona, we had the morning clear; but later the coach took us east along the coast road to the small town of

Castro Urdiales, which is town dominated by an enormous Gothic cathedral. We are not far from the Basque border.

In the 1790s, during the French Reign of Terror, Castro Urdiales became a refuge for French nobles fleeing the revolution, and close to the cathedral, well above sea level, is a deep narrow mooring space and we were told that the French refugees were able to embark here on an English ship that had been sent to rescue them.

Lower down where there is a plaza between the shop fronts and the sea wall, we enjoyed seeing Barry and Jane on a working carousel.

We returned via Laredo, which has one of the longest and loveliest flat beaches of fine sand in the region.

Day 5. After a leisurely breakfast, the coach took us west, beyond Santander, to the pretty village of Santillana del Mar, which is listed as a World Heritage Site, famous for its medieval buildings and cobbled streets, a village sometimes described as a living museum.

After a tapas lunch, and before we set off back, we went through Comillas to San Vicente De La Barquera, completing a day of art, history and the nature of the coast.

Day 6. A full day excursion took us to the Cabarceno Natural Park, one of the major attractions of northern Spain.

This is set high up in rocky terrain amid some very spectacular scenery, which is an ideal setting for this wildlife park, because most of the animals have exceptionally large areas in which to live and explore.

An exception to this applies to the brown bears, which have a large pen which includes large irregular rocky cliffs perfect for climbing and when we looked at them from ground level it quickly became apparent that some 30 or more bears were accommodated. This was obviously excessive, but understandable because the bears are feared and persecuted in the wild and many of the captive bears had been captured because they are now endangered in the wild.

The tiger pen was very spacious and largely flat grassland and there were several young tigers behind glass, looking out at the adults, but not being released into the arena, perhaps because the male tiger might seek to kill them if they are not his offspring.

At ground level we also saw elephants, hippos, giraffes and various antelopes.

Lower down in the northern corner of the park there is a 'station' for the overhead cable car system, which was a particularly special part of the trip. The aerial gondola system crisscrosses the park and at our second stop we found we were looking down into Santander town, which must have been about eight miles away. The gondolas took four to six passengers, and one could get off and on again at various 'stations'. Several occupied pens were overflown, and we could look down onto the animals without disturbing them – this applied to jaguar and leopard neither of which would have happily tolerated being viewed through wire fencing at their level. Using the cable car incurred no extra cost. We did not get time to visit the building that held the insect collection.

Day 7. Departing our hotel after breakfast the coach took us to nearby Cicero, where we boarded the FEVE narrow gauge railway for a spectacular journey through the Cantabrian hinterland to Bilbao, although Edward chose to stay behind. Bilbao is the capital of the Basque region and home to the amazing Guggenheim Museum with exhibits of architecture and modern art, which we were able to wander through. I think the coach drove to Bilbao without us, and that it was there to take us back to our hotel.

Day 8. A day of quiet relaxation.

Day 9. The coach took us to Santander in time for us to explore this port city before boarding the Brittany Ferry that would take us overnight to Portsmouth, from where the Woods coach would bring us to the taxi for home.

PATAGONIA, 2019

Heathrow Terminal 5 seemed remarkably empty and peaceful. We soon identified other Noble Caledonia travelers; we are in the right age group! After a very long buggy ride through deserted tunnels underneath the runways we eventually arrived at the gate for BA 777 and the plane left on time.

It was a 14-hour overnight flight to Buenos Aires, the cosmopolitan capital of Argentina with a population of about 3 million. We arrived on March 13th, our 54th wedding anniversary, and buses had been laid on to take us from the airport to a very nice hotel. The road into the city from the airport becomes a splendid main boulevard which for the last mile or so running down to the waterside has 10 incoming lanes allocated to specific types of vehicles and 10 outgoing lanes – a very impressive and very busy wide boulevard. Like any city there is a huge amount of traffic.

Next day there were three buses to take us to selected spots in the city; the tours were arranged so that buses two and three were routed differently to bus one so that no venue had to cope with more than one bus at a time. We were happy to find that Buenos Aires was a very green city, and impressed

to see huge, amazing portrait paintings on the ends

of several tower blocks.

The Plaza de Mayo – the main square – is named for the 1809 uprising against Spanish rule that led to independence in 1816. The plaza is surrounded by Jacaranda trees with blue flowers and the Silk Floss tree with pink flowers. The national flower is the Ceibo. The Pink Palace, which is in this square, is the residence of the President and nearby buildings within the same enclosure contain government offices equivalent to our Houses of Parliament.

On one side of the square stands the impressive Metropolitan Cathedral, which we looked around. This is where Francis Bergoglio was Archbishop for 15 years (1998-2013), during which time he became a cardinal in 2001. He was elected Pope Francis in 2013. The site was first built in the 15th. century and by 1620 a cathedral stood here, but it has changed much over the years and especially after a roof collapse in 1752. A small squad of soldiers marched over to the cathedral from the Palace to lay a wreath; this is apparently a daily ritual.

The Parque de Los Niños on the banks of the Rio de la Plata contains a huge silver sculpture depicting a multi-leaved flower, which was designed to open mechanically each day when the sun shone on it. It is now permanently open because on the death of its creator no instructions were found for maintaining the opening and closing mechanism.

We were also taken to the main cemetery which is another place of interest to residents and tourists alike; it contains substantial and expensive family mausoleums. Our guide made sure we saw the tomb with the plaque for Eva Peron.

Noble Caledonia arranged an evening meal for our whole party of some 90 people in a venue that had a stage at the far end where, after the meal, we had a flamboyant tango show when we could see that the Argentinian style of tango involves a surprising amount of leg kicking by both partners.

After our two nights in Buenos Aires, we had a very unfriendly 4 a.m. wake-up call to head down to breakfast and then to the airport for a flight taking us 1926 miles further south to Ushuaia in Tierra del Fuego. This is the main take-off point for ships sailing to Antarctica or to the Falkland Islands.

The flight was delayed, and, when we landed at Ushuaia we had a long wait for our luggage. Buses then took us to a large hotel to the east of the town sitting halfway up a small hill. This new and rather empty looking hotel was our lunch stop, but it also gave us time to walk in the garden and to climb the path to the peak of the hill, which was behind the hotel and offered us a view of the tail end of the Andean chain, where we could see a little snow or ice.

Looking south from the hotel we caught sight of our cruise ship "Island Sky" for the first time.

After boarding Island Sky that afternoon we sailed east and then turned south overnight towards the group of small islands making up 'Cape Horn'. This is actually named after the town of Hoorn in the Netherlands, because two or three Dutch ships tried to round the cape into the Pacific in very stormy weather and one, named Hoorn, was sunk by the heavy seas coming driving in from the Pacific Ocean adding to the tide race running from west to east.

On the peak of this small island is a white sign mounted where it is visible from the north and south. The sign has an empty central part cut out to look like an albatross in flight.

"I am the albatross that awaits you at the bottom of the world. I am the lost soul of mariners from all the world's oceans who perished while rounding Cape Horn. But they will not die in the storm-tossed waves. Today they fly on my wings for all eternity, in the final embrace of the Antarctic winds." (from Sara Vial, 1992).

There is also a passport office on this tiny island and many passengers had their first chance to use a zodiac to get to shore where they climbed endless steps to get to the top of the hill. We stayed on board, but the crew had our passports taken up those steps to the office to have them stamped along with those of our fellow travelers. Near the foot of the steps, we saw a few penguins but they were too far away for us to identify.

Next our captain, a Panamanian called Jose Fonseca, took the ship around the island anti-clockwise. When were south of it we met a small yacht with a British flag which was racing along to round the Horn from east to west. It is exactly this transit that was so often difficult; the large old sailing ships, whether they were naval or merchant, as they were occasionally delayed for as much as 2 to 3 months by the prevailing winds and stormy conditions. We could not have been luckier during our visit as the sea was amazingly calm.

This was not good news for Edward because it meant that the albatrosses were floating on the sea as the lack of wind deprived them of a lift to get into the air.

That evening, as the captain explained, we needed to head back north and rejoin the Beagle Channel and overnight we did this passing Puerto Willima and entering the channel.

Next day we had our very exciting first sighting of whales, which were humpbacks, found close to the entrance to Garibaldi fjord. There were either 2 or 3 of them, and their presence was given away by the air they "blew". They each blew two or three times before diving nose first leaving us a view of the tail fluke raised before the final dive. The black and white pattern is thought to be unique and pictures are brough together to learn where each whale goes.

Soon after seeing them the zodiacs were lowered. We had all had a lesson on how to step off the boat and into a zodiac and then sit on the inflated side of it. Potentially three of us on each side and one of the naturalist team, the zodiac driver, at the back with the tiller and the engine. Now, offered a zodiac outing for 1 ½ hours, we jumped at it.

While we explored the sides of the fjord, Island Sky steamed on towards the glacier at the head of the fjord. Our lady zodiac driver was a young German marine biologist, who was studying for her PhD and was passionate about all sea life. She has been instructed to keep a lookout for marine mammals during the voyage.

Almost immediately after embarking, where we were close to the left-hand shore, we found ourselves right up close to an entertaining group of sea lions – with young pups – some up on the rocks and some beside the boat. Most of them ignored us and refused to turn round and raise their faces. One group, deep in a cave, roared very loudly when our zodiac began to enter it. Our naturalist was careful to avoid getting too close.

Higher up on the walls, which were rather sheer here, we could see three Andean Condors perched on the cliff walls about 50 ft. above us. Lower on the cliff we spied a pair of Rock Cormorants and after we had moved deeper into the fjord, we found a family of Kelp Geese on the bank close to the water. The male is all white whilst the female and young have an attractive plumage which is dark brown with scattered white marks and an area under the tail completely white.

We crossed over to the other side of the fjord but found nothing there, so we headed towards the towering glacier at the end of this fjord. Island Sky was carefully stationed well back from the ice shelf, which was a cliff some 30 ft. tall that was occasionally calving in a small way. We boarded Island Sky at the stern and were rewarded with a glass of prosecco.

We exited the fjord and followed the strait to the port of Punta Arenas in the Strait of Magellan. We all landed by zodiac and the ship did not enter port. The original plan was for us to transfer to a catamaran which would take us eastward along this channel, which crosses back to the east coast of Tierra del Fuego, on what would be a short journey to Magdalena Island to walk amongst breeding penguins. However, at this time the sea was quite rough, and the coastguard stated that the water was too rough and closed the harbour denying us the chance to see the penguins – which was disappointing for those of us who had not seen the few penguins at Cape Horn. There is a small museum in town and a bus trip was organized to visit that. Just out of town to the east we found two ships, reproductions, one of which was of the Beagle. Here there were some Ashy-headed Geese at the water's edge. Unable to deliver the trip to the penguins Noble Caledonia hired two or three buses to take us some miles west to visit to see what was displayed where in 1584 there had been a first settlement by Europeans, on a headland close to what has become known as Cape Famine which is about 17 kms. west of modern Punta Arenas. I think all these first settlers were Dutch.

The buses had to stop about 1 km. short of our

destination and we had to walk from there, and eventually back again. The settlement failed, all 300 settlers perished due to the lack of local natural resources and the inclement weather. There is now a monument there to those who perished.

In 1843 an Englishman called John Williams attempted to re-establish the settlement near there, at what is now referred to as Fort Bulnes, but this also eventually failed and in December 1848 these settlers all moved to where Punta Arenas now stands. The early settlement buildings, those of 1843 I think, looked like rather primitive wooden structures built with bricks of earth sods.

The buses then took us back to Punta Arenas harbour, where we all crowded into a waiting room as the harbourmaster still considered the sea too rough, although our zodiac drivers were sure we could have got back to Island Sky safely. We waited, and waited – for several hours in fact, until the port was opened; in fact, the sea had calmed down earlier justifying the opening except that the reopening was announced after the water had become choppier again!

Out of all the zodiacs ours stalled halfway back to the ship and we had to wait for another of our naturalists could relaunch a zodiac and bring it out to us empty to lay it alongside so that each of us could swivel our bodies round and swing each leg over into the empty zodiac. Unsurprisingly we got somewhat wet as our zodiac returned to Island Sky, where, as usual, we were welcomed with hot flannels and champagne. It was later considered that the Harbour Master was trying to send Noble Caledonia a message because our ship had stayed out of the harbour rather than pay $250,000 (?) for the privilege of docking for the day!

A few of the birds seen were: Black-necked Swans, Chiloe Wigeon, Crested Caracara and Great Grebe.

From Punta Arenas we headed west by night along the strait and spent the whole of the next day wending our way north through narrows – requiring passage to Puerto Natales at slack water when it was safe to head in just before the turn of the tide, the caution being needed because the area of open water north of the narrows is very large and quite shallow so that it rushes through the narrows quite fast with growing rapidity. Coming back through is also slowest and safest before the outflow has gathered too much momentum.

We docked south of Puerto Natales, which faces Llanquihue Lake, South America's third largest lake. Buses took over and took us up to Puerto Natales where we lunched. From there looking east along the lake we could see a snow-capped volcano on the north side called Volcan Osorno. After lunch the bus took us to the Petrohue Falls not far from the foot of Volcan Osorno. to the south. Not far away to the south is another volcano, Volcan Calbuco, which is a stratovolcano and not pointed. It is more explosive in character, having exploded in April 2015 laying down a great deal of ash. Osorno has not erupted since 1869.

The bus near was parked just short of Lake Petrohue where the sandy shore was largely ash; some of our fellow passengers took up the offer of a boat trip around this small lake. There was a bridge over the falls from which there were attractive views downstream. We had hoped to see torrent ducks on the river at or below the falls, as they had been seen there two days ago. But we were not lucky.

We are confused about the next element of our journey. Puerto Natales is said to be the start of the road route to Torres Del Paine National Park, but some sources say that this is a drive taking more than 24 hours (and that it is better to fly in). However, we cannot recall having suffered such a long drive. One map we have consulted suggests that this long drive refers to a proper built -up road most of which is in Argentina, and which delivers you to the northern reaches of Torres Del Paine National Park. This same map includes a red line in

Chilean territory which is no doubt the route our bus took and was a dirt road. At several places along this road, we found caracaras looking for road kills.

Torres Del Paine National Park is a Biosphere Reserve listed by UNESCO in 1978 and in 2014 it was voted to be the 8th Wonder of the World by people from all over the world. The word "Torres" means towers, and this refers to the three sharp peaks in the mountain range, some of which reach 6,000 ft. We reached the park mid-morning and drove in to the entry barrier where we got out and stretched our legs. About a mile beyond the barrier is a building on the right that offers a look down at a narrow lake. Back on the bus again we ignored the left hand turn to Lago Grey and the new hotel there. Instead, we climbed up to a hillock, just below the peaks, which had another lake below us, and between us and the mountains, on which we could see ice in places. This was a popular photographic opportunity, but we were soon back on the bus retracing our recent steps and turning off down the road to Lago Grey, where we were all expected for a good lunch with a view down the lake to the far end.

Looking along the long thin lake we could see people far off walking on a sandy spit behind which we could see the grey glacier and in the lake some big recently calved blue "bergy bits".

While we were eating lunch the ornithologist member of our staff naturalists found a Magellanic Woodpecker in the group of pine trees just outside the entrance to the hotel. We heard of this and leaving our unfinished lunch on the table we rushed out to see it and had quite a good, but very brief view. It is almost all black, but it has its whole head crimson with bright yellow eyes. It is about twice the size of our familiar European Green Woodpecker.

Back in the bus again we returned to the area below the tall peaks but instead of walking up to the ridge we continued in the bus on a narrow road that passed by Lago Nordenskjold where there were a number of Chilean Flamingos (as well as a few other flamingos of a different montane species) and some Upland Geese. Along that route we saw some guanaco, which are like llamas but much smaller – these are the main food for pumas. We did not see a puma, but as subsequent films on television have shown us, their number is growing here in the park.

Quite soon we crossed the border into Argentina where we investigated a clothes shop and afterwards rejoined the bus which turned south almost immediately crossing the border back into Chile at a point a bit further south.

Driving back to Puerto Natales we saw Darwin's Rhea (a small cousin of the rhea and its more distant cousin the ostrich). The driver stopped the bus, and we were able to take a reasonable photograph of it.

Leaving Puerto Natales, Island Sky had to pass through the narrow channel we had come in by and the tide took us through very quickly; we then had to locate another narrow channel – called White Channel – and again be there at the time of slack water and in daylight; and in the afternoon we turned up another fjord to see the Bernal Glacier, before we came out onto the open sea.

Over the next night we sailed some 200 nautical miles and soon after lunch made landfall on the tiny island of Puerto Eden. It rains here most of the year. Almost immediately we noticed the tiny hummingbirds trying to feed in the rain on nectar from the native fuchsias – these were specimens of the Green-backed Firecrown and turned out to be the same species that I had photographed feeding on fuchsia nectar with Volcan Osorno in the background.

We saw few inhabitants of the island but learned that the school had 14 pupils. Sturdy flights of steps have been created over the rocks so that we were able to climb to the top of the highest point, perhaps 40 ft. higher, and on the way down we saw the very large Ringed Kingfisher.

Early, on our sea passage north, we were very lucky to encounter a Blue Whale – an adult can reach 35 meters in length and can weigh up to 200 tons, being the largest of living creatures on earth. Our mammal specialist spotted it, and most people heard the call and came out on deck to see it coming up for air. It then came really close to the ship and photographs were easily taken although not much of the body surfaced.

Our next stop was Chiloe Island, which is quite large. It is oriented so that its west coast is in line with the Chilean coast further north around Valdivia, and it has a sizeable harbour at Castro on its east coast, where we sailed in and disembarked. Castro is the island's capital. We were offered a choice of three activities: a tour of the many churches, a small bus to a natural park on the west side of the island and the opportunity to just explore the town on foot. I chose the popular tour of churches, while Edward went off to see the park with about six of our shipmates.

There are about 70 churches built as members of the framework of a "Circular Mission" introduced by the Jesuits in the 17th. century and maintained by the Franciscans in the 18th. and 19th. centuries. One church, which was entirely built of wood, was 280 years old and dedicated to St. Francis. The boat builders here were skilled in woodwork and were happy to be paid to construct churches. The abilities of the people of Chiloe as builders achieved their highest expression in these wooden churches, where farmers, fishermen and sailors all exhibited great skill in the handling of the most abundant building material available, which was wood.

We saw 16 churches which were outstanding examples of the successful fusion of European and indigenous cultural traditions; one was on Quinchao Island which we reached by a short ferry ride. Here potatoes are grown and served with every meal, including spaghetti!

From Chiloe Island, with all of us back on board and after dinner, we sailed east out of the harbour and then north before turning west to head out into the Pacific for an overnight run north up the coast to Valdivia Bay. In 1960 Valdivia suffered a strong earthquake some miles off the coast, which hit 9.5 on the Richter scale making this the most powerful earthquake ever recorded. It generated devastating tsunamis affecting the shores of Japan and Hawaii. Valdivia itself was affected both directly and by the tsunamis, and soil subsidence destroyed buildings, deepened local rivers and created new wetlands.

The Spanish-colonial forts around Valdivia Bay, were overcome in 1820 when Admiral Cochrane – previously of the Royal Navy, but recruited by O'Higgins, who was a Peruvian leading the growing opposition to the Spaniards – was originally asked to attack Peru, but priorities changed due to unrest further south. Provided with details of the fortifications of Valdivia Cochrane landed his sailors not in the bay, but south of it where they could climb the hill and along the ridge on the south side of Valdivia harbour to a point where they could take the battery below. They did so, and then fought their way east along the coast into the town, while Cochrane sailed his frigate in and bombarded the guns emplaced on the north shore. Nowadays, Niebla fort, built in 1671, is a tourist attraction and it was named after the Spanish Viceroy in Lima.

We anchored in the harbour and explored the town where there is a vast market for fruits and flowers close to the south bank of the river; in the water nearby was a huge walrus sitting on a platform and gratefully gulping down food thrown to him. There were also Black Vultures on the lookout for scraps.

In Valdivia we visited an Historical and Anthropological Museum which contained a very interesting collection of Mapuche artefacts and jewelry, as well as relicts and artefacts from the periods of German settlement which lessened Hispanic domination in the area. There was a large migration of German settlers in around 1840-50, including wealthy folk who were offered parcels of good, but uncleared land – sometimes very large parcels. One of the interesting exhibits in the museum is a beautiful "Siamese Twin" grand piano, which looked as though two pianos were fused together and sharing specially built casework.

The very large number of German settlers brought their own teachers with them and the pupils from the resultant private schools are taking all the well-paying jobs and the rest of the population, the native people, have become an underclass and a political problem.

Next day we were back at sea running steadily north towards Valparaiso. Over the course of the voyage, we have sailed almost half of the country's extensive seaboard, spanning approximately 2,700 miles from the tip of south America at Cape Horn to its boundary with Peru, where, north of Valparaiso there is the Atacama Desert and a very different climate.

We landed in Valparaiso and paid our mess bill and the ship's sailors transferred all our belongings to the coaches which were to take us to Santiago.

Valparaiso has limited beach space and almost all the buildings near the harbour back against cliffs and rise sharply up to housing at higher levels. We found an antique and frail-looking funicular and rode up in it to a high point where the better houses were well above and away from the port.

Having said goodbye to Island Sky, we left Valparaiso, and our bus took us to the Casablanca Valley, and the Rosario Valley where the Matetic vinyard is located, where lunch and 'degustations' had been arranged. This valley is considered to offer ideal climatic conditions for growing both red and white wines organically.

We were invited to taste both red and white wine and I found the white rather metallic. Interestingly the white wine was stored in large concrete vats, which I don't imagine the Swiss would approve! The visitors' restaurant was good, and we lunched there. The gardens with flowering plants and ponds and streams were delightful and a magnet for the birds on a hot day.

When we reached Santiago, the bus pulled up outside our hotel. We were given our room key and we got in the lift only to find out that we were not in the same part of the hotel as our fellow passengers; it turned out that, because I had registered for assistance on the flights out and back, it was presumed that we needed a bathroom appropriate for a disabled person.

In the morning our next problem was to find a money changer because we had something to post, and we had to walk into town to find one. Around midday buses appeared to take us to the airport for our flight back to Heathrow, this was uneventful.

We felt privileged to have been part of an amazing adventure.

THE ISLES OF SCILLY, 2019

There are some excellent coach companies in Sussex offering reasonable holidays, both in the UK and abroad. Edward and I decided to take a tour to the Isles of Scilly. The coach took us to Penzance from where we split up into groups to take small planes across to St. Mary's, the main island.

It was interesting to me to return here, and I enjoyed pointing things of interest to Edward like the seals along the shore. Various boat trips to the other isles were organized by the company. We joined the group going to Tresco gardens.

Now at the same time, our daughter Melanie and husband Steve decided to visit the Isles for her 50th birthday and we met in their hotel to enjoy a meal together. They were staying in a rather grand hotel at the top of the hill. Melanie and Steve were brave enough to venture into the sea for a swim and found it rather chill.

The isle of St. Agnes had a particularly nice little church with stained glass windows in memory of fishermen in a rowing boat and another of the lighthouse.

Edward and I decided to have some fun by renting electric powered bikes. We had never ridden such bikes but soon got used to them, suddenly shooting off at breakneck speed! We were fortunate with the weather and ate lunch out of doors and were soon joined by a sparrow who insisted on sharing my soup.

Our return journey was thwarted by the weather. Planes were not flying, which meant we had to take The Scillian for a rather rough and longer journey home. The poor coach driver had to drive us back through the night, but we got home safely, and all was well. Melanie and Steve had made their way home separately on a different day.

CORFU, 2023

This was the trip that decided us that we did not intend to do any more flights for overseas travel!

Our planning included making arrangements for me to have airport assistance, which actually meant from the station platform at Gatwick to the plane and I was glad not to have to walk miles and the benefits became more apparent when we were beginning the return journey.

We took a taxi from Corfu airport to our hotel, the Mon Repos Palace. We had a spacious room with a narrow terrace overlooking a bit of the sea. The island is not very large and the busy airport, which has just one runway for arriving and departing flights, is near enough that noise of the take-offs is very loud and very frequent.

There is a small swimming pool at the hotel, but although I did swim in the sea across the road it was not a very welcoming beach where one could swim easily, Across the road there is a low seawall along which there are occasional ladders with metal rungs that do provide a safe, but not easy, access to the sea. I tried this, but there was a mass of seaweed, and I had my legs nibbled by fish, which was not a very pleasant sensation. But swimming is certainly something the locals all enjoy.

We used the hop-on and hop-off buses to get around and see the island. The service is quite frequent, but the circuit has too few stops, so that quite a lot of walking is required. Happily, one stopping point is just opposite the hotel. One of the other stops is high in the hills where it overlooks the airport runway; another is down in the new harbour and there are probably only four or five others. The tickets are valid for the whole day. We used this facility on three different days. The maps suggest that there is a second Hop on Hop off service that goes down to the south of the island, where Edward had hoped to find some interesting wading birds. In fact, that second route service has been replaced; a "green" bus, of quite a different provider does have a route down there to the south of the island, but to take it you first have to find this bus company's central terminal, a fact that we learned too late to act upon it.

In one main square near the center, I sat down in the shade on a bench next to another lady and asked her if she lived on the island. "Oh no", she replied, "I come from Eastbourne in the UK"!!

Breakfast at the hotel was a help-yourself affair with quite a lot of choice and it was very adequate; Edward and I made good use of the delicious comb honey every day. I think we had one main meal in the hotel, but for most main meals we sought out a nearby restaurant and usually ended up with a fish dish – very good fresh fish each time.

The historic center of the town is proclaimed as a World Heritage Site, and it is supposed to have preserved its Venetian charm of yesteryear. Historically after the Venetians Corfu has been governed by England, France and Germany and, of course, Greece before and after the German occupation in World War II.

We took a guided bus tour to the north of the island where, as promised, we found a really good beach for swimming. It was popular, of course, and so it was crowded. It was next to where we were recommended to have our lunch, and once lunch was over, we found a spot and took the plunge into the crystalline waters. Well, I took the plunge, Edward found the sand was soft and the footing unstable and toppled into the water! So, we both got in, but getting out with our dodgy knees was much more difficult. We both had to ask for help from someone on the beach. A kind lady came forward and steadied me out after what was a lovely swim and Edward crawled out.

Somehow, we missed out on a launch trip to a cave around to the west from the mouth of the bay that we were in; missing the chance was probably due to the time it took for our lunch to arrive.

We had reached the north coast by rounding the eastern shoulder of the island; coming back led us up to the top of the surrounding hills, on a road which required one-way travel for much of it and thus took time. From the top there was a magnificent view over the bay where we had just swum in and indeed, far out to sea beyond; and from some places along the ridge, we could look towards the south of the island.

We enjoyed the holiday, but we found the island rather noisy from all the motorbikes – everyone seemed to own one. But the loud noise of the planes taking off was annoying. But the last straw was the flight home where the cramped seats are unsuitable for anyone with long thighs, and there was a seemingly unstoppable screaming baby.

The special assistance I got, and which benefitted Edward too, was to be hoisted up to the plane's galley entrance: much better than walking out and climbing steps!

Perhaps we are getting too old for all this!

ENVOI

Eastbourne is sometimes referred to unkindly as God's Waiting Room! We have the South Downs National Park just up the hill, a long beach for sea swims, countryside and enviable views. Many people with cars, including us, drive up onto the Downs to photograph Beachy Head or the chalk cliffs along the shore to the west and the sunset, and we and others often take up an evening picnic supper or tea to enjoy whilst watching the sun setting over the sea near Brighton. We love it. Of course, having been born here I just might be biased.

Edward and I have been fortunate to have each other for many years and we recently celebrated our 59th wedding anniversary. I just pray that the Morning Star, see Revelation Ch.2, v.28, will continue to shine on our children and three grandchildren.

ACKNOWLEGEMENTS

Without the encouragement and support of my family, this book would never have seen the light of day. Also, their collective memories were invaluable, as was the indefatigable and meticulous editing by my very dear husband. So, to them I give my heartfelt thanks.

I would also like to mention our computer wizard, and editor Amanda Sibley who has been the driving force for putting the whole book together and enabling the publishing on Amazon. Also my son Philip who has put much time and thought and AI technology into producing the book cover.

Finally, to all my friends who patiently waited and listened to endless updates on progress. Bless you all.